D0966892

Marketing Myths That Are Killing Business

#11/93

Fairleigh Dickinson
University Library
Teaneck, New Jersey

Marketing Myths That Are Killing Business

The Cure for Death Wish Marketing

Kevin J. Clancy
Robert S. Shulman

McGraw-Hill, Inc.
New York San Francisco Washington, D.C. Auckland Bogotá
Caracas Lisbon London Madrid Mexico City Milan
Montreal New Delhi San Juan Singapore
Sydney Tokyo Toronto

HF
5415
.C5278
1994
c.2

Fairleigh Dickinson
University Library

Teaneck, New Jersey

Library of Congress Cataloging-in-Publication Data

Clancy, Kevin J., date.
Marketing myths that are killing business : The cure for death wish marketing / Kevin J. Clancy, Robert S. Shulman.
p. cm.
Includes index.
ISBN 0-07-011124-3
1. Marketing. I. Shulman, Robert S., date. II. Title.
HF5415.C5278 1993
658.8—dc20 93-5891
CIP

Copyright © 1994 by McGraw-Hill, Inc. All rights reserved. Printed in the United States of America. Except as permitted under the United States Copyright Act of 1976, no part of this publication may be reproduced or distributed in any form or by any means, or stored in a data base or retrieval system, without the prior written permission of the publisher.

1 2 3 4 5 6 7 8 9 0 DOC/DOC 9 9 8 7 6 5 4 3

ISBN 0-07-011124-3

The sponsoring editor for this book was Philip Ruppel, the editing supervisor was Peter Roberts, and the production supervisor was Suzanne W. Babeuf. It was set in Palatino by McGraw-Hill's Professional Book Group composition unit.

Printed and bound by R. R. Donnelley & Sons Company.

This book is printed on recycled, acid-free paper containing a minimum of 50% recycled, de-inked fiber.

Dedicated to our children, Susan, David, Karen, and Molly, who will hopefully grow old in a world more free from cultural, political, religious, scientific, and, yes, business myths than the one in which we live.

Contents

12. Myths about Promotion 171

13. Myths about Public Relations 187

Acknowledgments

We started this project by combing through our last book, *The Marketing Revolution: A Radical Manifesto for Dominating the Marketplace,* for all the marketing myths explicit or implicit in our text.

We then asked colleagues at our former firm, Yankelovich Clancy Shulman, to submit their favorite marketing myth and a compelling argument as to why it is a myth. Lisa Carter, Henry Gamse, Doug Haley, Peter Krieg, Walker Smith, Steve Tipps, and Al Yesk all made valuable contributions.

We then turned to friends and colleagues in the academic community for their ideas. Paul Berger, Len Berry, Joe Blackburn, Leonard Geiser, Dick Harmer, Phil Kotler, David Lloyd, Tom Nagle, Michael Rouse, Richard Seclow, Stan Tannenbaum, Glen Urban, and Fred Webster were especially helpful.

By the time we had developed a proposal for Philip Ruppel, our wonderful editor at McGraw-Hill, the number of myths had grown from the 25 we'd found in *The Marketing Revolution* to 100. Our working title was *100 Myths That Are Killing American Business.*

Yet the more we worked on the manuscript, the more research we did, and the more people we talked to, the more myths we uncovered. Along the path to glory Ross Blair and Mike Hess of Information Resources Inc. and Mark Chesney of NCH Promotional Services were immensely helpful in sharing with us their own encyclopedic knowledge of marketing research and in providing access to their respective firms' recent findings.

We would also like to thank people who gave their time generously for in-depth interviews about different marketing issues that proved to be very useful in guiding our thinking. These include: Mark Begelman,

Office Depot; James Garrity, Compaq Computer; Richard Freeland, Pizza Hut of Indiana; Tom Melohn, formerly of North American Tool & Die; Bob Mansfield, AnalysisPlus Research; Jack Mitchell, Mitchell's; Jack Schoonover, Bill Wubbenhorst, and Mark Wiener at PR Data Systems; Robert Warrens, J. Walter Thompson; Lee Weinblatt, The PreTesting Company; and Marian Wood. We also thank our clients, whose intellectually stimulating discussions and marketing problems have fine-tuned our thinking and enriched our lives. We owe a special debt to Ray Lewis of Holiday Inn Worldwide, who has contributed mightily for almost a decade to our evolving thinking about marketing.

And no list would be complete without thanking our team at Copernicus: The Marketing Investment Strategy Group for their direct and indirect contributions to this book. This includes Ami Bowen, Eric Larsen, Lori Marvel, Susan Shulman, Tom Lix, and the effervescent Liz Wheeler. Also special thanks to Mary Zeigler of TR Productions for the exhibits used throughout the book.

A key player on our team and the most important contributor was Wally Wood—a business-writing guru. Wally is a friend, consultant, researcher, and gifted writer who worked closely with us on this project for more than a year, from ideation through to closure. His insights and his writing and interviewing talents were as essential to completing this project as they were to our previous book. His ever-ready comparisons of American life, work, culture, and business to their counterparts in Japan were indispensable to our entertainment, mental health, and expanding knowledge of international business.

We knew that if we were going to make *Marketing Myths* accessible to all businesses, we had to present our ideas in an exciting manner. The myths obviously are intended to do just that. Beyond the myths, however, we've ventured into a land where few serious business writers have gone—that of cartoons! They work for *The New Yorker*, so we thought they could work for us. We chose Ralph Owen—noted illustrator and ex ad guy (SSC&B). We trust that you'll chuckle at his artistry and our captions.

Finally, we would like to thank our team at McGraw-Hill, our editor, Philip Ruppel, and Peter Roberts, our editing supervisor, who played significant roles in bringing this book to life and to market.

Kevin J. Clancy
Bedford, MA

Robert S. Shulman
Westport, CT

Test Your Own Marketing IQ™

When in January 1992 our *The Marketing Revolution: A Radical Manifesto for Dominating the Marketplace* hit book retailer shelves, we were unprepared for the response.

We were pleasantly surprised by the reaction of chief executive officers, chairmen, and other senior executives in companies large and small whom we had soundly criticized in our book for their weak leadership in the marketing wars. Their words of encouragement in calls and letters convinced us that we were not the only people in town appalled by the poor performance of marketing programs in the 1980s and enthused by the promise of computer-assisted marketing strategy that our book was about.

We were especially pleased by the positive reaction from the national and business media. Newspapers, magazines, television, and radio ran more than 300 stories about *The Marketing Revolution* within a few months after publication—providing us with a much broader audience for our ideas than we had ever anticipated.

What intrigued us about the media reports was not just the large number of them and the favorable response, but the focus of their interest. After *The Wall Street Journal* published a story on our Marketing IQ test and the low scores achieved among a national sample of more than 1000 senior executives, and *AdWeek* did a cover story based on our discussion of marketing myths, we were beseiged with requests for follow-up stories from business publications throughout

North America, Europe, Japan, and South America. To our amazement, reporters wanted to discuss Marketing IQs and marketing myths—topics to which the *WSJ* and *AdWeek* gave more attention than we gave in our book. We discussed the measurement of IQs on four pages (out of 308), while we covered marketing mythology in depth (if you can call it that) in five pages and sprinkled it in perhaps a dozen more places.

In stark contrast, the business media mostly neglected the most important topics in *The Marketing Revolution*. Only *The Planning Review* (a publication of the Planning Forum, The International Society for Strategic Management and Planning) provided a much broader perspective on the book than IQs and mythology. Indeed, when we had first proposed the book to our publisher we had presented it as a definitive work on computer-assisted marketing strategy (the use of new computer-based tools for designing and implementing financially optimal marketing programs). Measuring Marketing IQs and discussing marketing mythology came later, when we began writing the book as a vehicle to communicate our ideas.

The reactions of CEOs, the media, and marketers from New York to Tokyo, Stockholm to Capetown convinced us, however, that much more could and should be written about these two topics. When executives asked us to test *their* Marketing IQs, our standard response became, "Wait a year or two and we'll tell you how to test it yourself." When they asked if we had a complete list of myths, our answer was, "No, but we're working on it."

Marketing Myths That Are Killing Business accomplishes both objectives. In the following few pages we present a simple 20-question test readers can take to evaluate their own Marketing IQs. This is a considerably shorter and different test of marketing intelligence than the one we described in *The Marketing Revolution*. This test is designed to give readers from any type of business organization a fix on what they know and don't know about marketing. (You will find the answers and a scoring key in the Appendix.)

Equally important, the test is based on the material in this book. Therefore, whatever a reader's initial Marketing IQ, a thorough, serious reading of *Marketing Myths* will improve the score. Readers can see their scores (and knowledge) jump from that of "death-wish marketer" to that of "marketing genius" with an investment of less than 20 hours' reading.

The reader can learn about the myths of marketing that are killing businesses throughout the world, because from Chapter 1 through Chapter 20 that's all this book is about. It was not our intent to write a "how-to" book on marketing. Rather, we use myths in order to tell our own story and to make an "easy read" that will inspire and assist current and future marketers.

Take the Test Yourself

The following 20 statements about marketing today may or may not be true. Read each statement and then answer "true" or "false." If you don't know, you're better off checking "don't know" rather than guessing and getting it wrong. In this test, as in the real world, you pay a penalty for a wrong decision.

Remember that this is a test—no cheating is allowed. You may not read the book or turn to the Appendix until after you have answered each of the statements.

1. Businesses in America were reasonably successful during the 1980s, enjoying real growth in sales of 2 percent or more per year.

   true______ false______ don't know______

2. During the coming decade, marketers will earn more profits from new brands than from existing ones.

   true______ false______ don't know______

3. A high share of market in a product category generally leads to economies of scale that result in a high level of profitability.

   true______ false______ don't know______

4. There is little agreement among marketers about what the hot new concept "brand equity" means.

   true______ false______ don't know______

5. A reasonable way to set the marketing budget is to take last year's figure and adjust for inflation.

   true______ false______ don't know______

6. Line extensions are a very risky way to introduce new products.

   true______ false______ don't know______

7. Focus group interviews are a serious marketing research tool that a manager can safely use to help make serious marketing decisions.

   true______ false______ don't know______

8. Businesses today invest more money in finding new customers than in further developing current customers.

   true______ false______ don't know______

9. The most profitable customers of a firm are usually its biggest customers.

   true______ false______ don't know______

10. Big companies generally make their marketing decisions after evaluating many alternatives in terms of profitability.

    true______ false______ don't know______

11. The more appealing a new product concept is to prospective buyers, the more likely it is it will be a success.

    true______ false______ don't know______

12. Every company should strive to hold on to all of its customers.

    true______ false______ don't know______

13. Location is the most important determinant of success for a new retail business.

    true______ false______ don't know______

14. One-hundred-percent customer satisfaction is *not* an intelligent business objective.

    true______ false______ don't know______

15. Media planners at major advertising agencies know a great deal about the relative effectiveness of print, television, and radio advertising.

    true______ false______ don't know______

16. Because pricing is such an important component in the marketing mix, most big companies have a serious pricing strategy based on serious pricing research.

    true______ false______ don't know______

17. Nielsen's television rating service—especially the new "people meter"—provides valid information about the number of people watching a particular television program.

    true______ false______ don't know______

18. Consumer and trade promotional programs tend to be more profitable than advertising.

    true______ false______ don't know______

19. Companies cannot quantify the effects of public relations programs. That's one reason why PR is a less valuable component of the marketing mix than advertising or the sales force.

    true______ false______ don't know______

20. Most marketing and advertising programs usually are measured in terms of their profitability.

    true______ false______ don't know______

Our cast, not in order of appearance.
Back row, left to right: Mr. Robinson, chairman and CEO of Consolidated Amalgamated. . . his marketing partner, Mr. Saver, founder and emperor of Saver Stores . . . Sharon, the marketing manager, and Sigmund, the market researcher at Consolidated Amalgamated.
Front row, left to right: Pierce, account executive and principal of Pierce, Brod & Schallo Advertising, Inc. . . . Lisa, wife of Pierce, housewife, and mother . . . Sam, the local retailer.

Introduction

In the early morning of October 25, 1415, 25,000 well-rested French knights and foot soldiers faced 6000 exhausted Englishmen on a soggy field near a town called Agincourt. The French that day believed a number of things:

- That the best of their nobility would quickly rout the weary English men-at-arms, a mere rabble fighting under the 27-year-old untested carouser, Henry V
- That the French massed-formation strategy—one that had changed little since the days of Caesar—would overwhelm a loosely organized, mobile force
- That heavily armored French cavalry and infantry were far superior to English longbows, despite the lesson that should have been learned at the battle of Crecy in 1346, when English archers had annihilated a force of 12,000 mounted knights
- That the rainy weather that had preceded the battle for weeks would have no bearing on the outcome

By mid-afternoon, the English were singing "Pro Nobis Domine" after a resounding victory, while the French asked permission to bury their dead. The French beliefs had turned out to be myths. Two hundred English were killed, in contrast to 10,000 French, including 5000 knights, "the flower of French nobility." Shakespeare called it "a royal fellowship of death." France, for a time, became the prize of the young Henry.

Like the French generals at Agincourt, marketing managers are often handicapped by myths, beliefs that lead them to make wrongheaded decisions. These result in the destruction of their forces and the death of that which they were entrusted to protect and preserve.

According to our dictionary:* a myth is "a traditional or legendary story, usually concerning some being or hero or event, with or without a determinable basis of fact or a natural explanation, especially one that is concerned with deities or demigods and explains some practice, rite, or phenomenon of nature." An alternative definition: A myth is "an ill-founded belief held uncritically, especially by an interested group."

This is what we mean by marketing myths. We're talking about unproved or false collective beliefs, with or without a determinable basis of fact or explanation, that executives use to justify some marketing practice, rite, or decision-making process.

Myths seem to arise out of a basic human need to understand and impose order on messy reality. In layman's terms, myths explain what's going on (or try to). The trouble starts when people draw erroneous conclusions from the reality they see around them. Take the story that land surveyor Robert A. Maschi contributed to the *Reader's Digest* not long ago.

Maschi was working at a golf course that was expanding to 18 holes. Clearing thick brush in an area he was mapping, he came upon a golf club an irate player must have tossed away. It was in good condition, so Maschi picked it up and hacked his way on. When he broke out of the brush onto a putting green, he found two golfers staring at him in awe. Maschi had a machete in one hand and a golf club in the other, and behind him was a clear-cut swath over 100 yards long.

"There," said one of the golfers, "is a guy who hates to lose his ball!"

There is a golfer creating a myth. The process happens all the time. It has happened since the dawn of time. Everyone can see that, allowing for hills and valleys, the world is flat. According to Vedic priests in India, circa 1200 B.C., 12 massive pillars supported the flat world; during the night the Sun passed underneath, threading its way between the pillars.

The early Chinese believed that a solar eclipse was a dragon trying to eat the Sun. The only salvation was to frighten the creature away: shout, scream, bang gongs, and make as much noise as possible. It always worked. Indeed, it works today. If you are in the middle of a solar eclipse, make as much noise as you can. The sun will return unharmed.

*For those who care and to save us from a copyright infringement suit, it's *The Random House Dictionary of the English Language*, 2d ed., New York, 1987.

Aristotle (384–322 B.C.), after carefully considering the flat-earth theory, concluded that the Earth was a sphere. But if he got the Earth's shape correct, he also believed it was the center of the universe. All ancient civilizations shared this general conceit and put themselves at the center of the center. The Egyptians not only thought Egypt was the center of the world, they believed the universe was long and narrow, much like Egypt. The Mesopotamians, whose empire covered an area more circular than long and narrow, thought the heavens more like a dome.

Aristarchus of Samos (c. 310–230 B.C.) seems to have been the first person in recorded history to come up with the idea that the Sun is the center of the universe. It was too radical an idea. No one else embraced the theory, and indeed Ptolemy's book, the *Almagest*, published roughly 150 years later, codified the belief that the Earth is center.

Ptolemy (120–180) may not have invented the Ptolemaic system, but he systematized it by saying that the Moon, Mercury, Venus, the Sun, Mars, Jupiter, Saturn, and the sphere of the fixed stars revolved around the Earth. Since, as everyone knows (and as every Greek mathematician knew), the circle is the perfect form, planetary orbits also had to be circular and the Earth was the center of the universe.

The idea began to fall apart thanks to Nicholas Copernicus (1473–1543). He mistrusted Ptolemy's system because it seemed inconsistent and cumbersome. Unfortunately for Ptolemy, the planets do not move regularly and steadily against the background of stars; at times the planets reverse direction. One example: Most of the time, Mars moves from west to east. We now know that its orbit lies beyond the Earth's and that it travels slower than Earth. As we overtake and pass Mars, it seems to perform a slow "loop" against its background of stars, a movement Ptolemaic theory has difficulty explaining. To do so, Ptolemy decided that Mars and the other planets moved in small (perfect) circles in their planetary orbits. Adding these little epicycles made the theory exceptionally messy.

Copernicus rejected the cumbersome Ptolemaic system in favor of his own, which put the Sun at the center of the solar system and thereby solved a bunch of problems (see Exhibit I.1). He wrote *De Revolutionibus Orbium Coelestium (On the Revolution of Heavenly Bodies)* but, afraid the Church might not subscribe to the work, did not publish it for years. Word got out, however, and Copernicus finally allowed the book to be published in 1543, the year he died.

His fears had been sensible. The Church in general was bitterly hostile. Martin Luther commented, "This fool seeks to overturn the whole art of astronomy. But as the Holy Scriptures show, Jehovah ordered the Sun, not the Earth, to stand still."

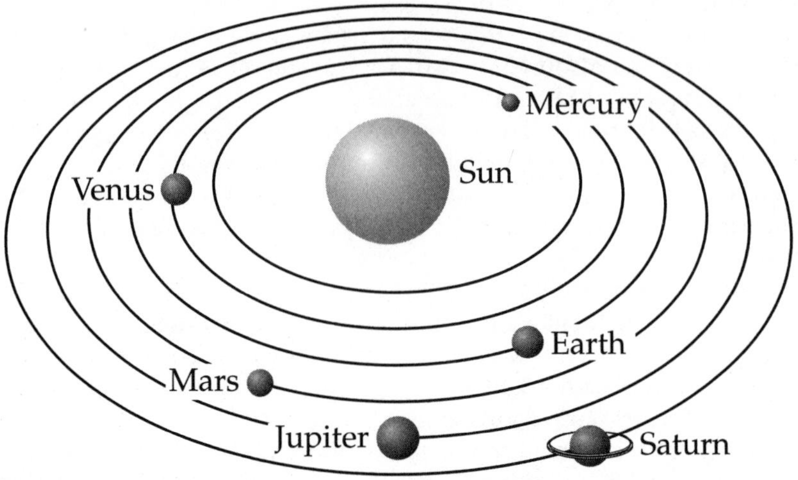

Exhibit I.1 The Copernican breakthrough—*De Revolutionibus Orbium Coelestium.*

With the advent of the scientific revolution in the seventeenth century, however, the Bible's authority began to develop cracks. Science insisted on observational and experimental evidence. A myth is a belief people continue to hold even when confronted with contrary evidence. Scientific theory is always provisional, always open to modification by new evidence. One measure of scientific truth is other researchers' ability to replicate experimental findings. There is no cold fusion unless others, following the same procedures, obtain the same results the original researchers claim to have arrived at.

Under the scientific method, you start with a theory about why something happens and design an experiment to see if what you think will happen does in fact happen. If it does, you may be on to something, although as Copernicus, Galileo, Darwin, and others have discovered, not everyone will agree. Even when, to the modern sensibility, the evidence is overwhelming.

Medicine is another example of a profession where myths have perpetuated themselves for years, despite inconclusive evidence on their behalf. In fact there are hundreds, if not thousands of examples of myths in medicine, even today. Take psychosurgery as an illustration. "Between 1948 and 1952, tens of thousands of mutilating brain operations were performed on mentally ill men and women in countries around the world, from Portugal, where prefrontal leucotomy was introduced in 1935, to the United States, where under the name of 'lobotomy' the procedure was widely used on patients from all walks of life," writes Elliot S. Valenstein in *Great and Desperate Cures*, a history of psychosurgery. The procedure was so successful that Egas Moniz, the Portuguese neurologist who created the operation, received the Nobel Prize for it in 1949.

While the operation became so popular for many reasons—including the ambitions and personalities of the surgeons involved—Moniz's original argument for the procedure was based, says Valenstein, "solely on a series of general, loosely connected, and essentially untestable statements" (much like the myths that follow in this book). The operation fell out of favor when criticism of lobotomy began to appear in the popular press and in professional journals.

Just as myths about lobotomies killed patients, myths about marketing are killing brands, products, entire companies. Like astronomy and medicine, marketing has been able to learn more and more about the world, and the new information has shown that many of the beliefs marketers hold—ideas that seem to explain how things work—are simply wrong. Yet marketers cling to their old notions.

This should come as no surprise. Consider medicine. The first medical school was established at the University of Padua in 1399. Since then physicians have studied extensively inside and outside the classroom. All this has led to today's training: four years of medical school, a year-long internship, a two-to-five-year residency, postdoctoral programs, licensing board and certification examinations. Many physicians begin to practice (an interesting word to describe what they do) only in their mid-thirties. Yet despite all this training in this almost 700-year-old discipline, myths are still pervasive.

Marketing, by comparison, is young. One J. Hagerty produced the first doctoral thesis on the subject in 1899, "The Distribution of Industrial Products." Almost 40 years later, in the first issue of the *Journal of Marketing*, Hagerty wrote, "Strange as it may seem to us now, relatively few seemed to be interested in the subject. For a long time it had been assumed that if goods were produced, they would be sold, and there was no need in studying the methods of selling them."

Several authorities attribute the dawn of modern marketing to the social and economic upheaval of the 1930s. As personal income plummeted and the demand for consumer goods and services crashed, the marketing function became more important. The firm's survival required that managers pay more attention to the markets for their products.

War and rationing, however, and the shortages of goods during and after the war years, put the full implementation of modern, consumer-oriented marketing on hold. Most observers attribute the origins of the "marketing concept" and "consumer orientation" to the 1950s, when companies recognized strong consumer demand—a "buyer's market"—and that goods had to be sold, not just produced. This recognition signaled the emergence of the marketing concept.

In essence, companies understood that marketing is the beginning of the sales process and integrated with every stage and every function in the firm. One standard text* identifies the marketing concept as "a company consumer orientation... All facets of the organization must be involved with assessing and then satisfying customer wants and needs." The company determines consumer wants, needs, and preferences, then produces products and services that satisfy these at a profit. The marketing concept recognizes that sales is just one marketing component, that "marketing" encompasses a much broader range of activities. The company places marketing ideas into the production process *before* it designs an item or product, rather than after.

Some suggest that major U.S. corporations did not fully accept this orientation until the early 1960s—the point at which the "consumerism" movement originated because companies were overlooking the marketing concept's tenets.

Yet even as the marketing concept developed, so did myths. They continue to abound because—unlike medicine—schools do not exhaustively train marketers, science does not drive the business, and the field is riddled with rules of thumb and old wives' tales, some of which are based on fact and some on people's imaginations.

Relatively few marketing practitioners have had the benefit of any serious marketing training. Few marketing practitioners, to start at the beginning, studied marketing as an undergraduate (in contrast to almost all MDs, who are required to take a premed program). Of those who did take marketing, most completed their studies in questionable programs under the tutelage of professors with little real-world experience. With the exception of perhaps 25 institutions, including Pennsylvania (Wharton), Indiana, Michigan (University of and State), Berkeley, Boston and New York Universities, Texas A&M, and the University of Illinois, we discount much undergraduate marketing education as suspect.

This problem could be ignored altogether if most marketing managers had an MBA (with a marketing concentration), or its equivalent from a graduate program keyed to real-world practice with professors known for their expertise in solving real-world problems.

In our consulting careers we've met only a dozen or so such managers. A goodly number of marketing professionals have skipped not only an undergraduate marketing education but relevant graduate work as well.

*Boone and Kurtz, *Contemporary Marketing*, 5th ed., Dryden, 1986, p. 13.

Of those who took an MBA, most completed three or fewer marketing courses, and those didn't focus on real-world practice. Rather, they covered the fundamentals of marketing (marketing management) and marketing theory, such as consumer behavior. If they also studied marketing research, the professors taught methodologies the students would rarely use. The tools professors teach in the classroom tend to be arcane, overly sophisticated, and mathematical. It's just not considered interesting to teach the kinds of things most marketing practitioners spend most of their time doing.

The material that marketing students study in class interests the professors because it's quantitative, because it's leading edge, because it's state-of-the-science. "State-of-the-science" changes somewhat from decade to decade, but in the past it has included multidimensional scaling (aka, perceptual mapping) and conjoint measurement (aka, tradeoff analysis). Today it's choice modeling, plus maybe meta-analysis and scale construction—not the tried-and-true, basic bread-and-butter tools that a practitioner uses in his or her everyday work.

A. H. Walle of Ithaca College recently commented that "the field of marketing is in the throes of a palace coup. For generations, narrow specialists with complex methodological expertise have held court. Now such gurus are falling under attack and losing their once-lauded clout." He goes on to describe "The Third Generation Idiot Syndrome: a 25-year-old graduate student who is studying under a 28-year-old assistant professor who wrote his dissertation with a 32-year-old associate professor. And none of them ever 'worked' a day in their lives. Today's business leaders are fed up with cloistered specialists whose mainsprings are driven by some kind of misplaced enthusiasm for scientific rigor for its own sake—practical significance of the research be damned." Although Walle's comments seem to us very extreme, they do strike a responsive chord.

Even when MBA students do learn some really good, high-powered stuff in the classroom (and this is certainly the case at the nation's most prominent business schools), by the time they've advanced far enough in their careers to apply these theories and techniques three, four, or even five years after graduation, they've forgotten what they learned. We've had clients who have graduated from top MBA programs, who have taken marketing research classes with wonderful professors, but whose knowledge was rudimentary because what they once knew they had lost over time. It was not reinforced through practice.

All this would not be a problem if marketing practitioners belonged to professional associations and completed crash courses given by their companies and outside organizations, including the American Marketing Association. Sadly, this is not the case. Marketing *research* practitioners tend to be professionally oriented; many belong to the AMA and take an occasional seminar and participate in professional conferences. But not marketing managers. Most managers have received little formal training before or after they begin to practice.

This of course points up a radical divergence between medicine and marketing: In medicine, young doctors apply what they learned in the classroom over and over and over, through internship and residency, until they can do it well. Only after a young doctor can diagnose and prescribe correctly is he or she passed on to the next level within the profession. Only when that physician has been thoroughly tested through licensing and board certification examinations is he or she fully accepted into the profession. That, regrettably, is not marketing's method.

Given that marketing practitioners are not trained well, it's no surprise that their patients—their products—often die. The death rate of marketing programs is so high that we have labeled the syndrome "death-wish marketing," our name for those misguided efforts by which managers, unconsciously or unknowingly, attempt to kill a product, a brand, or, occasionally, an entire company. Symptoms we've identified include the following 10:

1. The manager makes key marketing decisions on judgment alone, or on the basis of such circuitous reasoning as, "This is the way we did it last year...the way we always do it...the way we did it at P&G."
2. The company analyzes its competition as a guide to what opportunities to pursue. Looking to the competition for direction is death-wish marketing.
3. Top management demands short-term marketing results. The focus is on doing things quickly rather than on doing things right.
4. The corporate structure permits managers to develop and launch marketing programs that do not address real customer needs and problems with real solutions. Often, what sells internally ends up as the marketing program.
5. The company promotes marketing managers—often baby boomers more interested in being "different," "creative," "exciting," or "sexy" than in being smart—before they've had to live with the brands or programs they've launched.
6. The marketing plan rests heavily (or entirely) on suicidal research, including the most volatile, nonprojectable research tool in the world—focus groups—and other preposterous methods, including

"importance ratings," market segmentation studies done by telephone, and lengthy interviews done by mail to measure customer satisfaction.

7. The marketing decision-making process (and concomitant marketing research) considered *five or fewer* decision options—fewer than five targets, positionings, advertising executions, pricing levels, media spending, product/package configurations, etc.
8. Either there is no real analysis of marketing decision options or the analysis emphasizes what consumers think, believe, want, or say they would buy, with little or no emphasis on *profitability*.
9. There are no clear, specific objectives for the overall marketing program and its components—such as advertising—and no measurement systems for evaluating the performance of the program against objectives over time.
10. The marketing director does not know and is not interested in manufacturing costs and other costs outside his or her span of control, and as a result knows little about a marketing program's return-on-investment. Since the executive's remuneration is not based on profitability, this disinterest in, or inability to assess, ROI is not regarded as a problem.

While a company can probably survive when its marketing plans routinely reveal one or two of these symptoms, we do not think a brand can survive five or more. That is death-wish marketing. Such faulty planning can be worse than no planning at all, because executives think they're making sound decisions, unaware that they're operating on a basis of ignorance and myth.

If you know your boat's compass is broken, you'll steer by dead reckoning or by the stars or by compensating for the sun's position, and you may reach land safely. But if you don't know the compass is broken, you'll end up on the rocks or adrift in mid-ocean. If you believe the myths of marketing, your marketing plan will become just another statistic, one of those plans that we estimate dies every seven minutes.

But what *are* the myths of marketing?

We thought you'd never ask!

Marketing Myths That Are Killing Business

"I was doing fine—corner office, company car, executive dining room—and then they tied my salary to the return I could show on the marketing budget."

1

Myths about Business Performance

Conventional wisdom says that American business did extremely well during the 1980s. Business was booming. Sales were up. Productivity was improving. Everybody made a lot of money.

Finance, it was said, was the engine that propelled this phenomenal growth. Marketing, everyone knows, was less important to success, but that was okay because, happily, marketing is a subject that CEOs—particularly CEOs of major corporations—knew a great deal about. Consequently, marketing programs were strong, if not stellar, during this period of business prosperity. If there were any problems, the Japanese did it.

So let's take the following as our first myth.

Myth 1: American businesses were doing just fine during the 1980s.

Truth: Well, maybe in certain industries. The junk bond people did all right. Defense contractors did okay, as long as we were intent on defeating the Evil Empire. The computer software and knowledge industries mushroomed.

On the other hand, entire industries faltered—financial services (particularly the savings and loan industry), computer hardware, automobiles, footwear, shipping, retailing, steel—not to mention great names in American business: IBM, General Motors, Wang, Macy's, American Express, Citibank. Consider the collapse of some of America's best-known airlines, the disappearance of companies such as PanAm, Eastern, Braniff, Piedmont, Allegheny, and PSA.

But even knowing this did not prepare us for what we found when we looked at the two hundred largest *Fortune* 500 industrial corporations in 1980 and tracked them through 1992, correcting for inflation.

By 1992 only 141 of the 200 were left (that 28 percent decline says something in itself). The others had been sold or merged, corporations like RCA, Firestone, American Can, American Broadcasting, American Motors, Greyhound, Bendix, Norton Simon, Combustion Engineering, Uniroyal, SCM, and more.

But if you take the 141 companies existing in 1980, add the sales of those from 1980 they bought during the next 12 years (Philip Morris, for example, bought Kraft and General Foods; Chrysler bought American Motors; U.S. Steel bought Marathon Oil), and adjust for inflation, how much did sales grow?

They didn't. The average company's sales declined by a shade under 1 percent per year (0.2 percent, to be precise).

Since this is an average, of course, some did much better and some did worse. Those that did better include Campbell Soup, Merck, PepsiCo, Procter & Gamble, Quaker Oats, Scott Paper, and Whirlpool. Those that did worse include Beatrice Foods, Exxon, General Tire, International Harvester, Mobil, Union Carbide, and U.S. Steel.

Now strip out the mergers and acquisitions, however, and the organic growth for many companies—the business with which the company started in 1980—shrank by 3 percent or more per year. Stated differently, some companies have been able to report growth only because they've acquired other companies.

Apparently, profitability paralleled sales. Despite all the moving and shaking, buying and selling in American industry, once you adjust for inflation and mergers and examine real profitability growth...there wasn't any.

What about productivity?

While companies have been investing heavily in information technology—computers, software, telecommunications—something like $97 billion a year, they've used it mainly to speed up rather than transform office work. "With a few exceptions," write Thomas H. Davenport (Ernst and Young) and James E. Short (MIT Sloan School of Management) in the *Sloan Management Review,* "information technology's role in the design of nonmanufacturing work has been disappointing; few firms have achieved major productivity gains. Aggregate productivity figures for the United States have shown no increase since 1973."

American business did *not* do fine during the 1980s.

Myth 2: Many companies/brands/products/services failed to thrive in the 1980s and early 1990s because of the recession, Japanese competition, recalcitrant American workers, and other factors the organization could not control.

Truth: While these make convenient scapegoats, and while they may well have played a small role in individual situations, they are not the real culprit.

The Japanese are not the problem.

The American worker who is working longer hours for a shrinking paycheck is not the problem.

Moreover, total quality management, benchmarking, reengineering, and information highways will not in and of themselves turn around American industry. These are late-eighties buzz phrases that have already bloomed and faded. Consider IBM, a pioneer in every new fad of the 1980s, heralded by Tom Peters in *Search for Excellence* for its total quality management. Today many industry analysts and stockholders wonder whether IBM will survive the 1990s.

The problem with IBM and many other American companies is inadequate marketing, which we'll show in a moment extends to the very tippy-top of most companies. Many marketers or their bosses (or both) do not yet realize that the world has changed.

Today, almost all consumer markets are mature and fully penetrated at current price levels. Some product categories—detergents, cigarettes, soft drinks, cold cereals, and gasoline, to name five—are so saturated that the market structures exhibit what economists call "monopolistic competition." This apparent oxymoron labels a situation where no one brand dominates, where differentiation is not so much in product performance as in consumer brand perception, and where price competition is intense.

The only real growth comes from population increases, which never exceed 1 to 2 percent a year. To thrive as the marketer of a new or repositioned product or service, a company must either wrest market share away from established brands, entice new users into a category, or find efficiencies in manufacturing or marketing.

Notwithstanding these challenges, we're here to suggest ways astute companies can indeed thrive.

Myth 3: Finance should be the center of the business solar system.

Truth: Or that is what Wall Street hot shots would have you believe. After all, the 1980s was the era of the leveraged buyout, junk bonds, and M&A. Finance is the center because no money, no business. Every other business discipline—research and development, production, marketing and sales, distribution, human resources, information resources—orbits about finance.

During the 1980s, many otherwise intelligent managers *did* believe that financial manipulation was the answer to every challenge. (Corporations do not have problems; they have challenges.) American corporations spent the decade shuffling assets and downsizing. They acquired companies, fought acquisition, and struggled to make themselves indigestible by going private or assuming debt, or both. But finance has had its day. We propose a Copernican shift.

The purpose of a business is to create and keep customers, not to meet quarterly earnings goals, not to grow at a 7 percent compound annual rate. This is not just our idea. Theodore Levitt expressed it as well as it could be said in *The Marketing Imagination:*

> Without customers, no amount of engineering wizardry, clever financing, or operations expertise can keep the company going. To be the low-cost producer of vacuum tubes, to have the best salesmen of what's not wanted or wanted only by the few whose ability to pay won't even pay for the overhead—these can't save you from extinction. To do well what should not be done is to do badly.

Finance is not the center of the business universe; marketing is. As Peter Drucker says, "Because its purpose is to create a customer, the business enterprise has two—and only two—basic functions: marketing and innovation. Marketing and innovation produce results; all the rest are 'costs.'" If the company markets its products or services properly, it will meet quarterly earnings goals and grow at a healthy rate. If it doesn't, financial legerdemain will not generate earnings and growth indefinitely.

Myth 4: CEOs know a great deal about marketing. They've studied it, practiced it, become adept at it.

Truth: Most chief executive officers know little about marketing, and much of what they know is wrong. They subscribe to the myths that this book is out to expose. Most—with certain notable exceptions—do not understand marketing because they have not had to understand it.

While there was a time when manufacturers thought mainly about production, that time is long gone. Business theory in those days was simple: Manufacture a quality product and find people to buy it. In that era, chief executives with production backgrounds tended to dominate.

During the late 1970s and the 1980s, when the corporation's future appeared to depend on the proper manipulation of financial assets, organizations cast about for CEOs with financial proficiency. According to *Business Week*'s 1992 profile of 1000 chief executives, the largest group had finance in their backgrounds. Given their financial backgrounds, many CEOs naturally looked for financial solutions to company predicaments. If all you have is a hammer, every problem looks like a nail. But to survive in the 1990s, corporate chiefs will have to understand marketing.

To learn what top executives do know about marketing, we surveyed 1003 executives of U.S. companies with annual sales of $500,000 or more using a more complex version of the IQ quiz we hope you took at the beginning of this book. To keep the test simple, we employed a team of marketing consultants to develop 50 statements a respondent could answer with "definitely true," "probably true," "don't know," "probably false," or "definitely false." Half the items were correct—the right answer was "definitely true"—the other half were incorrect—the right answer was "definitely false." The statements fell into seven functional areas: marketing strategy, advertising, market segmentation, pricing, distribution, new product/service development, and marketing research.

To score the answers and to produce totals that resemble standard intelligence quotient scores where 100 is average and 160 is genius, we gave a 160 to the CEO who answered "definitely true" when the statement was correct or who answered "definitely false" when the statement was wrong. We gave a 120 to partially correct answers, when the CEO answered "probably true" to a correct statement or "probably false" to an incorrect one. We gave an 80 to don't-know answers, a 40 to mostly incorrect answers, and a 0 to totally incorrect answers.

The executives seemed to take the test seriously. They did not answer definitely true or false indiscriminately, or check "don't know" promiscuously. On the other hand, when they thought they knew the answer, they gave it. Take the statement: "Most pricing decisions are undertaken without any serious, formal research." Almost everyone thought they knew the answer and most were wrong. Only 14.6 percent gave the correct answer, "definitely true." Less than 20 percent of all pricing decisions in America today are based on serious research.

Once we had averaged the 50 scores we had a CEO's Marketing IQ, which could range from 0 (a dummy who got everything precisely wrong) to 160 (someone who knows as much about marketing as the people who wrote the questionnaire). If the average Intelligence Quotient in this country is 100, are American chief executives better than average in their Marketing IQs?

No. The average Marketing IQ of these CEOs is 79. This is a sobering figure when you realize that someone who answered "don't know" to every question would have obtained an 80. Marketing IQ scores did tend to rise with company size; people with greater marketing smarts are running bigger companies. Yet not one executive in our survey had a Marketing IQ above 120.

By now you know your own Marketing IQ.

Myth 5: Most marketing programs work.

Truth: In fact, few people know whether marketing programs work or not. And by "work" we mean not how much the company sells but how much it sells at a profit.

An investment in marketing should be like any other kind of investment. Nonetheless, not 17 marketing managers in America can talk intelligently about their marketing budget's return on investment.

We find this a mystery. Why are there so many professional managers who know far more about their personal investment portfolio's performance than about the investments their companies make in marketing?

Many readers will now pound their desks and mutter, "This isn't true! I know what I get when I spend money on advertising, consumer and trade promotion, sports or event marketing, the sales force, or any other ingredient in the marketing mix!" If you're right, if you do know, you're in the minority.

But *are* you right? Many readers will know something about the relationship between marketing elements—say, consumer promotion—*and sales.* But few people know anything about the marketing investment-to-profitability relationship. It's one of the best-kept secrets in American industry.

A few years ago we did a survey sponsored by the American Marketing Association among CEOs/presidents, marketing directors, and researchers of Fortune 1000 companies. Only a third of the respondents agreed with the statement, "Most marketing programs produce a reasonable return on investment." This was an unexpected revelation in a survey in which we expected considerable self-serving statements that make respondents look smart. This result was as surprising as if we were to find only a third of all physicians agreeing that "contemporary medical practices help people live longer, healthier lives."

Then we started to think about the issue.

Industry will spend more than $140 billion on advertising in the United States in 1993. That's more money than the total gross national product of many of the world's countries. And most of this is spent advertising established products and services.

How much does industry know about the ROI of this investment? No one knows.

We do know from past tests that when big companies increase advertising spending, sales increase less than half the time, and only on about half of these occasions (25 percent of all tests) does the sales increase justify the spending increase. Stated differently, only about 25 percent of the time is an advertising spending increase profitable.

We also know that when marketers change advertising campaigns, they hope or expect to see a sales improvement. Yet for 9 out of 10 campaigns, nothing happens at all.

If changes in advertising spending and changes in advertising copy do not have a positive effect on profitability, one wonders about advertising altogether. Could companies cut back on advertising and pocket the savings? No one knows for sure.

Companies have been doing something about advertising expenditures during the past decade, however. They have been reallocating marketing budgets from advertising to promotion—to consumer and trade promotion (price-cutting), and to sports and event marketing promotions (public relations).

Today approximately 75 percent of marketing dollars go into promotion, a reverse of the budget allocation 20 years ago. If our numbers are correct, that's a national promotion budget of $420 billion.

This must mean something. It must mean that promotion is more profitable than advertising. Not.

The switch from advertising to marketing to promotion does not mean anything at all. Promotion has simply become the MC ("marketing correct") thing to do. Just as debate has been squelched on college campuses because it's not PC ("politically correct"), so debate about promotion has been pushed under the rug in most corporate headquarters because promotion is MC. Indeed the evidence is in and mounting that buyer and trade promotions have a negative effect on profitability. They lower the price of the product, achieve a short-term boost in sales, and weaken the brand's image, and reduce both short- and long-term profits.

Price-off promotion policies have damaged entire industries, including automobiles, coffee, fast food, personal computers, and retailing.

And event marketing and sports promotion programs no more have a known positive effect on profitability than massive doses of vitamin E are a cure for homelessness. Marketers who buy megadoses of event and sports promotion are simply not sure what kind of return, if any, they are getting for their dollars. Again, it's just the MC thing to do.

Okay, you say, marketing does not work all that well for established products and services, but what about new products?

The story here is short and gloomy. Twenty-five years ago, the new product failure rate for packaged goods was approximately 65 percent. Today it's 90 percent. Only 1 in 10 new products will achieve sales and profit objectives—will survive the first two years of life.

Although no one knows the failure rates in other industries for sure, our experience and data suggest that no more than 20 percent of new products succeed in categories as diverse as consumer electronics, computer hardware and software, financial services, medical equipment and supplies, television programs, and Hollywood movies.

In some categories, the failure rate is much higher. In the fast-food restaurant industry, for example, only about 1 in 100 products introduced is regarded as successful. For prescription pharmaceuticals, the success rate may be closer to 1 in 1000. (Admittedly, in this industry when one hits big—Zantac and Prozac being two recent examples—it's like winning the lottery.)

American business, to recap, is experiencing serious problems: real growth in sales, profitability, and productivity have all been slow at best.

The main problem as we see it is that finance has been seen as the center of the business solar system and marketing, like manufacturing, R&D, human resources, and other functional areas, just another planet revolving around it.

The world is changing, however, and so is business. With the change is coming a new vision of what drives productivity and profits. We have labeled this vision *The Marketing Revolution* (HarperBusiness, 1992).

After the revolution, marketing—not finance—will be recognized as the legitimate center of the business solar system, and with this recognition will come the discovery that marketing is not working today as well as it might. The reason for marketing's failures, we argue, is that marketing is based today more on mythology than on science and knowledge.

Our plan in the remaining chapters is to separate the myths from the truths in marketing today. This knowledge should free managers of large and small businesses, goods manufacturers, and service providers from the conventional myths that hamper their marketing programs.

Our goal is better marketing, more profitable businesses, and a stronger America.

"Here at Consolidated Amalgamated we practice management by buzz phrase. Last year we were TQM. This year we're a Virtual Corporation."

2
Myths about Marketing Planning

During the 1970s and the 1980s, we saw a spectacular rise in strategic planning and marketing planning functions in companies throughout the land.

Managers widely accepted the idea that successful marketplace performance rested on a great strategy. They further agreed that a great strategy should begin with a clear knowledge of the problems buyers have in the product category.

Other elements in this process include a look at what the competition is doing, developing partnerships, improving brand equity, and more—not coincidentally, all subjects we cover in the following pages.

As we'll see, these myths are deadly because, when we subject them to empirical analysis, we find them to be false. Or at best only half-true, in which case they are even *more* likely to lead marketers astray.

Let's begin with results.

Myth 6: Short-term marketing results are what's important. Take care of the short term, and the long term will take care of itself.

Truth: During the 1980s, American companies, particularly packaged good companies, increasingly began to evaluate marketing managers based on short-term performance. They frequently asked, "How did we do last quarter?" or even, "How did we do last month?"

Unhappily, a company can measure the effects of product changes, advertising, and distribution strategies only over the long term—typically six months to a year or more. These powerful instruments in the marketing toolbox rarely impact short-term performance. So what can?

Trade and consumer promotions, such as coupons. In essence, giving the product to the retailer or to the consumer (or to both) at a price lower than normal. Doing this produces a one-time sales boost, but at the expense of profitability and brand image. Financial analysts are beginning to discover at the end of a year, or at the end of two years, or at the end of five that, yes, the marketing manager met his or her sales objectives month-to-month or quarter-to-quarter. But the manager did so using tools that were relatively unprofitable and damaged the brand's precious reputation. Consider ground coffee as an example of a category such activities murdered; in the 1960s it was driven by brand imagery, today it's driven by promoting price.

A short-term orientation over the long term turns out to be worthless.

Myth 7: Faster is better in planning.

Truth: For reasons entirely unclear to us, a company will waste years ignoring a marketplace trend—for example, a flagship brand's slowly deteriorating sales. Then, having acknowledged the problem (or challenge), management will decide that the situation needs to be dealt with overnight.

How long is "overnight"? If the business is small, it could mean literally overnight. If the business is a giant corporation, a major brand with a multimillion-dollar advertising, promotion, and sales budget, it could mean three (even six) months. Few major companies can progress from, "What advertising should we run?" to putting a new (and better) campaign on the air in less than three months.

The more important the brand, the longer it takes to do things right. But with a fast-turnaround, time-conscious orientation (perhaps because someone in top management has just attended a seminar on time-based competition), many managers on major brands try to make decisions quickly. Management sets an artificial deadline—"I want to see something happening by the end of June!"—and the hapless marketing manager has to say, "I would rather be wrong on time than right late."

One easy way to speed things up is to cut research altogether and make decisions based on judgment alone. As a result, we see company after company making important marketing decisions in a short period, only to see them reverse the decisions later because of disappointing performance. As a business sage once asked: Why is there no time to do it right, but always time to do it over?

An illustration: As the 1980s came to an end, American Express decided to drop its long-term advertising agency, Ogilvy & Mather, and go with Chiat/Day and a new campaign in a relatively short time from start to finish. The Chiat/Day commercials, in which the American Express card served as an icon, appeared on the air in record time. Two years later, American Express declared the campaign a failure, dumped Chiat/Day, and rehired Ogilvy & Mather.

Myth 8: Because marketing may be defined as "the discipline concerned with solving people's problems with products for a profit," most companies attempt to uncover consumer problems.

Truth: That's the definition, and there's nothing wrong with it. Indeed—and this is one of the more significant lessons of this book—if you understand the consumer's problem (or need), and if you design a product or service that fixes that problem better than anyone else, you address several marketing issues simultaneously.

You have addressed the product design or formulation issue, because your product *is* the problem's solution. You have, in a fashion, addressed the targeting issue, because the targets are those people who have the problem your product solves. You have addressed the positioning issue, because the positioning is what you say or do to differentiate your solution from other solutions to the problem.

Knowing people's problems in any given product category is a great way to start the process, whether you want to manufacture a new razor, open a dry-cleaning establishment, or market a credit card. But it begs the question: Is there some validated, standardized procedure to identify consumer problems? Do marketers have a mechanism the way every physician has a thermometer and every accountant a calculator?

No. As surprising as it may be, most companies do not clearly understand buyer problems in their product category. It may be even more surprising to learn that there is no firmly established procedure to determine consumer problems. Even Procter & Gamble (the corporation to which the above definition is widely attributed) has no validated, standardized procedure to measure the magnitude of people's problems in any P&G category.

This is like saying that the first thing a physician should do when conducting a physical exam is to measure the patient's height, weight, and body temperature, even though there are no tools available to determine height, weight, and body temperature.

True, marketers talk all the time about buyer problems, but the approaches they take for tapping into those problems are almost uniformly without any reliability and validity. They use focus groups, importance ratings, gap analysis, perceptual mapping, and other tools, none of which provides the marketing intelligence that executives need to make sensible decisions.

Indeed, there have been few attempts in the industry to establish procedures for measuring consumer problems. One is the problem-detection technology invented by the advertising agency BBDO. Problem detection, however, as we'll show later, has serious problems of its own when the problems are emotional rather than tangible.

We find it astounding that marketers are (figuratively) taking the consumer's temperature in so many different ways. They are employing so many different contrivances—from focus groups to gap analysis to problem detection and importance ratings—that to think the answers are comparable makes no logical sense.

Not that most companies even bother with these tools. The typical manufacturer looks at what's coming out of its research lab, at what its competition is selling, and at what its salespeople say will sell, and hopes for the best.

Even the rare company that actually begins with the customer and the customer's problems almost never explicitly considers profit when it evaluates a new product or service—and in our experience this is true for companies marketing to consumers as well as those marketing to other businesses. They have a touching faith that if they price the product or service "competitively"—that is, not so high that it drives prospects away—and if it sells at all, it will be profitable.

What about small businesses or entrepreneurs? They're not using sophisticated marketing research tools to identify consumer problems. Folklore has it that they go into business because they've recognized a consumer need through personal experience (wouldn't it be great to have a one-handed pepper mill...or an irresistible fishing lure...or whatever) and created a product or a service to fill it. (They can run into problems, because the need may not be big enough to support a business, or because they don't have the capital necessary to establish the business, or the managerial experience to run a business.)

But that's folklore. We think that most small business ventures got started, not because the founders saw a strong consumer need, but because they had some longstanding personal interest. The man whose hobby is making picture frames for his wife and friends decides he's going to give up his job as an engineer to go into the framing business. The restaurant manager, who knows nothing except how to run a restaurant, scrapes together the money from friends and family to open a Mexican bistro in Concord, Massachusetts. We'd like to think that people are sitting around worrying about the needs of their customers, but somehow we don't think so.

The most successful products are those that address real buyer problems, either with the product itself, or with advertising, or with both.

In the 1960s, as one example, many housewives were disappointed when they brought bananas home, peeled them, and discovered brown spots. One of the period's most successful advertising campaigns was for Chiquita Bananas, which talked about the care it took in packaging, which meant no bruises. A problem solved, a fortune made.

In the 1970s, one of the most widely acclaimed advertising efforts was Burger King's "Have It Your Way" campaign ("Hold the pickles, hold the lettuce, special orders don't upset us"). This talked to people who were tired of going into a fast-food restaurant like McDonald's and getting the same sandwich prepared and served the same way. Burger King permitted customers to order hamburgers any way they wanted—perhaps not the largest step forward in Western civilization, but it helped Burger King to achieve record sales and profits.

In the 1980s, Compaq computers addressed the buyer's need for higher levels of performance and more features in a personal computer. Compaq enjoyed a meteoric rise to become one of the dominant players in the industry.

In the 1990s we see Gillette's brilliant Sensor Razor addressing the problem many men have with nicks and cuts when they shave.

We're waiting for marketers to develop products to solve those problems that both personal observation and quantitative research show exist. Where, for example, is the movie theater for adults only, no noisy kids allowed? Where's the dog food that smells good? Where's the VCR that programs itself? Where's the PC that's easier to use than a Macintosh? Where's the microwavable product with the indicator that tells you when the meal is cooked? Where's the airline that carries the First Class passenger's suit bag and attaché case from curb to plane? Where's the....But you get the idea.

Myth 9: Small or entrepreneurial businesses don't need to follow a disciplined approach to understand the market.

Truth: The idea here is that large corporations, because they are often cumbersome, because they cover so much territory, and because they have the necessary resources, are able to impose a very rigorous and disciplined approach on the marketing process.

A small business—whether a $1 million restaurant or a $50 million scientific instrument manufacturer—does not have the time, money, knowledge, capability, access to resources, or desire to do studies to decide how to market the business, introduce a new product, open a new store, or whatever. The small business, so goes the argument, understands its market so well that it simply *knows* what to do.

The question: Is there something about size of organization that mitigates the need to take a more vigorous and disciplined approach to marketing research? The myth says there is. The myth says that smaller businesses don't need to take such an approach.

We argue that *every* business needs to take a disciplined approach to marketing.

New businesses fail far faster than established businesses. According to Dun & Bradstreet, approximately 60 percent of all new businesses fail within the first five years of their founding, a rate that rose during the late 1980s and early 1990s as the excesses of the decade and recession took their toll. This suggests an analogy between new business failures and new product failures: Either people are creating a lot of lousy new products and new businesses, *or* the approach to marketing them needs an overhaul.

We're in the camp that says business people are not bombarding the world with bad ideas. There are some bad new product and new business ideas, but most marketing failures are due not to crummy ideas but to weak marketing plans and poor implementation.

A new business, a small business, may not require the same degree of rigor and discipline a giant corporation requires. But if you're going to grow your business, you need to be following the same practices. What are they?

Assessing the environment. Narrowing and understanding your target market. Finding your proper positioning. Doing a competitive analysis and developing pricing, products, and merchandising—whatever. If you're a manufacturer, follow the preceding steps adapted for manufacturing. Continuously monitor your customers. Find out if they're happy, if they're satisfied.

Those are all things a business can do very inexpensively. Customers come through the store; ask them questions. Manufacturers have access to customer names; call them up. These are things a business can do all the time.

There may once have been a time when starting a successful small business was easy. If you were the only shoe store in town...if you were the only hardware store...if you were the first video store, it was relatively easy. But today, with a restaurant on every corner, with five shoe stores in the mall, with three video stores along Main Street, it's very difficult.

You have to be a marketer to survive. And if you don't want to take marketing seriously, don't waste your money on the business. You'll fail unless you have a brilliant concept.

One problem small business owners say they have is time. They tell us: "I don't have time to do the things you're talking about. I've got to run the business. I've got to make sales. I've got to deal with the employees. I've got to be putting out fires."

That's like saying, "I can't spare the time for a time management course." It's like saying, "I just had a heart attack, so I can't exercise." A comment like that usually predicts a business that's going to fail.

Every successful business we know takes time to work on market development. At the simplest level, market development means continuously improving your product, your service. One simple example is the local dry cleaner. These are increasingly installing computerized systems that tell them, say, that a customer wants his shirts lightly starched and on hangers. They have a computer-based accounting of everything each customer drops off, and, unlike the old system, they are unlikely ever to lose your shirts. The computer is a way to upgrade the service that brings about a more successful business.

But how many businesses have not improved themselves and died! Did this have to happen? No. But businesses will waste away unless they change and follow a disciplined approach to understanding their market.

Myth 10: One good way to spot marketing opportunities is to see what the competition is doing.

Truth: Why this assumption among executives that competitors know what they're doing? It seems to say that while we may be lost, our competition knows the way—an idea that grows more powerful when the competitor is big.

Compaq Computer's strategy was to match IBM's prices but with more innovative personal computers. That worked for a while, but in time a number of companies began selling PCs direct to customers, offering impressive service and support programs, and doing it at prices markedly below Compaq's. As Gary Stimac, who heads Compaq's systems division, told *Fortune* magazine, "We created a pricing umbrella that allowed all the clone makers to thrive. And when IBM lost touch with the pricing realities of the marketplace, we walked off the cliff with them."

Cautionary fable. Once upon a time, General Foods developed what amounted to chocolate-flavored Kool-Aid. The product developed tremendous momentum within the company, even though consumers were not overwhelmingly positive toward a watery chocolate drink. Discounting their research and hoping for the best, the company went ahead and introduced the product into three test markets.

Meanwhile Nestlé, working independently, had developed its own watery chocolate drink and had beaten General Foods into market test by a few months. When the Nestlé management saw the GF entry, it said, in effect, "We must be on to something! General Foods wouldn't go into test market if they didn't think the product had promise. We'll cut our own test short, go national, and position ourselves as the market leader."

Which is what Nestlé did, thereby managing to lose much more money than it would have lost if it had completed—and believed—its own test market research.

Knowing what one's competitors are doing, *and how successfully they're doing it,* is important marketing intelligence. But one ingredient does not a successful chocolate drink make.

Myth 11: Partnership marketing is a surefire way to increase profitability.

Truth: Partnership marketing—developing intimate relationships between a business and its customers, sometimes called "relationship marketing"—is no more a surefire way to build profitability than marriage is a surefire way to achieve personal happiness.

Unquestionably, there are some circumstances in which partnership marketing works. When the two partners are approximately equal in size and strength. When both partners have a corporate culture that fosters cooperative rather than adversarial relationships. When the power relationship is fairly equal, even though sales may not be. Indeed, the partnership works when, as one definition puts it, both parties see it as a strategic collaboration involving the commitment of assets and management resources, with the objective of enhancing the partner's competitive positions.

For example, Whirlpool Corporation built Sears Roebuck's Kenmore brand washers, dryers, and refrigerators for years. While the Sears business represented a large share of Whirlpool's total sales (at one time more than half), Sears could not dictate terms to Whirlpool because it could not have replaced Whirlpool with another supplier; the volume was just too big. Sears needed Whirlpool; Whirlpool needed Sears, and the partnership worked well for decades.

Does it always work? Obviously not. Wal-Mart made news not long ago by demanding more marketing information from suppliers than any retailer had demanded in the past. Wal-Mart needs, say, Procter & Gamble to complete its menu of health and beauty aid products. P&G, on the other hand, has an absolute need for Wal-Mart, because the retailer accounts for a significant portion of its sales. To the extent that P&G does not have an alternative to Wal-Mart, and to the extent that a Wal-Mart does not have an alternative to P&G, one would argue that theirs should be a happy relationship.

On the other hand, looking at it from an outsider's prospective, P&G has a greater need for Wal-Mart than Wal-Mart has for P&G. Why? Because few consumers who buy Pampers diapers or Tide detergent or Crest toothpaste or Bounty paper towels in Wal-Mart would travel to another store to find them if Wal-Mart discontinued distribution, because brand loyalty in those categories is not particularly high. Because few consumers are intensely loyal to brands in these categories, one can imagine a dissatisfied Wal-Mart turning to a P&G competitor (or establishing its own brands), making the competitor a better deal, and selling more of their product than P&G's.

Partnership marketing clearly has the potential to help companies become more profitable. The 1990 General Electric annual report held out the promise of such an arrangement:

> In a boundary-less company, suppliers aren't "outsiders." They are drawn closer and become trusted partners in the total business process. Customers are seen for what they are—the lifeblood of a company. Customers' vision of their needs and the company's view become identical, and every effort of every man and woman in the company is focused on satisfying those needs. In a boundary-less company, internal functions begin to blur. Engineering doesn't design a product and then "hand it off" to manufacturing. They form a team, along with marketing and sales, finance, and the rest. Customer service? It's not somebody's job. It's everybody's job.

In practice, lamentably, many companies abuse their "partners," just as in many marriages one spouse abuses the other. Particularly, if the benefits are unequal, one partner is likely to abuse the other. It is therefore a myth that a partnership automatically builds profitability. In good partnerships, just as in happy marriages, both partners have to give a lot to get something back in return.

Myth 12: In the coming decade, marketers will derive more profit from new products than from existing brands.

Truth: Believing this, companies believe they should devote a disproportionate chunk of the marketing budget to new products and to marketing them. They believe they can ignore their established products because they seem to hum along by themselves.

The myth implies that established-brand advertising is a waste, that a company should concentrate on new brands.

In truth, advertising for established brands often pays off in profitability even when it doesn't immediately increase unit sales. It reinforces a brand's differential status from competitors and reinforces many past and present satisfied users in their "existing favorable opinion of the product," in the words of Leo Bogart in *Strategy in Advertising*. "They must be given reasons and arguments to support what might otherwise be no more than an emotional tone of relatively low charge."

In any event, a company must make continuing efforts to maintain an established product's position in the marketplace—if the product's still there, it must have "made it," and it needs ad support to stay there.

Edgar Bronfman, Jr., the chief operating officer of Seagram Co. Ltd., told *Fortune* magazine not long ago:

> The general rule for marketers in the U.S. is that nobody needs anything more. This isn't the 1950s or '60s, when there was technical innovation. Now even when there *is* innovation, the next manufacturer catches up in one or two months. Succeeding is more and more an issue of marketing—having a more relevant proposition targeted more directly than your competitor. Absolut Vodka is a perfect example. It's not our product, but I wish it were. It's an incredible brand that's growing like crazy in a declining market. Absolut filled a void—the Chevas Regal of vodka.

The rule is that the difficulty and cost of gaining and adding new customers for a new product is usually much greater than the difficulty and cost of maintaining—perhaps even increasing—sales for an established franchise.

We are not discounting the importance of new products. Where you have the breakthrough new product in terms of advertising or product positioning or—preferably—both, you should introduce that product. But in most product categories, more than 90 percent of the sales and profits come from existing brands.

Simply thinking that the company must introduce one new product after another where there aren't clear consumer needs, where there isn't a clear positioning, where there isn't unambiguous product differentiation, doesn't make sense. The company could spend less money to mend the established product than what it would spend on a new product.

Unfortunately, we've now wandered into the area of baby boomer psychology and company culture. In most companies, working on a new product is glamorous; it's exciting; it's interesting. It's a lot more fun than cultivating a brand that's been around for 5...12...37 years. It's the same attitude that causes companies to spend more money acquiring new customers than trying to maintain their existing customers.

This attitude is another symptom of death-wish marketing (see Myth 29).

Myth 13: Brand equity is a marvelous new concept that every strategic plan should adopt.

Truth: "Brand Equity continues to be a `hot button' for the 1990s, and rightly so," enthused a recent announcement at an American Marketing Association conference that broke all AMA attendance records. "With increasing trade concentration, greater penetration of private label brands around the world, scanner-based measurement systems fostering short-term promotional activity at the expense of franchise-building advertising...it's about time we focused on...Brand Equity."

David Aaker, a professor at the University of California at Berkeley and author of *Managing Brand Equity*, illustrates brand equity's strength with the following story.

A colleague had placed three jars of peanut butter in front of subjects who had never tasted any one of the three brands. In blind tests, one of these—an obscure brand—usually won 70 to 80 percent of the votes as having the best taste; the two others consistently did not do as well.

Aaker's was not a blind test, however. His subjects could see the brand names, one of which—one of the less tasty—had a familiar popular brand name. The researcher asked the subjects to taste each of the three peanut butters and to select the one they liked best.

Aaker writes that these subjects chose the less tasty but recognizable brand over the other two by a 73 percent margin. Aaker feels that's a mind-boggling result, but it's one we've seen replicated with other products. When Armstrong tested a line of floor tiles against competitors' comparable products, for example, revealing the Armstrong name resulted in customer preference improving from 50 to 90 percent.

Most consumers assume (in the absence of clear and contradictory information) that if a brand is well known it tastes better, lasts longer, or is better made than an unknown, and if that were what brand equity meant to everyone that would end the discussion.

The trouble is that "brand equity" has no consistent meaning. Originally it was a financial concept, the goodwill a brand commanded and for which consumers (and investors) would pay extra. But the idea expanded until it became a pudding of all the assets a brand musters. In general it means that people have positive feelings toward the product.

The articles on the topic describe brand equity as if it had some common meaning on which everybody agrees, when in fact it has diverse meanings about which no one agrees. Ask several physicians, for example, to define quadruple bypass, melanoma, cesarean section, or trauma surgery, and they'll give you similar answers. Most medical terms have standard definitions that licensed physicians are required to learn. "Brand equity" has no such standard definition, and therefore practitioners invent meanings as they go along. Aaker has listed some: "name awareness," "loyal customers," "strong associations," and "perceived quality." Michael Amoroso, who heads his own marketing research firm, and Arthur Kover, a marketing professor at Fordham University, point out in a recent *Marketing News* article that brand equity also includes brand personality, brand bonding, user imagery, value, strength of feeling, and more. "So much more that the search for brand equity sometimes feels like whacking at a piñata. It is blind; it is hit or miss. When you do hit, you don't know if you want what showers down."

Finally, no one is sure how to measure it. Brand equity is a nice idea until you have to use it or act on it. Unless it acquires some consistent and useful meaning soon, it will pass quietly out of a marketer's working vocabulary.

Myth 14: "High" versus "low" involvement are useful terms to describe product categories.

Truth: Planners are fond of using "high" and "low" involvement to describe different product categories. High-involvement products require very different strategies than low. The idea is that "involvement" is a product characteristic, that at one extreme—paper towels, chewing gum, toothpaste—consumers pay almost no attention to what they are buying, while at the other—houses, video cameras, automobiles—consumers devote a great deal of time and attention to the purchase. So all high-involvement categories call for advertising that communicates a great deal of information about the product, while low-involvement categories need only constant reminders that the brand exists. Not surprisingly, firms use 30-second and even 60-second commercials and print campaigns for the former, and 15-second, even 5-second, spots for the latter.

In fact, involvement is a characteristic of *consumers,* not of products. Some people will spend almost as much time weighing the merits of different paper towel brands as other people spend choosing a new car. Consider the following:

Individual consumer involvement	So-Called Product Category Involvement		
	Low (e.g., toothpaste)	Average (e.g., new suit)	High (e.g., automobile)
Low	64%	34%	21%
Average	23%	45%	37%
High	13%	21%	42%

This table suggests that indeed, in a so-called low-involvement category such as toothpaste, 64 percent of the population are low in terms of purchase involvement. They're not particularly interested in toothpaste. They don't pay attention to differences between brands. They spend little time in the supermarket or a health and beauty aids emporium shopping for different brands.

In contrast, as much as 13 percent of the population are highly, one might argue almost neurotically, concerned about a toothpaste brand. This suggests that a low-involvement strategy may work very well for 6 out of 10 people in the category, but that there's a niche of high-involvement consumers who would respond to an entirely different toothpaste strategy.

At the opposite end of the continuum, take automobiles. Historically, academics and commercial researchers have regarded automobiles as a high-involvement category. The fact is, however, that only about 4 consumers in 10 exhibit high-involvement characteristics, and 2 out of 10 seem to buy automobiles with the same impulsiveness or lack of concern as others buy toothpaste. This suggests that the automobile category, like high-involvement categories in general, has different segments, people who respond very differently to different marketing strategies.

It's important for a marketer to know the relative distribution of low-, average-, and high-involvement customers in the product category, to decide which type of customer the firm wants to target, and then to develop a strategy based on that decision.

Myth 15: In most product categories, any brand that succeeds in getting placed on shelves will generate a good return on sales.

Truth: This myth is like saying in other words that, following the well-known law of physics, D equals S, where D is distribution and S is success.

For consumer packaged goods, just 12.8 percent of all supermarkets in the country accounted for more than half (53.4 percent) of all grocery sales in 1992, according to *Progressive Grocer* magazine. Many marketing executives believe that if those stores accept and carry their products, they've got it made.

The myth seems to assume that most consumers engage in high-involvement behavior most of the time. The basic model here is that Lisa wheels her cart down the supermarket aisles, stopping at every product category in which she's interested, picking up every different product she might consider, carefully examining the labels, processing their contents, calculating a price/value relationship, and making a decision.

This model says that in essence Lisa has a multiple regression equation in her head that helps her to make buying decisions. When she makes a decision and drops the item into her cart, she moves 10 more feet down the aisle to the next section and goes through the same process.

Of course if Lisa did this, the shopping experience would require a change of clothes. She would spend more time filling her shopping cart than John the Baptist spent in the desert. This simply doesn't happen.

Shoppers move through supermarkets, discount chains, pharmacies, and even malls with the speed of summer lightning. They reach out and grab the products they want far more quickly than one would think.

It is far more likely that prospects will ignore or overlook a new brand on the shelf than buy it. Lee Weinblatt, head of The PreTesting Company, Tenafly, NJ, has done extensive work with hidden cameras to learn how consumers actually behave in the supermarket. Putting tiny cameras in fake boxes on the shelves, Weinblatt has recorded the way real people behave in real stores. In one supermarket study, the cameras recorded shopper reaction to a promotion that offered a free box of plastic freezer bags—all the consumer had to do was pull a coupon from a dispenser for the product.

"It took two and a half days before someone just *looked* at the display," says Weinblatt. "We have it on tape, with time-and-date stamps. Nobody *noticed.*" Weinblatt adds that his tests in stores show that many shoppers fail to notice changes in product packaging. "We found that strictly relying on the box itself, in 9 out of 10 cases is an absolute waste. That's what goes wrong in a focus group. Everyone sits around a table, you come out and say, `Here's a new Diet Coke,' and ask, `What do you think?' But who says, when shoppers are rushing down an aisle, that they'll even *look* at the Diet Coke?"

Myth 16: The way to develop a strategy to invigorate a brand is to begin with an analysis of where the product falls in the product life cycle.

Truth: It is true that many strategic planners and management consultants develop brand strategies depending on where they believe the product is in its life cycle. The implication is that the product life cycle, like the human life cycle, has a natural beginning, middle, and end.

But where would one put the following brands and products on a product life-cycle curve?

Kodak cameras

Del Monte canned fruit

Wrigley's chewing gum

Nabisco crackers

Gillette razors

Coca-Cola soft drinks

Ivory soap

Campbell soup

Colgate toothpaste

They were all the leading brands in their product categories in 1923 and they are all the leading brands today—except Colgate toothpaste, which has slipped to second place over the last 70 years.

Although we can always identify any given product's birth, it is not so easy to determine middle age or senility. Some products have a life cycle of about three years and others have life cycles that exceed a century. What is the life cycle of chewing gum? The electric refrigerator? The videocassette recorder? The cigarette?

Associated with the product life-cycle concept are the recipes and standardized ingredients—much like a liturgical sequence—specifying "what needs to be done" to reach full, mature product success and eventual decline. The authorities usually agree that, depending upon the product and strategy, a company should use heavy advertising and penetration, premium, or skimming pricing policies, and should search for the most efficient and effective distribution system for the life cycle's "youth" or growth stages. Then, in maturity, the company can cut back the advertising, pare the prices, and maximize profits.

But the product life cycle is really nothing more than a generalized, conceptual planning device. The standardized tactical/strategic moves ordained at each level do not fit every product category or product.

How do you know what stage of "the life cycle" you're in? You can guess or analyze historical sales data, but neither approach is likely to yield a gold prize.

As Leo Bogart states in *Strategy in Advertising*, "The homilies about...objectives and expenditures [at different life-cycle states] may be counterproductive." A clever and powerful ad campaign may "give an ancient and enfeebled brand a new injection of youthful vitality." Campbell Soup and its agency BBDO once ran a campaign for the heavier soups in the Campbell canned soup line (some of which had been around for 50 years) called "The Manhandlers." Soup sales, which had been declining for years, stabilized, then began to rise. We call that "producing sex after death."

The product life cycle, akin to the family life cycle, is a useful conceptual tool for, perhaps, broadly outlining and attempting to anticipate market development. But it certainly does not provide the exact recipe and correct ingredients to magically "invigorate" a product.

With human beings, we know that they live on average to be 77 and that old age begins at approximately 65, so it makes sense to talk about the Seven Ages of Man. It might be useful to talk about a product's life cycle, but if you don't know whether you're gauging the life of a mosquito, a human being, or a whale, it's very difficult to do anything with the concept.

Myth 17: The faster technology changes, the more valuable the brand name.

Truth: After all, purchasing agents didn't get fired for buying IBM. With a rapidly changing field like computers, a company can count on the big, successful corporation. It can count on the prestigious brand name, on the market leader. It can trust them.

On the other hand, in high-technology categories such as personal computers, the technology is changing so fast that brand name is becoming less important. Product differences seem to be diminishing, and people are perceiving the product as simply a box.

As the product evolves, prospects ask: What box can I get with the most features per dollar? And: Who cares who makes that box? Even though Apple may make an absolutely wonderful box for the dollar in 1993, there's no guarantee that Wally Wood Computer, which does not exist in 1993, may not be making the best box for the dollar in 1996.

Dell Computer did not exist until 1984, a time when IBM was the biggest force and Wang a dominant player. Today IBM and Wang are suffering, as are Digital Equipment, Prime, and Data General. IBM's focus on mainframes didn't keep up with the strong trend toward networking PCs, and in the PC category, IBM just wasn't smart enough, or fast enough. As technology changes rapidly, customers value the new products more than the brand name.

Kodak, to cite a different example, has been a terrific brand name in the photography industry—a business based since the mid-nineteenth century on chemistry. But Kodak may not be a major player in the twenty-first century—its brand name may become as extinct as Tyrannosaurus rex—unless it adapts quickly to the next generation of picture-taking using electronic imaging.

In product categories like toothpaste or detergent or even automobiles, on the other hand, categories in which the technology is not changing as rapidly, one can count on a preferred brand or market leader to be reasonably successful from decade to decade.

Myth 18: Most marketing plans are adequate blueprints for success.

Truth: They're not, and here's what's wrong with them.

We look at many marketing plans in our work. This table provides a rough estimate of what we find in them.

What's In/What's Out of the Typical Marketing Plan

Factors	Prevalence in marketing plans	In-depth coverage, if included	Probability of success, if missing
Demographics	90%	50%	40%
Market share/sales	90%	80%	10%
Competitive analysis	90%	90%	50%
Consumer desires/needs/problems	80%	40%	80%
Consumer lifestyles/values	20%	10%	70%
Political/economic factors	10%	20%	25%

In other words, virtually every marketing plan we see includes demographics, market share, and competitive analysis (the 90 percent in the "prevalence" column).

Almost as many plans, 80 percent, include a discussion of consumer desires, needs, or problems, although companies often measure these in bizarre ways, as we discuss in Chapter 9, Myths about Positioning.

Very few, however, consider consumer lifestyles and values, or political/economic factors.

Moving on to the next column of figures, among plans that *do* include demographics, about half give the topic in-depth coverage, but we estimate that 40 percent of the time it would not be a serious omission if demographics were missing (the last column). In many product categories the consumer demographics are obvious, and brand profiles are strikingly similar.

On the other hand, we believe an analysis of consumer desires/needs/problems and lifestyles/values is critical to a marketing plan's success. Yet among the plans we see that consider these issues at all, only about 32 percent (80% × 40%) give adequate coverage to desires/problems and only about 2 percent to lifestyles/values.

The "Probability of success, if missing" column reflects our judgment as to how serious the omission can be. Factors vary in seriousness. If a car is missing a backseat, that's a problem, but it's not serious. If a car is missing a steering wheel, that's a very serious problem and the probability of success is low.

Similarly, if the marketing plan is missing the political factors, that's a problem, but in many industries it's probably not critical. (On the other hand, if your company is in the defense or health care industries, it might be crucial.)

If the plan does not consider consumer desires/needs/problems or lifestyles/values in depth, that is a problem and it is serious. Unless a marketer knows a great deal about the needs, desires, problems, lifestyles, and values of the company's customers and prospects, it's difficult to conceive of a successful marketing strategy at all.

Myth 19: Market share determines profitability; firms should always strive for market leadership.

Truth: From the late 1970s through the 1980s, a Harvard Business School discovery changed the way many companies did business. The "discovery" was a strong positive correlation between market share and profitability across a broad range of industries, companies, and business units. Market leaders, this research found, enjoy rates of return that are three times greater than those of businesses with a market rank of 5 or less.

This view came with the imprimatur of academic respectability. After all, the PIMS (Profit Impact of Market Strategy) program—a database of 450 companies and more than 3000 business units that was loosely connected to the Harvard Business School—had first brought this relationship to the attention of general management. Moreover, the Boston Consulting Group (BCG) had transformed this "discovery" into their (now) well-known "experience curve," promoting its virtues around the globe. As a result of this discovery, its dissemination and deployment, companies began an almost mindless pursuit of market share. Big meant better in everything.

One particularly odious implication—a spin-off of the experience curve—is that a company could "buy" market share. Big discounts, for example, or heavy trade promotion could artificially create market share dominance, which in turn, it was argued, would yield the economies of scale essential to a high ROI.

Today planners are not so sure about anything concerning market share and profitability. There is no disagreement that it is positive, but there is plenty of debate concerning the magnitude of the relationship and what it means.

What seems to have happened is that proponents of the share-equals-profits connection, both consultants and corporate strategists, appear to have read the headlines but not absorbed the whole story. Bob Buzzell and Brad Gale, in their wonderful 1985 book *The PIMS Principles,* point out that "this evidence that the [share/profit] relationship exists, does not, however tell us *why* there is a link between market share and profitability. There are at least four possible reasons: economies of scale, risk aversion by customers, market power, and a common underlying factor." What could this mysterious underlying factor be?

More recent evidence suggests that the relationship between share and ROI is much weaker than was previously discovered, *if* you remove from the analysis common contaminants of both share and profitability. "Perceived Product Quality," for example, is a dimension correlated with both share and ROI. If you ask the question "What is the relationship between ROI and share, holding product quality constant?," you substantially reduce the original bivariate share-profitability correlation.

Thus, one mysterious underlying factor is product quality. Because it is related to both market share and profitability, ignoring it in any share/profitability analysis (which researchers did for years) inflates the apparent correlation.

Other common underlying factors that have been suggested are market differentiation, management expertise, competitive stupidity, and just plain luck.

Then there's a new school of thought which argues that if whatever is left of the share-profit correlation is causal, then the causality is the reverse of what has been argued for almost two decades. The more profitable companies, this hypothesis runs, can afford to make the investment to build share dominance.

This is not an illogical (nor an untestable) proposition. So the debate goes on, but our myth, you'll recall, was that market share dominance inevitably leads to greater profitability, therefore market share is king.

Certainly, we've seen many industries in which companies have chased market share more vigorously than corporate profitability. Witness the heavy emphasis on promotional programs among food products, automobiles, airlines, and health products. As we will discuss in Chapter 14, promotion can drive market share, but with a concomitant loss of profit.

To illustrate our point, here is Roger Enrico, the chief executive officer of PepsiCo Worldwide Foods speaking to *Fortune* magazine about an industry dear to his heart:

> The soft drink industry in the 1980s tended toward the mindless pursuit of market share. Managing share without profit is like breathing air without oxygen. It feels okay for a while, but in the end it kills you. So in the nineties you'll see a greater emphasis on operational excellence and cost control. We're telling every employee, "Yes, market share is important, but only as a measurement of the sustainability of the profit stream." In 1992 we may still be No. 2 to Coke in U.S. volume, but we expect to be No. 1 in share of domestic industry profit.

Market share is neither king nor queen. It may even be the court jester. At best it's a rough proxy for ROI; at worst, it's an alluring attraction on the road to decline. Most important, be careful not to confuse it with the real thing: return-on-investment.

Myth 20: Effective marketing plans should be based on the premise of continuous year-to-year improvement—what the Japanese call *kaizen*.

Truth: Maybe, but only after you throw out last year's plan and adopt a clean-slate approach.

"Clean-slate marketing" is our analogy to zero-base budgeting. The marketer assumes nothing about the environment or the consumer. It is as though the company and the product were starting fresh. Clean-slate marketing asks about everything: "Why are we doing this? Should it be done at all? How do we know? Should it be done differently? What's changed since we started? What's different?"

Clean-slate marketing demands that a manager demonstrate the profit-directed thinking that went into every marketing decision: targeting, positioning, product design, pricing, budgeting, everything.

Only with clean-slate marketing can an organization avoid slipping into a rut and mindlessly repeating the mistakes of the past.

"Based on my P&G experience, if we run a `Buy One—Get One Free' event for our new line of cars, we'll really move the needle!"

3

Myths about Marketing Department Organization

What's the best way to organize the marketing department (or, with a smaller organization, the marketing function)?

Asking the question that way assumes that a best way to organize the department exists at all—an assumption we reject. In our experience, a new CEO or marketing director comes into the company and the first thing he or she wants to do is to reorganize on the basis of some new, improved vision of how the whole thing should work. We also know that when a management consulting firm comes through, whether it be McKinsey or Booz Allen, no more than about 22 nanoseconds pass before its consultants conclude that the department needs to be reorganized.

We have clients who seem to spend 90 percent of their time working on reorganizations, while marketing plans and their execution are in a state of quasi-limbo as people change offices, titles, and responsibilities, export functions, rewrite job descriptions, and basically try to figure out what they should be doing. Depending on the corporation's condition—and Citibank, General Motors, American Express, and IBM are notorious examples of this syndrome—all this activity is akin to shifting deck chairs on the Titanic.

Perhaps our first myth should be the one that says it's important to reorganize the marketing department (if not the entire company) every three years. But perhaps not. There is nothing intrinsically wrong with reorganizing the department in response to changes in the marketplace. But it is wrong if it distracts management and employees from the real job and doesn't contribute to marketing productivity. We wish that marketing directors and management consultants would spend as much time thinking about improving the process and execution of marketing programs directed to prospects and customers and the company's products and services as they do reorganization. If they did, marketing would not be in the sorry state it is today.

So rather than talk about the myth of department reorganization, let's stop in one of the offices along the corridor, where the brand manager is at this very moment planning this year's marketing campaign based on the following myth.

Myth 21: The important thing is to get the marketing program launched now rather than build consensus.

Truth: That may be the attitude of certain corporate cowboys, those from the David Glasgow Farragut School of Business.* These are the suits who believe it is possible to ignore what's going on internally because once the marketing program is out in the world, everyone will see what a success it is.

They believe that building consensus within the organization before the marketing program's launch is not important. What is important is to get it into the real world, and consensus will follow.

The truth is, of course, that if you can't sell the marketing program internally, you can't get it into the world in the first place. Since a marketing manager or a brand manager develops the marketing program, the more help, cooperation, or input he or she receives from the strategic planning group, marketing research, senior marketing management, financial management, and senior management, the more likely it is that the plan will be a success. Everyone is working to see that it happens.

On the other hand (and this seems so obvious from the outside that we're always startled when we come across it in our consulting work), if the marketing manager develops a plan with minimal input from others in the organization, the plan is much less likely to be successful. This is akin to a platoon leader plotting an incursion beyond enemy lines that doesn't call for air or artillery support.

True, marketing managers cannot go ahead without *any* support from the organization, but certain enthusiasts do try to go ahead with minimal support. The attitude, we think, connects to the last myth in this section. It's the conviction that "I know I'm right...I know it's dif-

*Farragut of course is best known for his order at the Battle of Mobile Bay: "Damn the torpedoes—full speed ahead!"

ferent…I've got a brilliant idea…just let me execute it." Some cowboys do remain in American business, but remember that in the Wild West, most cowboys died without distinction.

Myth 22: We don't need a corporate marketing and research staff when we can push the marketing function down in the organization.

Truth: This is a volatile myth that changes from one period to the next, as fads in organizational behavior come and go. In a couple of years—perhaps by the time this book reaches your hands—the myth will have taken a 180° turn and will be saying that organizations should centralize the marketing function.

The reality, unfortunately for those who like simple truths, is that the marketing function can be complicated. Since strategic planning in the marketing function cuts across different business units, it should be organized at the highest level of the corporation and should serve as a strategic planning and consulting organization to all of the firm's divisions. (This advice works better when an organization has several divisions than otherwise.)

At General Foods, 20 years ago, all of the marketing people working on Maxwell House coffee could count on the fact that they had a large marketing research/strategic planning staff in a central location that could help them to address individual issues that might arise. This staff also worked to ensure continuity in the company's marketing and advertising.

In the late 1980s and early 1990s, as more and more companies tried to streamline operations (i.e., cut costs), they went through these large, centralized marketing/strategic planning staffs like a combine through a wheat field, and pushed the marketing function down onto the strategic business units level. On the theory that those closest to the customer known the market best—true, as far as it goes—each division, each unit, each brand is ultimately responsible for its own marketing.

In time, these corporations will discover that this structure too has flaws. No individual brand, unit, or division has the budget, insight, vision, or the time the corporate marketing staffs of the 1970s had for the company as a whole. As the marketing director of a $120 million SBU of a corporation selling business products recently remarked to us, "I'm not sure what I'm supposed to do. All I have is about 15 minutes a week to spend on marketing planning, with no help from anyone else in the organization. Everything has been passed down to my level."

Not long ago we had a personal experience with the consequences of decentralization and staff reductions. A multimillion-dollar marketing organization's marketing director asked us to investigate the relationship between the company's advertising investment and sales. In essence, he was asking a very smart question: What is the optimal advertising spending level?

To help our client address that question, we asked for information. We wanted advertising spending by brand, by media type, by quarter, over a five-year period. We wanted sales data—actual figures for the company, estimates for the competition—by brand, by product type, by quarter, over a five-year period. We wanted to know about new product introductions, price changes, and the whole nine yards on competitive activity, all the information that would help to answer the question.

We were amazed to learn, about a week after our request, that none of this information was available. A year earlier, the company had dissolved its five-person competitive information unit; no one since had gathered the figures. We then asked for the historical data, the figures the competitive information unit had accumulated before it went away. The company couldn't give us that either, because unfortunately, when it shut down the business unit, the files and resources had just disappeared into some corporate black hole. Our contact explained, "They're in storage, somewhere."

In a decentralized organization, some of the efforts of the strategic business units cannot be the same as the overall company's efforts. The company will be like the knight who leaped onto his horse and rode off in all directions. In time (one hopes) management will learn that marketing success requires both centralized and decentralized organization. But most importantly, it takes better marketers.

Whether the marketing is organized at the corporate level or the individual SBU level does not make much difference to the organization's success, if the company is pursuing death-wish marketing. It does not make much difference how the department is organized, if the people in the department don't know what they're doing. The company can organize the department 50 different ways and the end effect will be about the same.

We do believe a company needs some combination of both corporate and, for lack of a better phrase, individual brand marketing. The organization does need to push marketing responsibility down to the individual brand level, because otherwise it may lose touch with a particular brand's situation. But if it pushes the entire responsibility down, the individual units do not, by definition, have the resources to look at the entire market. (Nor, in our experience, is the marketing director of one SBU much interested in another SBU marketing director's challenges and opportunities.)

Some readers will argue that what we're proposing may be more expensive than either a central or decentralized marketing system. Functions, titles, budgets may overlap.

That may be true, but if (as we anticipate) this new vision replaces death-wish marketing with intelligent, effective marketing, the company's surplus productivity should more than offset any increased expense.

Myth 23: It is important to promote brand managers quickly, because otherwise the company will lose them.

Truth: One of our observations over the years (perhaps less frequent during the last few recession years than during the 1980s) has been that the average tenure of a brand product manager is approximately 20 months. How common is the tendency to move on? For about half the new product and new service launches on which we've worked, the marketing team at the project's end was considerably different from the one we had at the beginning.

This would not be a significant problem if, in fact, the players were well trained, extremely bright, and interchangeable. It would not be a problem if they had demonstrated a high level of job performance, if, in short, they had shown an ability to develop a successful marketing program for an established product or to launch an outstanding new brand. Regrettably, this is not the case. The players, while bright, are not interchangeable. They cannot develop successful programs. Indeed, most marketing programs don't work.

In major universities, by contrast, professors usually don't win a tenured associate professorship—if they win one at all—until at least six years after they've completed their doctorate (which takes approximately four to eight years to earn). The general rule is that it takes six or more years past the Ph.D. to demonstrate a level of performance in research, teaching, and university service commensurate with the respect and responsibility that go along with a permanent academic appointment.

In hospitals, a young physician does not take primary responsibility for surgery until he or she has been a surgical resident or chief resident, which comes six to eight years after college. Law and accounting firms commonly require seven to ten years of service after law school before they promote someone to partner.

In universities, hospitals, law and accounting firms, a careful evaluation process monitors the professor, surgeon, or partner in terms of what he or she knows and doesn't know. A system of checks and balances assures that, all other factors holding constant, only the best and the brightest make it to a position of professional competence. Medical boards and bar and CPA exams help to ensure that some level of competence across organizations is maintained.

In marketing, a discipline not characterized by a high level of training either before or on the job, and increasingly driven by time constraints, the notion seems to be that brand managers should be promoted quickly or the organization will lose them to other companies.

We may be just whistling "Dixie" here, but it seems to us that individual companies should promote brand managers only when they have demonstrated a given level of competence by designing and implementing successful marketing programs. No marketing manager should be promoted before he or she has had time to demonstrate the ability to launch a successful campaign for an existing product or to introduce a new product.

The common phenomena of people leaving a new product introduction in midstream to be promoted on to another brand, or of an untried executive being hired away from another company, make little sense. It's like promoting the doctor before you know whether the patient will live, or promoting the lawyer before you know whether she can win a case.

Myth 24: When the organization needs new marketing talent, the place to recruit it is from packaged goods companies.

Truth: Once upon a time, the latest developments in marketing unfolded at packaged goods companies. During the 1950s, 1960s, and 1970s, you saw new ideas hatching right and left in the packaged goods industry. Ideas on marketing planning and decision making, advertising and promotion, marketing research and media evaluation, and more.

Not surprisingly, a broad range of consumer durable, service, and business-to-business marketers recruited executives from packaged goods marketers—General Foods and General Mills, Lever Brothers and Colgate Palmolive, and a host of other companies whose goods dominated prime-time television.

Five years at Procter & Gamble was considered the equivalent of an MBA from a top business school, and in those days few managers had MBAs from anywhere. If you had that P&G or GF pedigree, you could do no wrong. Any idea, no matter how revolutionary, seemed to make a certain amount of sense if it had been tested and institutionalized at one of the packaged goods giants.

From on-air testing of advertising copy to front-loaded media plans, seven-step new product development systems to simulated test marketing, if it wasn't invented by one of the Big Brand companies, it probably wasn't any good.

By the early 1990s, the world of marketing had changed dramatically. Durable goods and service marketers, pharmaceutical companies and business-to-business organizations have in many ways caught up with (some would say surpassed—we don't agree) their packaged goods counterparts (see Exhibit 3.1).

Our own work with the marketing IQ test—discussed in Chapter 1—revealed no difference between packaged goods and other marketers in terms of marketing savvy. This was a surprise to us. Moreover, the experiences we relate in this book pertaining to professional surveys we have designed and undertaken to assess the state-of-our-profession, suggest comparable attitudes and beliefs among marketers in different sectors of the economy. Thus our own sense is that today packaged goods marketers and marketers of other types of products and services are more similar than different.

However, we note some new developments occurring faster in non-packaged goods firms than we would have imagined two decades ago.

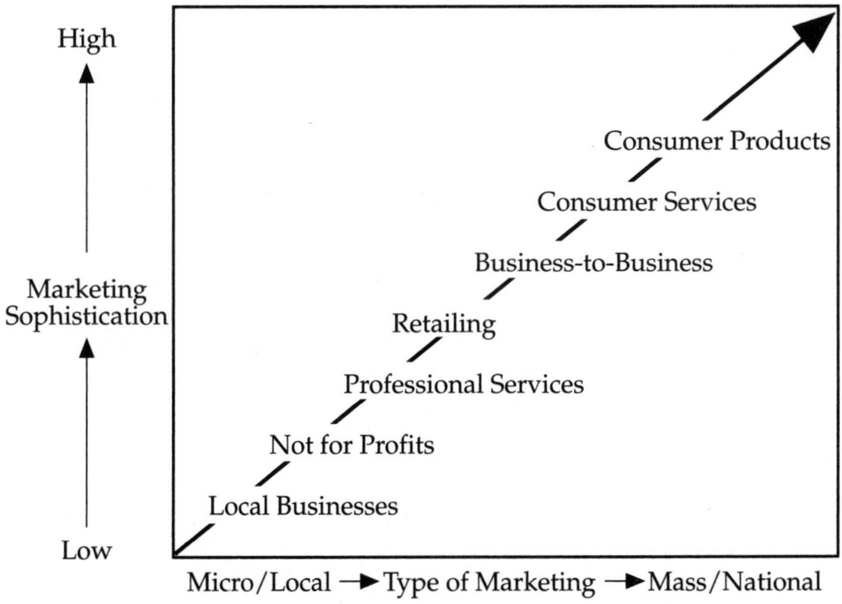

Exhibit 3-1 Relative sophistication of different types of marketers.

Direct marketing, as an illustration, particularly of the database-driven, one-on-one variety, is booming outside of packaged goods, as is the problematic quest for brand equity, customer satisfaction and loyalty, marketing partnerships and strategic alliances, and other new concepts.

Packaged goods firms, some critics point out, are not just *not* leading the way, they are stuck in a time warp—clinging to old ways of doing things, holding on to concepts, processes, methods that should have been discarded long ago.

Indeed, many of the marketing myths explored in this book were started at packaged goods companies and spread like chicken pox to other industries. Because the tribal traditions at the packaged goods firms are so strong, however, and the myths so deeply ingrained, they seem harder to change than at, say, telecommunications, personal computer, or financial services companies.

Admittedly, in the past, when companies needed marketing talent, they looked to packaged goods companies. Today, however, talent can be found in companies large and small in every industry. The trick is to find smart, creative, well-trained, hard-working, and experienced "professionals" with high marketing IQs who are not intellectually paralyzed by the myths of the past. Who are flexible enough to keep abreast of breaking developments in the field. And who capitalize on new trends and ideas to lead their brands into the future.

"I want the campaign on the air in five weeks! I'd rather be wrong on time than right late!"

4
Myths about Marketing Decision Making

During medical training, a surgical resident works under an expert's supervision while he or she operates. Some of these operations are failures. The patient dies. Perhaps the patient would not have died if the experienced surgeon had performed every aspect of the operation perfectly. The harsh fact is that a person gains knowledge only by having many experiences where an action is tied to an outcome.

In the marketing profession, if a young executive were to work on, say, 20 new products, a third of which were successful, a third so-so, a third failures, and if experts in the field were to train the young marketers to analyze the reasons for their successes or failures—the way every surgeon in a hospital is required to stand and defend the surgical procedures used—we'd be training people to make good marketing decisions.

But the typical new product manager does not work on 20 cases; the typical new product manager works on 2 or 3. In most cases, the outcome is clear; the patient—the product—will die, and no one will know why. There will be no formal autopsy. Marketing executives cannot build on their successes or learn from their failures, because they simply don't know what caused them. In most cases they don't have anyone looking over their shoulder to tell them. Indeed, as we pointed out in Myth 23 in the last chapter, before the typical brand manager even knows the outcome, she's moved on to another brand, another company.

We're not training people to make good marketing decisions.

"We've tried to match authority with responsibility, which is real hard for most companies to do," says Richard Freeland, president of Pizza Hut of Indiana. Companies give managers responsibility, but don't always give them the authority to remedy problems. "They'll get burned by some bad manager," says Freeland, "and rather than train the manager out of the problem or fire him and get somebody else, they'll put in a new rule." Over time, rules grow to compensate for the organization's worst manager. The rules frustrate the good managers and they leave.

"Believe me, it's very frustrating for a manager to have responsibility but not authority," says Freeland. "It's also very motivating if he can and does do something to solve a problem. He goes home feeling good." In Freeland's case, his marketing myth-busting business, with 39 stores mostly in northern Indiana and approximately 1600 employees, is one of the most successful franchises in the fast-food industry; average store sales are double the national Pizza Hut average while profits are almost three times the average.

True, most established companies do have a marketing decision process or procedure. Some are explicit (such as "The Amalgamated Consolidated Seven-Step Process for New Product Development"), some are implicit. The task may be as simple as picking a target, or as complicated as revitalizing a dying brand or creating a new product category.

The one tiny problem with these processes, as we'll see, is that they are all fundamentally flawed. The way things generally happen today is that companies (large and small, consumer and business-to-business, selling products or services) pick and evaluate relatively few alternatives—three to five. Three to five (or fewer) new product formulations, advertising positioning strategies, corporate image concepts, package designs, etc. Indeed, for some decisions—market targeting, as an example—firms seem to impulsively select a single target without evaluating any alternatives.

In the case of a new product or service one can easily demonstrate (as we did in *The Marketing Revolution*) that there are tens of thousands, or more, different product formulations or service configurations from which a company may choose. There are a comparable number of different ad campaigns, corporate image strategies, product names, and so forth.

If there were some rational, cerebral process that helped marketers to screen these zillions of ideas down to two, three, or sometimes as many as five, this approach would make sense. But in most companies that sophisticated screening technology does not exist, and what passes for "screening research" is really just another word for "quick and dirty." Today, in most cases, people are simply forced to choose from two to five alternatives. Typically these possibilities are really not very different from one another, and not much different from what already exists in the market. The likelihood of finding a winner is slight.

So let's make that this chapter's first myth.

Myth 25: You can make the right marketing decision for a new product or service, target group, positioning, or ad execution by evaluating a few alternatives and picking the winner.

Truth: The truth is that for every decision in the marketing mix there are scores, hundreds, thousands of alternatives, so that to randomly select two or three is just plain dumb. Let's take a new product. How does the system typically function?

The vice president of marketing charges a brand manager with the mission of trying to develop a new product in a given product category.

Different companies have standard ways of doing this as part of the corporate culture. It generally starts with a review of different types of research the company has done in the past...some focus groups...concept screening among a hundred people dozing off in a Long Island mall. Out of all this the company comes up with three concepts, as if some law of marketing says you always need three concepts.

The company then does some more serious research on the three concepts, followed by an evaluation of two or three different product formulations (or service designs) for the winning concept or concepts.

In the case of a consumer packaged good, this is followed by an in-home concept/product use test. While the company is collecting data, the advertising agency is creating advertising. The company then tests two or three alternative ad campaigns, using criteria only modestly related to sales. Of course the ad agency's only information was the data the company had at the beginning of the process; it does not include results from the in-home tests. And without this, how good can the campaign be? But it's a kind of ritual companies go through.

They go through it, we believe, because it's comfortable. When they follow rituals, managers do not have to think. No one does. If you knew, as people knew in the early days of this century, that when you got up on Sunday morning you would go to church, sit in your pew for three hours, return home, listen to Sister Susie play the piano, sit and read until dinner at five o'clock—chicken on Sunday—it would be comforting. One would not have to think about what to do next.

In many companies—perhaps all but a few—most employees do not have to think about what to do next. The marketing system is a series of predetermined, culturally defined steps or rituals based on tradition, not science, in much the same way as the Apache rain dance was a necessary ritual to end a drought but had nothing to do with the creation of rain. The vice president of marketing measures the brand manager by how well he or she executes the dance, not on the basis of marketing performance.

If the steps have been well established, for, say, performing a tonsillectomy, and if a doctor can do them well, that's wonderful. If one doctor can do a tonsillectomy in 18 minutes with the same safety and concern for the patient, and at the same performance level, as the doctor who takes 32 minutes, no one would disagree that the first surgeon is more efficient than the second.

If the established steps invariably lead to the patient's death, however, then one has grounds for grave concern. In marketing, even when the steps don't lead to the patient's (that is, the product's) death, it's due to luck as much as to science.

Thus far we've been talking about the difficulty in making a few decisions; consider the marketing plan as a whole. To introduce a new consumer or industrial product or service, marketers must make at least a dozen key marketing decisions. These include the market target, the product positioning, product design, pricing, distribution type and level, advertising message, media spending, media mix, media schedule, promotion spending, promotion mix, and promotion schedule.

Suppose for the sake of illustration that the company has only seven alternatives for each of the dozen decisions. In the real world, of course, a company may have fewer than seven for a given decision—but it also may have many more. But to keep this simple, if there are only seven options for each of the marketing mix's dozen ingredients, how many different programs could a marketing manager develop? What do the escalating sevens total?

Not 12 × 7, or 84 different programs.

The answer is twelve to the seventh power, or 13,841,000,000 different marketing programs. That's 13.8 *billion.*

Now before you remind us, as one reviewer who suffers from "chronic irritability syndrome" recently did, we know that not all of these decisions are independent of one another. If, for example, one of the market targets is people without any money, you might not want to consider evaluating the highest-price strategy among this group. We know that. But we also know that there are not 7, but 70, or even 7000 possibilities for each decision. We are trying to illustrate a point:

There are many, many, many, many possible programs that a company might develop.

Among all these possible programs, a few would be total, unmitigated, Maggie-bar-the-door disasters. Most would be neither a success nor a disaster (but probably would not be successful enough to meet the typical corporation's sales and profit hurdles either). A few would be total, unqualified successes. In other words, you'd end up with a standard bell curve.

But what are the odds that a marketing manager will pick one of the resounding successes from the 13.8 billion choices...even working late at the office? Virtually zero is the right answer, which is why most new products and most repositioning efforts fail.

As an aside, our experience is that the people involved in research and development and in engineering are very bright. We give them credit for their ability to come up with manufacturing-driven products or engineering-driven products more often than the marketing people come up with marketing-driven products.

If we could find a way to have marketing and manufacturing and engineering work together, so that marketing actually provided a blueprint to engineering or to R&D, we'd be more likely to have product successes than failures.

Myth 26: Profitability is the guiding criterion when marketers pick a target group, positioning or advertising strategy, new product, price, or marketing plan.

Truth: A marketing professor recently suggested in *The Journal of Marketing* that this is not a myth at all. That marketers and marketing professors already know this, and that projected profitability *is* the basis for marketing decision making today.

That professor needs to get a grip and ride out into the real world. He could not be more wrong.

Like the professor, there is no marketer in the country who would not say that he (or she) isn't obsessed with making profitable decisions for his brand. In fact, there are few marketing managers in America who explicitly consider forecasted profit as the foundation for their marketing decisions. Rather, they make these decisions on marketing alternatives on the basis of warm feelies, not profitability.

Consumer attitudes, for example, measure the extent to which people "like" a particular option. Another popular measure is behavioral intention, that is, the extent to which people say they "will buy" a particular product.

We call these "warm feelies" because when the information is positive it makes management feel warm all over. "Prospects say they `like' our fresh-squeezed taste!," or "They `intend to buy' our new software package! We've got a winner!"

Why is this a myth? Because, as we just discussed at interminable length, a company must evaluate hundreds...thousands...tens of thousands...eleventy-jillion alternatives for every marketing mix decision. (The computer makes this possible, time-wise and money-wise.)

Moreover, the company must evaluate all these alternatives in terms of profitability, not appeal...not demand...not share...not sales. Obviously, the company must have sales (the new product no one buys is not a happy product), but the company must have sales with profits (a new product people will buy only when the company loses money on each sale is not the formula for long-term prosperity).

Myth 27: Companies evaluate different marketing options on the basis of attitudinal criteria (what people want, what they like, what they say they will buy) and seasoned judgment, because profitability is too difficult to measure.

Truth: Often we will suggest to a client that a decision might be evaluated in terms of profitability. Take the targeting decision, for example. We argue (as you'll see in Chapter 8) that the company wants to find a target market that responds to its marketing efforts, buys or uses more of the company's product, is growing, is responsible for making buying decisions, and is one the marketer can reach through media.

The client will routinely say, "Yeah, but those are soft criteria. They're not the kinds of criteria we could take to our financial people—our own gnomes of Zurich."

To which our response is routinely one we borrow from Peter Drucker, the intellectual beacon of management, and Leonard Lodish, Professor at the Wharton School: "I'd rather be approximately right than precisely wrong."

Yes, the criteria a company can use in a marketing study may only approximately hit the mark in terms of tapping into profitability. But it's better to hit the mark approximately than to ignore it altogether. It's better to hit the mark approximately than to use criteria that don't take profitability into account at all, such as how many people "like" this product, or how many say they "will buy" it.

Myth 28: Management judgment based on experience is the best way (if not the only way) to make key marketing decisions.

Truth: In October 1992, we participated in a meeting with domestic and international marketers and researchers and gave a presentation on why it is necessary that marketers use more science in their decisions.

A senior manager from a major international bank stood up and said, "This is ridiculous. You're taking decisions away from executives. You're taking away their prerogatives. Only seasoned marketing decision makers can make good judgments."

Another executive in the room snickered and asked the manager to explain a *Wall Street Journal* article that morning, which reported that his bank had lost $350 million that quarter. "If managers' decisions are so good, if their judgment is so good," he asked, "why were so many decisions obviously so bad?"

We do not say executives must abandon the essential inputs to great marketing: creativity, sound management judgment, and experience. They are absolutely vital. We do not believe in slavish obedience to the numbers alone. On the contrary, we are increasingly convinced that American business must *balance* science and subjective insight in marketing.

Myth 29: The key to successful marketing is in being "different," "creative," "exciting," "sexy," or all four.

Truth: For many American marketing executives, being different, being creative, being exciting, being sexy is associated with superiority. These young Turks have a certain look and attitude that says, "I am a success."

A large percentage of the marketing and middle managers are baby boomers. These are people who, until recently, have been more interested in being creative than in being right. We say, beware the young marketing manager in the Armani suit wearing the Ralph Lauren glasses; he often has the chief symptom of death-wish marketing, a belief that style is more important than substance, packaging more important than content.

Take as symptoms of this syndrome two small examples. The prices of exotic autos like the Lambo, Countach, Ferrari P40, Boxer, and the like are tumbling. They've been getting sexier and sexier, but who really wants to pay over $200,000 for a car you can never take out of second gear, is uncomfortable, and has less and less utility?

On a less lofty note, the Buick (Regal) Grand National was supposed to be a unique "roadworthy" replica of its real Grand National racing counterpart. Buick gave it a completely different and distinctive color and ornamentation, wheels, tires, and the like, to produce the "go fast" image. But they used a production Buick V-6 turbo engine with fuel injection and valve changes that gave the engine an anemic 200 HP—slightly less than a '58 Chevy. The disappointing performance, a terrible dependability track record (due to the new injection system, etc.), and a foolishly high price tag made this piece of "marketing creativity" a total flop after two seasons

What marketing executives truly need is intelligence guided by seasoned judgment. They must be aware of the many options available to them for their marketing plan, be aware that profitability can—and should—be an important decision-making criterion, and be committed to a relentless search for truth and excellence.

Myth 30: A reasonable way to set the marketing budget is to take last year's figure and adjust for inflation.

Truth: This is a myth, because the statement assumes that the way the company set the budget last year made sense.

In fact, corporations often set budgets based on fatuous criteria such as: "Let's set our ad, research, promotion budget as a certain percentage of sales."

Why do it that way? Because everybody in the industry does it that way. But that's no real reason, just a habit. Each year management simply tweaks the figures a little. These tweaks may be based on the inflation rate. They may be based on whether the company wants to increase its market share by a third of a point. They may be based on the current year's sales rate.

Setting a budget based on an advertising-to-sales relationship is of course only one way to decide to make a silly budget decision. Other approaches that we'll talk about include using one of a variety of share-of-spending-to-actual or desired-share-of-market formulas, setting budgets based on what competitors are doing, what the ad agency did for its last client in the category, and just guessing.

If the company set the marketing budget in terms of some sensible criteria in the first place, adjusting it periodically might make sense, assuming that marketplace conditions haven't changed. But that's not the way it usually happens.

Marketing, as we pointed out in the last chapter, requires a tabula rasa or "clean-slate" approach. Top management should ask the marketing manager to demonstrate how the budget translates into short- and long-term profitability. If we spend $50,000 on this promotional program, or $5 million on that advertising campaign, what do we get for our money?

Often we don't know for sure. A sophisticated corporation will try to model the outcome (one reason that computer spreadsheet programs are so popular). If the organization does set up the systems, it can measure the year's results. But that's a clean-slate approach: Prove you need the money, and show how it will result in a particular performance level. If the marketing manager can only say, "Gee, we spent $500,000 last year. I want to spend $500,000 plus 2 percent this year," that's a witless approach.

Let's say we're launching a new product. We have done some serious thinking and have determined that if we obtain a 50 percent awareness level our new product is likely to succeed. How do we know that? Because we have a long, rich history of new product introductions where we have tracked awareness and performance, and, on average, 50 percent is a good number.

Now the marketing planner comes along and says, "We need a $35 million advertising and promotion campaign." What's the connection between $35 million and 50 percent awareness? Forty-two people in America know, and they're not talking.

If the planner can say, "Our experience shows that $35 million will buy 2964 gross rating points in prime-time, 30-second spots. Two thousand, nine hundred and sixty-four GRPs over the course of a year will produce a 50 percent average awareness level," this may make sense. (For one thing, it's very close to what we do when we use sophisticated simulated test marketing models.)

But to simply say, "Give me the money. Trust me, it's going to produce the number" makes no sense. Although in marketing's defense, this is the way industry commonly sets budgets.

That does not have to be the way. As we've suggested, big marketers can use serious modeling approaches and marketers large and small can estimate the right budget using a simple approach such as the one Professor John Little at the Sloan School at M.I.T. described in a famous article in the *Sloan Management Review.* The approach employs "decision calculus," which is less intimidating than its name.

In our version of a decision calculus, the marketing manager first plots current sales and marketing spending on a sheet of graph paper.

The *X* axis indicates sales, the *Y* axis indicates marketing spending. Next, based on the manager's experience, she estimates what sales level the company would obtain if it doubled the spending. Third, she estimates the sales level if the company were to increase the spending level astronomically, if it were to spend more money than it could ever afford. Finally, she estimates the sales level if the marketing budget disappeared, if it went to zero.

The graph now has four data points: sales with zero marketing expense; current marketing expense; double marketing expense; and a budget only the U.S. Senate could contemplate. The manager then estimates (or has a statistical program do it) a best-fit line through those points. She can then solve for the optimal marketing spending level.

Marketing management should think of ad money as an investment like any other; it needs to be handled carefully and wisely, after serious deliberation and intelligent analysis. While decision calculus is a judgmental approach, it's a lot more rational then simply saying, "Let's take 7 percent of sales plus 0.3 percent for inflation, because that's what everybody's doing in our product category."

Myth 31: Getting the right decision-making process or system in place is what's important; the details of execution will take care of themselves.

Truth: Execution is often more important than process. Let's illustrate this point with a recent consulting engagement. A business-to-business marketer engaged a major management consulting firm to do a "best practices" study for marketing decision making. The consultants identified six companies in related industries that were supposedly famous for their marketing savvy and six companies notorious for their failures. Interviews were completed among multiple players in each of the dozen companies to uncover how marketing decisions, and the advertising and new product decisions among them, get made.

The results dumbfounded the consultants. There were few differences between the "superstars" and the "dimwits" in terms of marketing decision processes, and those small differences, the consultants believed, had nothing to do with marketing performance.

Enter Clancy and Shulman. The management consultants brought us in to render a second opinion on their methodology and findings. The results of our analysis surprised even us, and we're not easily surprised.

All twelve companies did indeed have the same general processes for making marketing decisions. All, as an illustration, developed marketing plans that talked about objectives, targeting, positioning, product design, customer satisfaction, etc., etc. What separated the losers from the winners was not the decision-making process but how the companies implemented the decisions—the execution.

The kind of systematic, profit-directed execution discussed in Myths 25, 26, and 27 and reflected in *The Marketing Revolution* (a cloudy reflection, we'll admit) characterized the winners; death-wish marketing would describe how the six losers implemented their processes.

Smart decision-making processes *and* intelligent execution are both essential to survival in the 1990s.

"We tried pupil dilation research, galvanic skin response, Ouija boards, and Tarot cards. Now we've come up with a multiplex hyperplane, logic-free model that uses double dipsticks to make national projections based on eight people."

5
Myths about Marketing Research

Marketing research can be as simple as chatting with customers, as complex as surveying a nationally projectable sample of customers and prospects. Marketing research tells marketing management about the problems people have with products, with services, with companies. It helps management estimate the market's size, position a product, advertise it, and price it.

Just as marketing research can be modest or elaborate, managers (often in smaller organizations) may find it intimidating or (often in large companies) rely on it unduly. Marketing research is a tool; like any tool, one can use it appropriately or ineptly.

The tool comes in many shapes. Survey research—the most common type of *serious* marketing research—does have one built-in problem: Sample sizes must be large enough to make stable projections. If it is possible to forecast national election results plus or minus 3 percent by polling a random sample of 1000 Americans, how many people must you poll to forecast a state election with the same level of precision?

The sample still must be around 1000 people, whether the state is California or Rhode Island. Although this is not intuitively obvious, it's a law of sampling statistics that can be confirmed by talking to any statistician. This issue comes up when a company looks at the research budgets and says, "Well, since we can't afford to interview 1000 or even 500 people, let's do a survey among 75 and hope for the best." Because the results will be drivel in most cases, and since we don't know any way to adjust drivel to make it useful, the company is better off spending the limited research budget on something else.

A family that owns a business, for example, could sit around the dining room table and discuss their firm's best target...or the best positioning...or what they could do to improve customer service.

Three people could talk about marketing issues in a small organization and hit upon as good a solution—certainly a more cost-effective solution—as a full-blown market study. We do not think an organization needs to commission a survey every time it has a market research challenge, particularly a survey that has more problems than promise.

Which leads to this chapter's first myth.

***Myth* 32:** Small or entrepreneurial businesses can't afford to research and plan strategy the way big businesses can.

Truth: This is a straw man. No one says that a small business should operate the way a major corporation operates. This is like saying that small businesses cannot afford a national television campaign the way big businesses can. It's true, but so what?

The challenge, as we said above, stems from the fact that a representative sample of a market (assuming the total size of the population of consumers or buyers is large, more than a few thousand people) requires a survey of at least 200 people. That's true whether the business is a $100,000 retailer or $500 million manufacturer, the research still requires a stable, representative, projectable sample of buyers.

So the issue may be that the business can't afford to do the same type of studies. What it can afford is something more modest, yet still scientific and reliable.

What's hidden in the myth is the idea that small businesses *don't need* to do research and plan strategy the way big businesses do. Which of course is not true. They do. Every business requires research.

What it does not need is what we have called elsewhere death-wish research. It should not turn to focus groups as the alternative, or hire a consultant to conduct a concept test or gap analysis—marketing research tools that, as we'll soon see, have questionable value.

***Myth* 33:** A company should spend a fixed amount of the total marketing budget on marketing research, year in and year out.

Truth: This is another marketing rule of thumb that time and tradition have turned into precept. In some companies, the amount is 2 percent. In others, as much as 5 percent. In many, less than 1 percent.

In fact there should not be any fixed relationship between the marketing budget and the marketing research budget. It should vary with the brand's needs at a given point in time. If the company's strategy is to milk the brand—or grow the brand—the budget will vary. Perhaps a cigarette marketer—offering a mature product with a huge total marketing budget—should spend one-tenth of 1 percent on marketing research; a software manufacturer—with a radical new design in a growing product category—should spend 8 percent of the marketing budget on marketing research.

More important, we say managers should stop thinking: "How am I going to squeeze the money for more marketing or marketing research out of this year's budget?" Because this is the wrong question, the answer will inevitably be wrong.

The money has to come from a different place. Management has to look at the money differently. Market research money is an investment the company must make to grow the business. Managers who adopt the clean-slate marketing approach will think about budgeting in an entirely different way. What needs to be done?

A company needs the marketing research it requires to develop, execute, and monitor intelligent marketing plans. It needs to be able to scan the marketing environment we talk about in the next chapter. It needs to be able to identify and describe the market target. It needs to be able to develop the product's positioning. It needs to track the performance over time.

Sometimes, if an organization has never done these chores, all this may require a major investment in a given year. Once made, however, it may require only a marginal investment in the second or third year to monitor the system. To buy a house, you may have to come up with a 20 percent down payment on the price just to move in; once settled, your annual upkeep may be only 3 percent of the price.

Does it make any sense to do, say, positioning research one year, targeting research the next year, and pricing research the third year?

No. The patient is on the table. The product's life is at risk, its plan is at risk, the company is at risk, and the marketing manager, the researcher, the consultant are operating. They must do what needs to be done in order to help the patient to survive and prosper.

Myth 34: The only way an organization can obtain marketing research is to buy the services of a professional marketing researcher, a consulting firm, or both.

Truth: Every marketer would love to have the expertise of a BBDO Advertising or a Copernicus or a McKinsey & Co., to help them with a marketing challenge (not to mention their marketing problems). But the fact is that these talents are available only if you have a sizable budget. So how does a small marketer get help to develop a marketing program cost-effectively?

Almost every marketing professor at every business school in the country is on the lookout for real-world projects for his or her students. University budgets are increasingly tight. Professors sometimes don't even have the money to make copies of questionnaires that they would like students to use for a class project.

Along comes a small to medium business to ask a marketing department professor to work on a marketing project, for which the company will pick up the out-of-pocket costs. The students do the work, the professor supervises, and everyone benefits. It may even result in a publishable academic paper, and sometimes the results of these projects can be astounding in terms of the cost benefit to the client.

Harvard and Boston Universities periodically give a marketing course called "Consulting." The faculty seeks out projects large and small within the community on which the students can work. In one year, BU students worked on projects for American Express, Greyhound, Perrier, Raytheon, a local bookstore, a local hotel, and a chain of shoe stores. In each case the faculty and the students discussed the client's problem. They established a budget appropriate to the business size. The professor assigned three to seven MBA students as a consulting group to work on each project. The students completed interviews, analyzed the data, presented the findings to the client, and left behind a written report.

Some of the results were momentous. One Boston University MBA project, designed to help American Express develop a campaign among young professionals, led to one of the most successful advertising programs in the company's history and ran for years. The American Express project cost around $15,000; the local hotel project around $600. This is a far cry from the $300,000 and $2 million projects we are accustomed to doing for clients.

This is not to suggest that the $5000 student-run project will have the same level of thoroughness as the $500,000 project undertaken by the internationally famous consulting firm. But considered from a cost-to-value angle for the small-to-medium business, the student project often turns out to be a very worthwhile investment. The local dry cleaner or pharmacy doesn't need to hire a big-time research firm to undertake a project.

A related but different way to accomplish the same end is to contact the university and speak to an assistant professor or lecturer—he or she at the lowest level—in the department. Ask such professors if they or a graduate student are willing to put together a team of undergraduates or MBAs to work on a project that has some commercial value. Given that these juniors in the academic ranks need real-world experience to put on their resumés and to test the latest theories and methodologies, they would love to have somebody cover the cost of collecting the data and doing some statistical analysis—minor costs from a marketer's standpoint, but major problems from an assistant professor's.

Myth 35: Research practitioners are well trained in the common tools of the trade.

Truth: This is sometimes the case. That's why we call someone "professional." But it is not always the case, and that's what makes such a blanket statement a myth. We recently had a bizarre experience which made us realize that the honorific "research professional" covers a multitude of sins.

A major advertising agency sent us a questionnaire it had received from a major advertiser. The prospective client was seeking agency insight into different research tools and technologies. This is a standard practice when advertisers are looking for a new agency.

The agency called us to see what tools or expertise we had that they could use to address the client's questions. This particular questionnaire consisted of 10 different areas of marketing research. When we received the list we had to laugh, because the advertiser wanted to know the agency's experience with both "tradeoff analysis" and "conjoint measurement." The advertiser listed these as separate items, when in fact they are different names for the same tool. The list also included "multidimensional scaling" and "perceptual mapping" which, again, are synonymous. Apparently neither the advertiser nor the agency knew that the 10 techniques were actually 8.

The list also included a little-used and generally irrelevant analysis called "canonical correlation." Asking a prospective advertising agency whether it knows something about "canonical correlation" would be akin to asking a physician whether he can tell you something about the company that manufactured his examination room table. Even if he did, it wouldn't tell you anything about his medical competence.

(Canonical correlation, for those who care, and now that we've brought it up, is a form of analysis between a set of independent variables and a set of dependent variables. Let's assume you have age, education, socioeconomic status—that is, a set of demographics—and you have coffee consumption, beer consumption, cigarette consumption—a set of behaviors. Canonical correlation permits you to find the patterns linking the two sets. It's a tool marketers probably use in 1 out of every 5000 market research analyses, and it probably should be used even less.)

Other items on this list included econometric analysis, galvanic skin-response testing, and strategic planning models.

At first we thought the advertiser's questionnaire was a practical joke concocted by a researcher with too much time on his or her hands. But it was not a joke at all; we checked. The advertiser was serious, and the agency was equally serious. It was the proverbial blind leading the blind. One can almost imagine the advertiser working late with a marketing research textbook, trying to identify difficult topics on which to quiz the agency.

This is not so surprising. The fact is that most marketing researchers, unlike medical, legal, or accounting practitioners, have had very little formal training in marketing, marketing or social science research methods, statistical analysis, model building, computer science, or related fields.

True, many of them are very bright and quickly pick up what they need to know to do their job. But few are professionals in the common sense of the term.

Myth 36: Most marketing research tools in widespread use have demonstrated reliability and validity.

Truth: When we say "marketing research tools," we're talking about things like concept testing, product testing, and advertising testing. By "reliability," we mean that if you replicate the test you'll obtain essentially the same results. By "validity," we mean that the tests measure what they purport to measure.

When marketing researchers and social scientists talk amongst themselves about the reliability of their measuring instruments, their scales, their questionnaires, and the like, you often find them saying—we're paraphrasing here—"In contrast to the work of physicians, engineers, psychologists, and other applied scientists, and in contrast to the instruments they use, our work and our instruments have relatively modest reliability and validity."

The New York Times recently reported that one of the minor medical myths of the nineteenth and twentieth centuries has been debunked—the idea that 98.6°F is the normal human temperature. New research has established that the normal mean temperature is 98.2°, and that the normal range for adults in the study was 96 to 99.9°. Nevertheless, one can take an oral or an anal thermometer and measure that temperature reliability. A patient's temperature read at 9:00 a.m. and at 10:00 a.m. will rarely vary by more than one-tenth of a degree.

Our point in bringing this up is that we as a profession know relatively little about the reliability of marketing research instruments, and even less about their validity. Despite the fact that companies spend billions of dollars on marketing—$140 billion on advertising alone—we do not have the reliable instruments we see in other disciplines. We don't have the devices to measure the marketing equivalent of a hurricane's wind speed or an earthquake's tremors.

For example, it is relatively easy to create a test to evaluate advertising copy. Dozens of companies offer their proprietary methodologies. But it is very difficult to prove that the test really measures what it is supposed to measure, and that what it measures is relevant to sales and marketing.

You might measure copy and prove definitively that people do recall certain kinds of ads, headlines, or illustrations. But recall may have no relevance whatever to whether people buy the product or not.

We once consulted to Richardson-Vicks on a copy testing project. They had tested a Formula 44 television commercial that produced exceptionally low scores. They had employed what was called an "on-air" testing method. Interviewers would call approximately 200 people who had watched a given program the night before and ask them about the commercials the program had carried. The percentage of people who remembered something—anything—about the commercial was the "recall" score.

At that time, 24 percent was an average score. This particular commercial brought in a 13. Agency and client executives fretted over this low score; what did it mean? They thought, based on past experience and their professional judgment, that it was a better commercial than the score had indicated, so they tested it again. This time the score jumped to a 45. Thus, over a couple of months, two tests generated both the lowest and the highest recall scores Formula 44 commercials had ever recorded, and both for the same commercial.

No one knew exactly what to do with that information except to say, "Well, clearly the commercial isn't as bad as the first test said it was."

(In those days, researchers routinely tested commercials on different programs, because they felt the program had little or no impact on commercial recall scores. As we'll be seeing in Chapter 11, there *is* a link. Commercials aired during programs people like enjoy much higher recall scores than those aired on programs people like less. While no one knew this at the time, it is the most likely reason for the score's fluctuation.)

That experience made us think. If this basic tool the industry uses to test advertising copy is not reliable, what do we know about the reliability of other tools that researchers commonly employ? Relatively little.

Further, given that the relationship between reliability and validity is a little like the relationship between walking and running—you can't have a valid instrument unless you first have a reliable instrument—we certainly don't know much about validity.

As an illustration of this point, until recently, we didn't know whether copy-testing scores are related to sales performance. We now know that certain types of copy-testing measures are related to sales for a few widely used, established packaged goods brands. We don't know it for anything else.

Myth 37: You can count on interviewers to ask a survey's questions precisely as written, and to write down the respondent answers exactly.

Truth: Sounds pretty basic, doesn't it? Every survey study uses a questionnaire of one kind or another. Researchers hire companies who do the actual interviewing, and they assume that the interviewers, because the research firm pays them, will ask the questions exactly as they appear on the questionnaire and will write down the answers verbatim.

Not true. We once did a study for a major brewer, and to ensure the quality of the data we asked that the interviewers tape-record all the interviews. We thought that this would put the interviewers on their guard, and guarantee the accuracy of the questioning and of the handwritten responses.

When the data came back, we decided to compare each respondent's written interview with the recorded interview. We were dumbfounded by the variances that we discovered. Interviewers tended to improvise, asking the questions in a way with which they felt comfortable and/or in a way they felt respondents would understand the questions best. In many cases, how interviewers asked a question and how we had wanted them to ask it were quite different.

This is not a trivial issue. Tiny word changes make huge differences in respondent answers. If different interviewers are each editing the questions, they might as well be working from different questionnaires.

We also learned that many interviewers took short cuts and interpreted responses when they put the respondents' answers on paper. In some instances, the responses on paper were dramatically different from the responses on the tape. Finally, the interviewers asked questions that in some cases they weren't supposed to ask.

All this suggests that researchers must be constantly aware of the problems involved with survey data. They should build checks and balances into any study to ensure the highest-quality information. They should monitor interviewers to ensure that they ask the questions exactly as worded and record the answers exactly as presented to them.

Myth 38: Data analysis is far more important than data collection.

Truth: This pervasive myth in the research industry has some interesting correlates:

- Companies buy data by the pound, with a misplaced focus on how much each completed interview costs. Everyone in the industry knows at least five Sigmunds who want to record on their resumés that they saved their company oodles by persuading research firms to reduce data collection costs. Under "Accomplishments" the resumé reads: "I reduced data collection costs for a market segmentation study from $52.00 an interview to $31.50, by switching from an in-home personal interview to telephone."
- Companies give little care or concern to how the data is collected. All that matters is that it's collected quickly.
- The industry pays data collectors poorly (salaries under $35,000) while it pays data analysts well (salaries over $50,000).
- Telephone interviews are increasingly replacing the more serious personal, in-home or in-office interview
- Companies often bring to bear rocket science analysis, including the latest high-powered statistical models and methods, on relatively worthless data. In truth, the quality of the data collected in any research study determines in large part the study's value. Just as a house built on a foundation of sand will not stand, a research conclusion or management implication constructed upon research data of questionable integrity often will not stand up to harsh reality.

Obviously, circumstances occur in which a "quick read" (a research euphemism for "fast and cheap") of the market to check an awareness level, or usage incidence of a particular product, or reactions to a new campaign or political candidate, may be defensible. But the growing trend toward making serious marketing decisions based on dumb data, poorly collected (often in shopping centers or by telephone and by mail), is a frightening development, and another symptom of death-wish marketing.

Myth 39: The focus group interview is a serious marketing research tool a manager can use safely to make serious marketing decisions.

Truth: Corporate marketers like focus groups. Compared to other kinds of research, they are cheap. They can mean a diverting junket to a warm or entertaining location (Las Vegas, Disneyland). They seem to give voice to the real feelings and real reactions of real people. They can and do provide a marketer with insights into how people feel about a new product, what a print ad communicated, or what language consumers would use to describe a new service.

All this suggests that we too like focus groups, and we do...when they are used correctly. Focus groups can be a helpful first step in a serious research process.

But when the first step becomes the *only* step—which has become the case at many companies around the world during the last decade or so—someone has to blow the whistle.

Focus groups as the only step are not just a symptom of death-wish marketing. It's professional malpractice.

One problem with focus groups is that you don't know who you're talking to. Because researchers do not (*cannot,* in fact) select participants scientifically to represent the population (or the target market), corporations are basing multimillion-dollar marketing decisions on the opinions of a small group of unpredictable people with time on their hands who happen to be wandering through shopping malls with nothing better to do. Recruit your focus group participants on a different afternoon or in different mall, and the results may be (and often are) completely different. You might as well consult a Ouija board.

Once the researchers have assembled a group, dozens of irrational dynamics at work skew what the participants have to say. One man likes to hear the sound of his voice and pontificates at length. A woman wonders whether she's giving the "right" answer. Another is uncomfortable confessing her true feelings—if only about a bar of soap—in front of strangers. Still another has no opinions about soap whatsoever but feels obligated to say something. These factors mean that the information the group leader draws from the participants may have little bearing on a product or service's true potential.

Faulty dynamics can exist on the other side of the two-way mirror as well. A major packaged goods client of ours once wanted to know if the world was ready for fruit-flavored potato chips. After sitting through some focus group sessions, the corporate research director was convinced that the chips would be a disaster. His assistant, who sat at his side during the sessions, concluded just the opposite; he submitted a report which suggested that the company had a winner. (More investigation, and the research director's view prevailed.)

Richard Grinchunas, president, and Tony Siciliano, a vice president of A&G Research Inc., made this same point not long ago in *Marketing News* magazine. In focus groups, they argued, the client takes away what he or she wants to take away. In focus groups, "There are no facts. There are only verbatims."

Why do people participate in focus groups? To give companies their opinions? To get out of the house? Three researchers, Peter Tuckel (associate professor, Department of Sociology, Hunter College), Elaine Leppo, and Barbara Kaplan (president and executive vice president, respectively, of In Vision Inc.), found in two studies that money is the main reason.

In an open-ended question ("What would you say was the main reason why you decided to participate in the [last] focus group you attended?"), over half of the 504 respondents who had participated in recent group studies said "money." The authors concluded in *Marketing Research* magazine that "individuals who emphasize money to the exclusion of other factors tend to be less committed to the research." Our own suspicion is that most respondents would be astonished if they knew how seriously American business was taking their responses.

Some clients and agencies claim that they have held so many focus groups that surely by now the results must be quantitative—that it is possible to project the findings. This is insanity! In fact, there is no way to turn qualitative (exploratory) research into quantitative findings that can be projected. It is like trying to convert a patient's statements about her condition into degrees Fahrenheit. In a quantitative research study, researchers interview respondents independently. They measure and tally these opinions precisely. A manager can confidently use only results from properly conducted quantitative, projectable research, using tools with demonstrated reliability and validity to substantially reduce the risk of proceeding in the wrong direction or in a direction that will have little impact.

After the Bush 1992 campaign debacle, Martin Puris, the President's top advertising executive and president of Ammirati & Puris, winced perceptibly when an *Advertising Age* reporter mentioned focus groups and their role in political advertising planning. "Sure, you have to use them in a campaign," said Puris, "because there's no time for in-depth research, but you have to use them as a tool, not as an end. You can't submit your strategy or major concepts to 12 people in Des Moines and then run with the answer, good or bad. In the ad business, we'd never use focus group research the way these people do. It was appalling." It also helped to cost President Bush a second term.

Focus groups, as we've said, have their place. But their widespread overuse and abuse have confused American marketing managers (and politicos) as to the difference between qualitative, exploratory research and quantitative, projectable research.

Don't mistake focus groups for a serious decision-making tool. Focus groups are to serious research what bumper stickers are to philosophy. Only a manager who is an *agent provocateur* (working for the enemy in your company) or one unconsciously compelled, positively driven to make the wrong decision, would use this lightweight tool to guide a major decision.

If you want to talk to a real person, talk to your mother. It's cheaper than a focus group, and you know exactly who you're talking to.

"No, I'm afraid that `Shopping is as much fun as root canal without Novocain' is not one of the choices."

6
Myths about the Marketing Climate

If we were planning a trip on a sailboat between New York and England, we would want to take advantage of all available knowledge as to winds and waves and currents. If in fact we could sail along in possession of such information, we would arrive quickly, comfortably, and safely.

If, on the other hand, we chose to just charge into the wind and the waves and the currents and the storms, we would arrive exhausted. We would be wet, we would have been banged around; it would have taken a very long time, and maybe we would not have gotten there at all.

So smart marketers should be in the business of tracking the weather before embarking on a voyage. This is not to say there aren't some brands that can fight the weather and go counter-wave, counter-wind, counter-current—do something unusual, and stand out for that reason.

Take the sailboat analogy: Sometimes a Dennis Conners can work on a hunch that there is a better wind to be found someplace else, and sail off to the total amazement of more conservative skippers, who will stick with the weather report. And Conners may win. But the number of counter-weather performers who will win is small, and it has as much to do with luck as anything else.

We're saying that you want to be aware of the weather and that there are many, many different forms the weather can take. The myths we're going to talk about here have to do with two different types of weather report. One has to do with changing population characteristics, with demographic variables. The other has to do with consumer values.

Myth 40: The U.S. population is becoming more diverse as men and women, rich and poor, young and old, black and white, Protestants, Catholics, Jews, and other religious groups have less and less in common.

Truth: The media burden us every day with how different men and women are, how different the rich and poor are, how the older generation has different values than the younger, and how blacks and whites are moving in different directions.

It may make good copy, but it's simply not true.

For years we've been tracking American society's homogeneity versus heterogeneity in terms of attitudes and beliefs, values and behavior patterns. The evidence clearly shows that homogeneity is becoming the rule rather than the exception. The differences between genders, socioeconomic groups, age groups, and races are attenuating over time, primarily because of the mass media, mass public education, and the rising level of education.

Women in the 1990s, for example, complain that their husbands are not as warm and affectionate and romantic as they might be. They argue that men are not as helpful around the house and with the housework and with the kids as they ought to be. These swipes have considerable merit; a lot of what women say is true.

On the other hand, men today are quite different from their parents. The attitudes of men and women today toward gender roles are far more similar with respect to values, beliefs, and behavior patterns than were the attitudes of people only a generation ago.

The fact is, the American population is becoming more homogeneous. When we take a complete test battery like the National Opinion Research Center's General Social Survey—which taps into how people feel, what they value, how they choose to spend their leisure time, how they plan to raise their children, the number of children they plan to have, and the like—the results show that different segments within the population are slowly becoming more similar than different.

Take the major issues of the 1992 presidential campaign. As we all know, a critical factor was the economy, something President Bush apparently could do nothing about. Bill Clinton took some comfort in the fact that even as he was being inaugurated the economy seemed to be improving due to causes beyond his control.

The one campaign issue that turned many Americans against George Bush was the one over which he did have some control: freedom of choice. This was the antiabortion plank in the Republican Party platform.

As long as such attitudes have been tracked, a history that goes back to the 1930s, American society has been growing much more liberal in terms of people's attitudes toward abortion. Differences between people who are upscale and those who are disadvantaged, between blacks and whites, and between Protestants and Catholics are diminishing over time. In the 1950s, abortion was anathema to Catholics, both in terms of attitudes and behavior. In the 1990s, Catholics cannot be differentiated from other population segments in their attitudes toward abortion.

The fastest-growing segment of the American population is the Asian-American. Some people wonder what the United States cultural landscape will look like in 50 years, with this terrific increase in the number of Asian-Americans.

But while this population group is growing rapidly, it is also adopting mainstream, middle-class American values faster than any immigrant group since German Jews. In the school system and in the job market, Asian-Americans are increasingly undifferentiated from Caucasian-Americans. Increasingly they are surpassing Caucasian-Americans in school and job performance. If anything, the acceleration of Asians into the U.S. population will accelerate the increased homogeneity of the population generally.

The implication of this is that there is a growing potential for mass marketing. If mass television is in decline, it is because it has become so expensive and fragmented vehicles more economical. The pundits who tell us that the days of mass television campaigns are over, because the population is becoming so disparate, are off the mark. They are like a weather-person telling people they should flee town because a hurricane is coming, when in fact the weather will be clear.

Myth 41: Knowing consumer values will not help us to understand how people will behave in the future, or how to motivate them to buy our product.

Truth: Values are the things people believe in, the qualities they hold dear, that are important to them. People have beliefs with respect to the family, to morality, to leisure time.

We have met marketing executives who acknowledge that consumer values can be interesting but who believe they are irrelevant. (This is one reason why, as we pointed out in Chapter 2, so few marketing plans discuss consumer lifestyles and values.) Knowing someone's attitude toward honesty or toward leisure time, they feel, does not help them to understand the future any better.

When consumer values change, the marketing environment changes, and the first company to recognize the change can be enormously successful. In the mid-1980s, a friend told Mark Begelman over a drink that he was selling astronomical quantities of office products to a membership discount warehouse chain. He wondered if there were any merit to developing an office products superstore that could cater to the small business market. Could one apply the operating principles of the warehouse club to an industry in which the channels of distribution had ossified?

At the time Begelman was in the office products industry, and a lightbulb went off over his head. Extensive consumer research had found that 27 percent of all consumers said they would shop at an office products store that offered discounts up to 40 percent off list price; another third said they would be very interested.

The industry, however, was dominated by 18,000 independent mom-and-pop office supply stores that were out of sync with their customers. For example, while 67 percent of the customers said that price had led them to choose one office products dealer over another, only 12 percent of the dealers said that price had led customers to choose a dealer. "It became very obvious to me," says Begelman, "that an opportunity existed to tap into the small business market, to treat the smallest customers as if they were an IBM or a General Motors in terms of purchasing of office products." In 1986 Office Club was born in California, with Begelman as president and CEO.

By the time Office Club merged with Office Depot in 1991, with Begelman as president and COO, the chain had 51 membership warehouse stores in nine western states. Office Depot, a marketing myth-busting organization, is the largest office products superstore chain in North America, operating—at the end of April 1993—303 stores in the United States and Canada, with plans to open approximately 60 new stores a year in both 1993 and 1994. Total 1992 net sales were $1.7 billion (up 33 percent over 1991), while net earnings were $39 million (a 161 percent increase).

Myth 42: Status-seeking remains an important motivation for people, and an effective way to differentiate products and services.

Truth: Conventional status symbols are fading, a change that began to occur before the most recent recession. Americans are beginning to sense that what you know, and how you spend your leisure time, is more important than what you have. The idea that, as the bumper sticker said, THE PERSON WHO DIES WITH THE MOST TOYS WINS, has been discredited.

Personal, customized, individual accomplishments—writing a book, climbing Mt. Everest, learning Japanese—will be much more powerful in the mid-1990s than the conventional symbols of success—a 6000-square-foot home, a $20,000 Rolex watch, a gas-guzzling power boat.

Twenty years ago, many Americans thought that a woman wearing a full-length sable coat and a three-carat diamond, and driving a Ferrari convertible, represented the pinnacle of success. (Not every single person, of course, but enough to set the country's mood.) More and more, these external symbols of wealth and status are a sign that you're a jerk.

Such display is not the only behavior diminishing. Smoking a pack of cigarettes before breakfast, belonging to two clubs, drinking three martinis at lunch, lining up four trash containers at the curb, and raising five children were conventional behavior for social trend-setters in the 1950s; today they are increasingly socially embarrassing.

Conspicuous consumption is decreasing, and it's not clear whether it's coming back or not. This is not because people cannot afford to consume conspicuously. Rather, people feel they have other more important things to do with money than to spend it frivolously. Our research has found a need for deeper social connections, particularly with one's family; a need for greater emotional enhancement; a desire for more meaningful social commitments and community involvement; and living what is increasingly called a "self-examined" life.

We have found that Americans are starved for leisure time, for having time to do things by themselves, for themselves, or with their families. Almost half (47 percent) of all Americans told us they have only a little or no free time. More than two-thirds (69 percent) of the public would like to slow down and live a more relaxed life, while only one out of five (19 percent) would prefer to live a more exciting, faster-paced life.

Significantly, while all Americans feel these pressures, women are especially affected. They are near the breaking point when it comes to juggling the demands of family, jobs, and children.

This yearning for the simple life has wide-ranging consequences for marketers. Consumers no longer feel the need to buy the "best" or most expensive products; they are saying that there are better things to do with their time and money. Status and prestige are increasingly seen as mere surrogates for quality while convenience, reliability, and price value are in the ascendancy.

Myth 43: People like to shop; it's a form of recreation.

Truth: Are you kidding? People *hate* to shop. Shopping may once have been a form of recreation among certain women, but no longer. (Teenagers cruising the mall are not what we would call "shoppers," that is, people who are looking for products they will actually "buy," i.e., exchange money for.)

People do not like to shop; it's one reason why catalog retailers—L. L. Bean, Land's End, Eddie Bauer, Norm Thompson, and hundreds of others—have grown so. Prodigy Information Service's appeal in certain markets is that it permits subscribers to do their food shopping without leaving home; just type up the order on your home computer.

A consumer study, sponsored by MasterCard and conduced by LAR Management Consultants and Yankelovich Partners and released in January 1993, found that 17 percent of all Americans (all right, it was really a nationally projectable sample of 1000 consumers between the ages of 18 and 74) described themselves as "disenchanted shoppers." Another 22 percent were "low-interest shoppers."

"Affluent customers used to love to shop till they dropped," says Jack Mitchell, one of the owners of Mitchell's, a myth-busting clothing store in Westport, Conn. At one time, customers would stop by Mitchell's for a cup of coffee and a leisurely afternoon. "It's totally changed," says Mitchell. "They'd rather cocoon with their spouses, or go somewhere, or do something for themselves." The changes have forced Mitchell's to know its customers so well that, when they do come in, the store knows what they do and what kind of clothing they like, and can service them efficiently. Mitchell's, a privately owned, 25,000-square-foot store that sells both men's and women's clothing, has annual sales over $12 million. "You have to be proactive. You have to keep in touch and let them know when new things come in. Then people love it."

In general, we have found decreased consumer involvement in the buying process. Consumers want to spend as little time shopping as possible. They show less active interest in variety or novelty, particularly when it comes to foods, than in the past. According to Yankelovich research, in 1987 almost half (49 percent) of all Americans said they were actively looking for new foods; by 1991 this had dropped 10 percentage points. In 1987, almost 30 percent of all consumers said they were actively looking for new department stores in which to shop; by 1991 the figure had dropped to 15 percent.

Myth 44: Companies can safely ignore the environmental issue.

Truth: Actually, the environment continues to rank among the most important social issues in the country, right up there with quality of education, medical costs, crime, drug and alcohol abuse, and AIDS.

Think of the things we are doing today that would have been unthinkable 10 or 20 years ago: sorting our trash into different bins—tin cans, aluminum cans, clear glass, green glass, newspapers, magazines, and recyclable plastic. Reusing metal coat hangers, plastic shopping bags, and paper sacks. Having a choice between plastic and paper bags at the supermarket. Throwing paint on people wearing fur coats to make a statement about animal rights. Not buying aerosol products because they damage the ozone. Fearing hypodermic needles and medical trash on ocean beaches...but being able to swim in Lake Erie in downtown Cleveland and to eat the fish that's returned to rivers and streams.

Our research indicates that almost two-thirds (62 percent) of all Americans say they usually save cans and bottles for recycling; more than half save newspapers. Almost a third of all consumers say they look for environmentally friendly brands when they are shopping in the supermarket and drug store. When they have a choice, they buy the product with the least packaging.

Since, lamentably, the environment will not improve dramatically or quickly—at this writing, yet another oil tanker has run onto the rocks and is spilling crude oil onto Scottish beaches—consumers will continue to regard the environmental issue as grave. Manufacturers who ignore it do so at their peril.

Myth 45: The "middle market" for products and services is dying.

Truth: The implication of this myth is that products and services need to be positioned at the high end or the low end of the market to be successful .

Let's start by saying that in the 1980s marketers believed (with some validity) that the marketplace was polarized. A product had to be—so ran the thinking—at one extreme of the value chain or the other. An item had to be the cheapest in the market or it had to be the most prestigious, the most luxurious. What defined the high end was not always price, although price was important; high class included status as well.

In the 1980s there were cheap, cheap, cheap products, and prestigious products, and consumers could flaunt them both as badges. They said to the world: I know how to buy something as inexpensive as possible to get the job done...or I can afford the very best, the most luxurious. It was cool to wear a Swatch watch or a Rolex. A company could market a product successfully for $25 or $25,000, but not in between. There was a cachet associated with being at one extreme or the other.

Marketers thought that to be between the two extremes was to be in the middle of nowhere. It was poor marketing to be in the middle. A company in the middle of the value spectrum doesn't stand for anything.

Then a dramatic shift in social values took place in mid-decade. The baby boomers—the group that has driven much of the last 40 years' social change—began to realize that they had fought to be extremely competitive in the early eighties. Much of their urge to get their lives together, to make money, to be immortal, had driven them to be really smart shoppers. It also (slight exaggeration) drove the middle market out of business.

By the end of the decade and the beginning of the 1990s, more and more people were saying, "Wait a minute, there's more to life than conspicuous consumption. There's more to life than finding the absolutely lowest price on the things I want." Consumers are beginning to feel they want a more balanced life.

Balance is the key. If you want to put your life in balance, where is the fulcrum? In the middle. As a result, the consumer's decision to be in the middle suddenly became smart, desirable. Such a stance told the world, "I've streamlined my life. I don't want to make a serious effort at shopping all the time. I'm going to buy brands I know and trust."

The brands consumers know and trust tend to be those in the middle of the market—brands such as Budweiser, Chrysler, Ford, Holiday Inn, Kellogg, and the like. This is one reason why we (the authors) foresee a resurgence in middle brands, because consumers feel that buying them is a smart decision.

Buyers are becoming more practical. They're streamlining their lives, seeking substance and value in products and services, avoiding traditional status symbols. They have thrown off their need to be at one extremity or the other. Right now (the pendulum can always continue to swing) most consumers look for a good balance of price and value rather than, at one frontier, the lowest possible price, and at the other, the highest prestige. As a result, the middle market is thriving in most product categories.

Myth 46: Brand loyalty is dead.

Truth: It may be ailing, and marketers may yet be able to kill it, but it is far from dead.

Brand loyalty, we should say at the outset, comes in two flavors: attitudinal and behavioral. Attitudinal loyalty reflects how buyers feel and think about your product or service, what share they give you in their hearts and minds. Behavioral loyalty, in contrast, is about action, about behavior, about what people do; what share they give you of their product category purchases or their time.

Marketers want and need *both* flavors. See Exhibit 6.1 for an example of both types of loyalty as they relate to people and relationships between them. A "high" level of attitudinal and behavioral loyalty (lower right-hand of the box) suggests a happy marriage—something every firm would like to have with its customers. The concern, however, is that "low" levels of loyalty (the upper left-hand of the box) are becoming more common, that the relationship between companies and their customers is becoming increasingly impersonal and distant.

The contemporary marketplace is awash with generic products, competing brands, and line extensions. In this climate, the big scare is that brand loyalty—consumer loyalty to an established brand—is

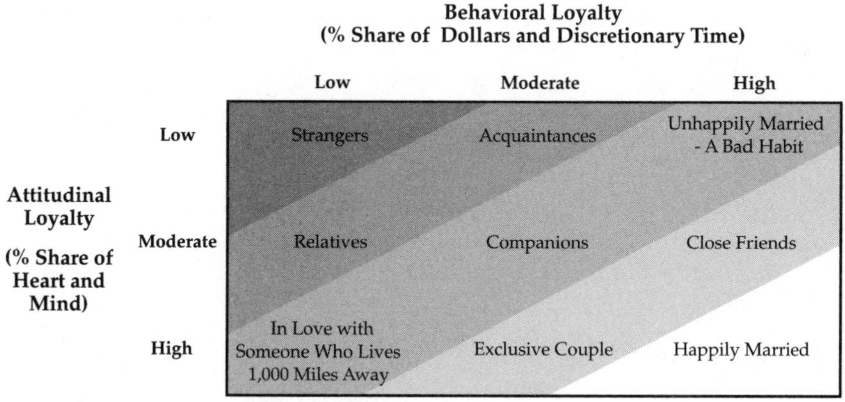
Behavioral Loyalty
(% Share of Dollars and Discretionary Time)
Low
Moderate
High
Low
Strangers
Acquaintances
Unhappily Married
- A Bad Habit
Attitudinal
Loyalty
(% Share of
Heart and
Mind)
Moderate
Relatives
Companions
Close Friends
High
In Love with
Someone Who Lives
1,000 Miles Away
Exclusive Couple
Happily Married

Exhibit 6-1 Two types of brand loyalty.

going to go down the tubes. A recent *Newsweek* article states, however, "Diminished brand loyalty is the trend of the moment; whether it will be the trend of the next time the robins return only the trendiest of trend spotters dares guess."

As consumers streamline their lives, branding becomes a dominating factor in consumer decision making (where brand is a factor, at all). Brands offer consumers a shortcut to identify products and services with high value—hardly a new idea. Seven out of ten American consumers agree with the statement, "I buy the same brand over and over again without really thinking about it." Almost 6 out of 10 agree that "I don't have time to investigate the quality of different brands, so I usually just buy the same brand I bought last time." And almost three-quarters of all consumers agree that "once I find a brand I like, it is very difficult to get me to change brands."

There really is no "crisis" associated with brand loyalty. It is simply the case that many companies held fast to their old brand status/image/positions during the 1980s, and their names—Listerine, Nieman Marcus, and IBM—began to slip away. The latter company lost sales to cheaper (allegedly just-as-good) catalog or mail-order personal computers.

It is also true that too many marketers are killing their brands with promotions, decreased advertising spending, and line extensions.

On the other hand, Toys 'R Us stocks only name brands, and they owe their success and their consumer patronage to their brand-name policy. Sears Roebuck gave up on its private label (Kenmore) appliances and added brand names to its stock.

When people believe "brand" means something more than a name, when the brand becomes a resumé reflecting accomplishment, performance, and superiority, they go for them. Brand loyalty is hardly dead.

"I know Chevrolet is `The Heartbeat of America,' but do you really think Chevy Electronic Heart Pacemakers is a good line extension?"

7
Myths about New Products

While new products and services can be a company's lifeblood—consider Rubbermaid and 3M, two companies famous for their flow of successful new products—they can also be a drag on profitability. Consider the statistics we cited at the beginning of this book. Introducing one failure after another does little for a company's morale or balance sheet.

Because new products are so important to so many companies, they have propagated an entire flock of myths, starting with the following.

Myth 47: Most new products fail.

Truth: Why do we now say this is a myth, when up to now we've stated this as a fact every chance we've had?

Because the products (or services; when we use one term we mean both) are not always the problem. The strategies for developing them and taking them to market also fail.

If the new product development effort was guided by smart strategic thinking, and the new product introduction was directed by intelligent market targeting, positioning, and pricing, the probability of success is very high.

In our experience, new products fail for five reasons (we've compressed a lot of information into these five). First is a weak, poorly articulated targeting and positioning strategy; 3 out of 10 failures fall into this category. Second is product/service dissatisfaction, the failure to meet and exceed consumer expectations and competitive offerings; this accounts for another 3 out of 10 failures. Third is an insufficient level of new product awareness, a problem due to weak or inadequate advertising, not enough sales effort, and the like (20 percent of the cases). Fourth and fifth are insufficient promotion and inadequate distribution (10 percent each).

These figures reflect our experience with new packaged goods and services, and our attempt to force all failures into one category or another. Yet the general finding that the product itself accounts for less than one-third of the failures is, we suggest, a discovery common to a broad range of industries.

Since the product itself is not the main reason for the failure, there's a felicitous corollary to our analysis. Many new products that fail upon introduction into the marketplace can be resuscitated. Often it's a matter of fixing some problems with the marketing plan, adjusting the positioning strategy, increasing the promotion and distribution or reformulating/redesigning the product. This is very good news. It means that a seemingly dead patient can be revived, to go on to live a healthy life.

Myth 48: New product failure rates have declined as companies have become more effective marketers.

Truth: Fifty years ago, more than half of all new products introduced succeeded (by succeeded, we mean the product was still on the shelf, still in distribution, two years after introduction). Products that did succeed could expect to be around 50 years or more. As we pointed out in Chapter 2, many products introduced at an earlier time are still market leaders today.

Twenty-five years ago, 65 percent of the products that packaged goods companies launched succeeded, and many of these products are still around today. In 1993, as we write this, only 10 percent of new products are successful, and for those that are successful, the life expectancy is only about five years.

Of course these statistics vary from one category to the next, but not as much as you might think. In the fast-food category, only about 1 percent of new products are successful. In high-tech categories, the life span of a new product is especially short; one estimate puts the average personal computer's life expectancy at 13 months.

Today, almost all consumer markets are mature. Whatever real growth there is comes from population increases, which never exceed 1 to 2 percent a year. To survive, a new product must wrench market share away from established brands.

In the past, a few brands shared most of the volume in most product categories. These markets were what economists call "undifferentiated oligopolies"—a few dominant brands, and virtually no price competition. As the markets grew, consumers eagerly looked for and companies enthusiastically provided the product diversity that new entries represented. Since the dominant brands were often slow to adapt, new brands were able to win market share.

Today, product categories are so saturated that market structures exhibit what economists call "monopolistic competition." This apparent oxymoron describes a market in which no one brand dominates, where product differentiation is not so much in product performance as in brand perception, and where price competition is intense. These are not ideal conditions for a new product that must build its brand image from scratch.

The trade is another new marketplace power. As recently as the early 1980s, retailers tended to be passive channels for product distribution. Today, retailers are an active, powerful marketing element. They have provoked considerable price competition among manufacturers. They insist on slotting allowances (money to put your product on their shelves) and failure fees (money to make up what they would have earned if your product had sold properly). These protect them against the flood of new products. Add these costs to the high advertising and couponing expenses and it is difficult—sometimes impossible—for new product marketers to generate an adequate margin, one that will pay for the marketing program and return a profit.

Finally, marketers have watched advertising's productivity decline in the past decade, particularly network television's (more on this in Chapter 10). When there were only three networks that between them reached 96 percent of all American homes, network TV was critically important to building brand awareness and to telling consumers that new products were available and desirable.

Traditional marketing communications has lost much of its effect through media fragmentation, the splintering of communications budgets, and the prevalence of promotional pricing.

All of which suggests to us that new product failure rates have increased as companies have become less effective marketers.

Myth 49: If a man can write a better book, preach a better sermon, or make a better mousetrap than his neighbor, though he builds his house in the woods the world will make a beaten path to his door.

Truth: So Ralph Waldo Emerson said, and perhaps at the time—the middle of the nineteenth century—it was true. It has not been true for a long time, but the "better mousetrap" fallacy is alive and well.

Professor Philip Kotler has written that many manufacturers still believe that consumers will favor products that offer the most quality, performance, and features. The organization should therefore devote its energy to making continuous product improvements; the Japanese even have a word for this, *kaizen*.

Kotler, the S.C. Johnson & Son Distinguished Professor of International Marketing at the Kellogg Graduate School of Management, Northwestern University, points out that while a consumer may be looking for a way to rid her house of mice, she may not want a mousetrap at all. She may prefer a chemical spray, an exterminator, or a cat.

Some companies—taking Emerson's adage thoroughly to heart—have actually built better mousetraps and failed miserably. One inventor created a high-tech laser mousetrap that cost $1500. It did not sell well.

But even a better mousetrap that retails for $1.98 will not sell unless the manufacturer packages it attractively, distributes it to stores (or through catalogs) where consumers can buy it, brings it to the attention of the people who need it, and convinces them that it is indeed a better mousetrap.

Consider as a cautionary tale Steven P. Jobs and the NeXT computer. Since Jobs virtually had created the consumer/home computer industry with the Apple and the Macintosh, the world expected something spectacular from Jobs' next computer, which turned out to be the NeXT computer.

The machine was slick, with a black magnesium housing and a CD-ROM reader (for Compact Disk—Read Only Memory), the first to be included in a desktop computer. Reviewers said it was even more user-friendly than the Macintosh, which was very friendly indeed.

But if the NeXT was user-friendly, Jobs and his partners (Canon and Ross Perot put up $200 million) never made it clear exactly what the machine was or who its customers were supposed to be. Was it a personal computer, a high-end version of the Macintosh? Or was it a work station, a low-end version of the Sun Microsystems machine? Was it for students? Business managers? Engineers?

When he introduced the NeXT, Jobs said the machine was a "scholar's work station," whatever that might mean, and said that the target market was to be institutions of higher education exclusively. But at $10,000 apiece, the distinctive black box was a tad rich for that market. There was another problem: Scholars need software, and NeXT, which was not compatible with either Apple or IBM, offered little.

NeXT decided to try the business market and made a deal with Businessland, at the time the leading personal computer retailer. But it takes more than a deal with a computer retailer to sell the corporate market, and neither NeXT nor Businessland did very well. Businessland went bankrupt for reasons unrelated to NeXT computers, although if NeXT had been a runaway sales success it might have made a difference.

NeXT next decided that what it really should be doing was to compete with Sun, the work station market leader. To do so, NeXT added a direct sales force, which proved surprisingly successful. NeXT finished the fourth quarter of 1992 with revenues of $45 million and its first-ever operating profit.

That might have been the turning point, but it was not. The NeXT machines, dazzling as they were when first introduced, were already falling behind the competition, a comment on how quickly technology moves in the computer industry. In February 1993, Jobs announced the sale of the NeXT hardware to Canon Ltd., one of the company's original investors, which intended to market the machines under its own name.

Jobs said at the time, "We understand we could work really hard for the next few years and emerge as a good second-tier hardware company. But people are telling us there are just three competitors for the software, and we have a chance to become a first-tier software company."

The idea that a product can sell itself runs deep. Kenneth Olsen, the former chairman of Digital Equipment Corp., which lost $636 million in fiscal 1992, has been quoted as saying, "You only need marketing if there is something wrong with your product."

Every company needs marketing, if only because one of the things marketing will do is help management see how to change the product so that the market does not pass it by.

Myth 50: A company cannot *create* markets.

Truth: This is a misreading of the marketing concept, notes Professor Frederick E. Webster, Jr.

The marketing concept was defined by Professor Theodore Levitt in his influential *Harvard Business Review* article, "Marketing Myopia":

> Selling focuses on the needs of the seller; marketing on the needs of the buyer. Selling is preoccupied with the seller's need to convert his product into cash; marketing with the idea of satisfying the needs of the consumer by means of the product and the whole cluster of things associated with creating, delivering, and finally consuming it.

The problem arises, says Webster (who is the E.B. Osborn Professor of Marketing at the Amos Tuck School of Business Administration at Dartmouth College), when executives interpret the marketing concept to mean that the height of marketing sophistication is to identify and respond to *existing* consumer needs and wants.

That is a myth because it assumes that consumers (individual people, business executives, government officials—everybody who spends money for products or services) can always identify their needs and wants. What made Fred Smith (Federal Express), Ray Kroc (McDonald's), and Steve Jobs (Apple) so extraordinary is that they identified needs people did not know they had. They created whole new industries

Here, Webster adds, is a major shortcoming of excessive reliance on market research: Customers can't tell you much about something they want, if they don't know about it or if it doesn't yet exist. Conventional market research is not likely to reveal really exciting breakthrough business opportunities.

The more breakthrough the product, the more broadly must the company search for consumer problems. For example, if a product is a new brand in an existing category, all the company has to do is talk to people about features and benefits of the existing products to see how the new product will fare. It is not as difficult to research Comet Bathroom Cleaner ("Removes Tough Soap Scum *and* Hard Water Stains") as it was to research the first consumer microwave oven.

If you are the Radio Corporation of America in 1935 and capable of inventing television, you have to think of entertainment very broadly. To do the research properly, you would start searching for problems that have to do with entertainment. These might suggest that maybe it would be good to bring radio with pictures into the home. (Then again, it might not. After all, it was Darryl F. Zanuck, head of 20th Century Fox Studios, who said in 1946, "Video won't be able to hold onto any market it captures after the first six months. People will soon get tired of staring at a plywood box every night.")

If you're looking at a product in an entirely new product category—paper towels before there were paper towels, disposable diapers when diaper services were at their peak, a plain paper copier when offices got by with carbon paper and mimeograph machines—the research becomes a little trickier, but you can do it.

If Xerox had done a problem-detection study in 1965, it might well have found two things: They were asking companies to spend thousands of dollars on a machine that solved a problem companies felt they had already solved with carbon paper. *And* the existing solution wasn't very good; it was time-consuming, messy, and inadequate. We argue that such a study would have shown the need for a plain paper copy machine.

Myth 51: A company must offer the highest-quality products.

Truth: This myth has a corollary: The higher the quality, the greater the chances of marketing success. After all, isn't that the tactic the Japanese employed to lay waste the American automobile industry?

Compaq Computer prior to 1992 is a perfect example of a company that followed this policy and got into deep trouble. James Garrity, Compaq's director of marketing communications, North America, says the company grew originally because customers perceived Compaq as an IBM-compatible product with better than IBM quality. But over time the elegance in engineering went from being an asset to a liability. Engineers were encouraged to take a high-quality product and make it better. The internal expression was "creeping elegance." The improvements drove up the cost, which did not correspond to the value offered. The company's prices were out of line with the rest of the market, says Garrity "because the rest of the market was delivering what customers were looking for—adequate quality at a respectable price. Not the ultimate in quality at a high price."

After a 1991 management change, CEO Eckhard Pfeiffer's marching orders were dramatically different. He said in effect, "Engineer to a price. Take a customer view of the world. What is the price point that will motivate a customer to look at our product? Then you guys, who have the reputation for being the best engineers in the world, figure how to build this product at this price." Two small examples of cost savings that came out of completely fresh thinking: Compaq thought that it could buy power supplies for much less than it cost to build them. It found that it did not need to run new computers for 96 hours to test them. "There were ways through sampling and testing to learn enough in the first hour of testing to obviate the need for the last 95 hours," says Garrity, "and that made a dramatic impact." In June 1992, Compaq introduced 45 new computer models (for a total of 76) as well as across-the-board price cuts of as much as 32 percent, bringing the price differential between Compaq's machines and low-ball clones from 35 percent to 15 percent.

What happened when Compaq stopped searching for perfect quality? Sales zoomed to $4.1 billion in 1992, up 25 percent from the year earlier. Net income did better: $213 million in 1992, up 63 percent from 1991's figure. And even more remarkably, operating expenses as a percent of sales declined from 25.7 percent in the fourth quarter of 1991 to 16.4 percent in the fourth quarter of 1992.

American companies are fixated on how to guarantee the highest product-quality levels. In recent years, management consultants have made "zero defects" the corporate watchword at consumer and industrial firms from coast to coast. The underlying theory is that absolutely perfect products will lead naturally—almost inevitably—to maximum profitability. (Thoughtful readers will recognize this as a version of the "better mousetrap" theory we've just trashed.)

We've found, however, that across a broad range of categories, customer satisfaction with products is curvilinearly related to profitability. That is, as the customer satisfaction curve rises, the profit curve drops. Why? Because extremely high product quality levels are often unnecessary (they represent overkill) and the cost of delivering them is exorbitant.

Buyers of consumer and industrial products often fail to discriminate between excellent and absolutely perfect products. If the cost is low to bottle, bottle soft drinks in cans with no variation in carbonation, to design a piece of software that is totally bug-free, or to manufacture a machine part that breaks down once in a century, the company should do it. But the fact is that for many products the cost of moving from excellent to perfect is often enormous.

(At the same time, of course, there are situations in which every product must be perfect; bungee-jumping cords, parachutes, and jet engines come immediately to mind. If the buyer can, and will, discriminate between perfect and excellent, and if the difference between the two means pain, dismemberment, or death, we think a company should go for perfect.)

For these reasons, a company that automatically invests in perfect-quality products is not necessarily making the best investment. Rather, a corporation should seek a financially optimal balance between customer needs and expectations on the one hand and, on the other, the firm's resources and capabilities and the costs of maintaining quality standards.

It is not necessary to build a car that *never* has a mechanical problem—even $40,000-plus, brilliantly engineered German and Japanese luxury performance sedans have occasional problems that require a visit to the local dealer.

Myth 52: The key to company profits—not to mention personal promotion—is to create new products.

Truth: When we were running the Yankelovich organization, the marketing and sales executives were constantly pressing for new products. The company was a consulting business dedicated to providing business-to-business services to large corporations, and it seemed that every salesperson wanted to have one new product to talk about every year.

One year our sales manager told us that we had to have a new product to take to Clorox, one of our best customers and one of the smartest marketers in the country. We said we didn't have a new product, but we agreed to travel to the Bay area to chat with Clorox about the products and services we had been delivering for a number of years, products Clorox had not yet bought.

We were amazed to discover that Clorox marketing managers and researchers—well informed about the Yankelovich products and services they had purchased—were aware only of the services they had used. Since Clorox at the time was buying perhaps 10 percent of our products and services, it meant that 90 percent of the things we had to offer were, for all practical purposes, new to them.

Coming home from that meeting, we decided to survey our customers and prospects to learn what they knew about us. We found many customers who knew less about our firm's products than we would have thought (or liked). We certainly found far more prospects who knew relatively little about our products and services than prospects who knew everything about us. Based on this research, we told our salespeople that it was more effective to invest the firm's money to communicate information about the products we already offered than to invest in new services. As a result, we began to see more customers buying more products.

If a company's customers have good experiences—they know what the company is like, they know what it can do—presumably they will buy other products or services. Assuming the company offers a range of services it can sell to those customers, it does not have to create more.

A problem can arise, however. As more and more companies decentralize their marketing down to the strategic business unit level, they will have salespeople who will be paid to sell a particular product or service and not to represent the entire company. Say you are in the scientific instruments business; one division sells air purification equipment to hospitals, another sells chemical analyzers to hospitals. If each group is not rewarded for cross-selling the other's products, it's not only conceivable but likely that your hospital clients will use one of your products but not the other.

For most organizations, it is more cost-effective to sell more products or services to the existing customer base than to pressure R&D to create new products.

Myth 53: Line extensions are the least risky way to introduce new products.

Truth: Another version of this myth goes something like: Because line extensions are easier to develop and introduce than completely new brands, they are the most profitable.

Like many of our myths, this one may have been true once (which is why people believe it today), and it may still be true in certain special circumstances. Brand extension strategies often offer great market potential—a strong brand name can give immediate recognition to an extension, with savings in advertising and promotion. It's also a classic way to ensure brand/market continuity as the core brand matures, maintaining sales and profit levels.

On the other hand, a brand extension can be risky for the following reasons.

1. The brand name is sometimes slapped on a disappointing product. This does damage to the core brand's reputation. As an example, the "Cadillac Cimarron" was actually a Chevy Cavalier with leather seats and some luxury appointments. It was aimed not at the Cadillac buyer but at the less affluent who wanted a Cadillac at a lower price. It ceased production, but not before it hurt the Cadillac image. New Coke was another example. The product was as embarrassing to Coca-Cola executives as discovering that you have left for work without your pants on.
2. The core name may be inappropriate for the new product (and vice versa), even if the new product is well made and performs as intended. A good example is Toro's electric, hand-maneuvered "Toro Sno-pup," a spinoff from its line of heavy-duty snow blowers. The core name should have legitimized the line extension. Instead, consumers thought the name indicated a weak, far less effective snow removal machine—as it was. But it was intended for "cleanup"—light snow on walkways and porches—and for the apartment or condo dweller, with its light weight and compact storage. It bombed until Toro dropped the "Sno-pup" name, made its positioning/usage clearer, and separated it from Toro's main line of snow blowers and tractors.
3. Through overuse, the core name may lose its unique positioning in

the consumer's mind, leaving an apparently "loosely" connected bunch of brands, with the appearance of being in the same general category.

Brand extensions have run amok. They have been turning consumers into feature shoppers and retailers into shelf-space auctioneers. What's a feature shopper? Someone who buys a product only for a certain feature. In 1980, for example, Kotex offered Maxi Pads for feminine protection. Today there are Maxi Regular; Super Maxi; Thin Maxi; Thin Super Maxi; Ultra Thin Maxi; Ultra Thin Long Maxi; Shaped Maxi; Overnites; Curved Maxi; and Curved Super Maxi.

What's the problem with this? There are a couple of obvious ones. A big single brand is now a portfolio of smaller pieces, which makes the company's management task much more complex. It means that more and more products are chasing a relatively stable amount of shelf space. As we learned in Economics 101, when demand increases and supply remains constant, prices rise. Sure enough, retailers are charging manufacturers to put new products onto the shelves and, if a product does not meet sales or profit goals, they are charging manufacturers an exit fee.

Consider ConAgra's Healthy Choice line of frozen entrees, one of the most successful new product introductions of the 1980s The products were well prepared, tasty, nicely packaged, and came with a very strong positioning strategy.

Then ConAgra made a fatal error: They began slapping the name Healthy Choice on a broad range of products including desserts (ice cream), soup, pizza, and low-fat ground beef—relatively few of which met even minimal standards for product success. As a result they tarnished the Healthy Choice brand name and ConAgra's reputation among retailers and consumers.

Other examples? Cadbury—associated with excellent chocolate—brought out Cadbury's Smash instant potato product, dried milk, soups, and beverages—all a giant step away from the brand's key association—and failed. Woolite's Tough Stain rug cleaner conflicted with the brand's image for washing delicate clothes. Similarly, SOS Glassworks glass cleaner evoked negative associations, given the brand's famous scouring pads.

One of the biggest line extension disappointments recently is Crystal Pepsi. Here's a product we called a flop before it left the starting gate. Not only are sales below expectations but it is having a negative ruboff on the Pepsi image.

Brand extensions erode consumer loyalty. Since 1975, the NPD Group, a Port Washington (New York) research firm, has maintained a database of 50 brands that were first, second, or third in their category when the firm began its study. Joel Rubinson, the firm's chief research officer, says that although consumer loyalty (as measured by share of requirements among a brand's own buyers) has declined somewhat overall, it has declined significantly more for brands that exist in categories with increased levels of "feature segmentation." It also declined significantly more for brands that decreased, rather than increased, advertising support. (We'll talk about advertising in detail in Chapter 10.)

Line extensions are particularly risky because they tend to cannibalize the present product. The pattern has become common across different industries. Marketers, eager for quick success, introduce the line extension to a major brand. The "line extension manager" introduces the new entry, diverting resources away from its parent. The extension may achieve its sales objective and the manager is rewarded. Then the parent brand goes into a slow decline and the diagnosis is cannibalism.

Net incremental profits—not sales—should be the criterion for evaluating line extensions. And when a company takes NIP into account, line extensions often prove to be far more risky than most marketers have been led to believe.

Myth 54: The way to make incremental improvements in a product is to test the new version against the old.

Truth: This is one of those ideas that seems to make a lot of sense. Suppose we have an exceptionally successful frozen condensed five-juice fruit drink, and the production people point out that we could save a tenth of a cent a can by cutting back on the high-fructose corn syrup we're using as a sweetener. That's not a lot of money in and of itself, but add up all the millions of cans we sell and not only does it become a lot of money, it drops directly to the bottom line.

But what will it do to sales? Let's find out. We test the new formulation against the old and learn that 98 percent of all consumers can't tell any difference. The sales decline is more than offset by the material savings. We make the change.

Next year, with the price of cherry juice going through the roof, we test a formulation with less cherry juice against the current product and find essentially the same thing: Most people can't tell the difference.

Next year there's a problem with the pear crop, but now we've got a routine. Reformulate and test. As before, few consumers can taste any real difference between the new, cheaper formulation and the current product.

The fallacy here is that almost everyone could taste the difference if the company were to test the most recent version against the original. These incremental adulterations slowly, slowly weaken the product. Consumers drop away not because they taste any real difference between one version and the next but because they sense something is wrong.

We've seen this particular wheel turn a complete cycle. Sales eventually fall far enough to attract management's concern. A new product manager takes over and replaces all the ingredients slowly removed and runs a "New! Improved!" campaign to attract customers back to the product. Sometimes the effort works, but even when it does, the expense tends to be more than the savings the company realized during the years of adulteration.

When the effort *doesn't* work, of course, the product dies.

Myth 55: A product that scores high in a concept test will be a sure winner in the market.

Truth: On its face value, the statement seems to make sense, but it assumes a number of things.

It assumes that the concept test is reliable and valid, but, as we discussed in Chapter 5, we know relatively little about the reliability and validity of much concept testing.

We do know that most companies do their concept tests among small, nonprojectable samples of people we have described as roving through shopping malls with time on their hands. To gauge the new concept's appeal, researchers ask these lost souls questions based on a one- or two-paragraph description of the concept. Often the description does not include a name or a price. And most of the time the company does not present a competitive frame; that is, it asks people to rate the concept in a contextual void.

Such research is patently nonsensical, and no one should expect it to yield surefire marketplace successes, even when the concept scores high.

True, new forms of concept research constantly evolve. We were amused by the American Marketing Association's program for the January 1992 conference on attitudinal research. We think the program, generally the most prestigious of the AMA's annual marketing research conferences, might have been relabeled "Death-Wish Marketing and How To Do It." One wizened veteran observer of this conference has facetiously suggested that the more bizarre the methodology, the more word-of-mouth advertising and awareness it generates. The more advertising and awareness, the more companies adopt it. In our industry, he says, a harebrained idea has yet to get in the way of success.

Today some companies are heralding bizarre concept-testing tools as methodological breakthroughs. Indeed, one concept-testing tool is based on exposing a small, nonprojectable sample in a single market to 100 different concepts, presented in no particular order, and making sales potential forecasts for each of the concepts. These are preposterous research tools; if marketers use them, they are much more likely to yield failure than success.

So, point number one: The myth assumes that concept-testing research is reliable and valid, while our experience is that much concept-testing research, particularly the kind utilizing these new technologies, is neither.

But assume for the moment (as most companies assume every day) that the concept-testing procedure is valid. Assume the company hires a leading consulting firm such as Bases, ESP, Novaction, or even Copernicus. Assume the questions are valid, the stimulus makes sense, the research procedures are commendable, the sample is projectable, and all the rest. What happens next?

Often the pieces don't add up. The advertising, the distribution, the other elements of the marketing plan are flawed. In most instances, only about 30 percent of the variability in new product performance can be explained by the new product concept itself. Or to put it the other way, 70 percent of the variability (or 70 percent of the time) the reasons for a product's success or failure lie outside the concept itself.

This naturally suggests that high concept scores in and of themselves do not answer the question on everyone's lips: Will the new product be successful or not? Even if the research is strong and the marketing program is solid as well, the product may not be a success for the reasons we discuss in the very next myth.

Myth 56: The more appealing a new product, the more likely it will be a success.

Truth: By "more appealing," we mean the research shows that many people—scads and scads—say they intend to buy it. This is a common finding and a common fallacy.

One of the most interesting discoveries our research has turned up is that the most appealing product concept is always the least profitable.

Why? Because, at its most basic level, the most appealing concept is a quadruple-scoop ice cream cone with chocolate sprinkles—for a dime. The product has enormous consumer appeal, but is no way to make money in the ice cream business.

That's the extreme, an example all managers grasp immediately. Unfortunately, they do not always understand that their new or repositioned product is like that dime cone—it has consumer appeal but it loses money. Or—somewhat more commonly—the product will not actually lose money, but will not be making what it could.

A current example of this problem can be found in the automobile industry. Cars are now so loaded with safety and antipollution equipment, powerful engines, antilock brakes, and super stereos—all features that are very appealing—that they cost too much, $18,000 on average, compared to $9000 a decade ago. So people are staying away from the showrooms and sales are way down.

This problem would be of only academic concern were it not for marketing's heavy focus today on "appeal scores." "How did the concept perform in terms of 'top box' purchase probability ratings?" the product manager asks, confident that purchase interest and profits are moving together. The higher the score, the greater the manager's interest in the offering.

Here, for example, is a simplified version of three hotel concepts: management's favorite, the most appealing to the consumer, and the optimal.

An Evaluation of Three Different Hotel Concepts

	Alternative concepts		
	Management's favorite	Most appealing	Optimal
	Configuration		
Restaurant	2 Restaurants	2 Restaurants	1 Restaurant
Staff service	Moderate	Excellent	Excellent
Pool	Yes	Yes	Yes
Fitness center	No	Yes	No
Room size	Small	Large	Moderate
Business service	No	Yes	No
Bath size	Small	Large	Moderate
Shuttle	No	Yes	No
Rate per night	$50	$30	$60
	Performance		
Trial	29%	65%	34%
Market share	4.3%	7.1%	5.2%
Sales revenues	$100MM	$160MM	$125MM
Costs	$120MM	$310MM	$95MM
Gross margin	($20MM)	($150MM)	$30MM

Note that management's favorite would have lost $20 million in the first year, while the most appealing concept—with much greater trial and market share—would have lost $150 million. The optimal concept, while obtaining neither the trial nor the share figures of the most appealing concept (although somewhat better than management's favorite), is much less expensive than the other two and therefore profitable.

Sadly, what interests prospects the most—the concept that earns the highest purchase interest score—is a temptation marketers must avoid.

"The world is changing. We need to take a serious look at our targeting decisions. Instead of targeting 18-to-49-year-old women, let's address our efforts to women 25 to 54."

8
Myths about Targeting

The targeting decision is one of the first issues a marketing manager considers. By "targeting decision" we mean identifying people we want to direct our marketing efforts toward. Who are the folks who should buy our product or service?

One of marketing's great mysteries to us is why so many companies devote so little time to this decision. In some firms, no time at all. The decision is made as quickly as buying a favorite brand of cigarettes, the result of a bad habit of many years. They think they know who the target should be, and they go after it without much research or evaluation. And like that quickly purchased pack of cigarettes, it's a habit that can kill you (or your market position).

We should differentiate here between two different targets: the product's buyers and nonbuyers. In other words, between what one might call "customer targets" and "prospect targets."

Industrial marketers, business-to-business marketers, and direct marketers tend to focus on whether the buyer is a prospect or a current customer rather than on a general target (that is, both customers and prospects).

Packaged goods marketers, in contrast, often develop an overall strategy that covers both. They want the heavy consumers of, say, beer, and they don't differentiate between their own consumers and the competition's. The challenge is to encourage nonbuyers to try your brew and to buck up current buyers so they remain loyal.

One of the great advertising campaigns of all time was "The one beer to have when you're having more than one." It propelled Schaefer Beer from a relative unknown in the New York market to being the fifth-largest selling beer in the country, in spite of the fact that it was distributed only on the East Coast. That classic advertising campaign focused on heavy users, the 20 percent of beer drinkers who accounted for 80 percent of beer sales.

Yet the Schaefer campaign was successful *not* just because it went after heavy users—a point often lost on many students of marketing—but because it was the only beer making that particular claim.

Schaefer positioned itself as "consistently good-tasting, beer after beer," a position no other beer had claimed, and this was a key reason for its success.

At the time, heavy beer drinkers were a relatively homogeneous group. They tended to be working-class and lower-middle-class blue-collar men who were actively involved in spectator sports or participating in sports or both. The Schaefer media, copy, and promotional strategies talked to those people with those interests, and it worked exceptionally well. We would say that in this case, Schaefer's heavy user strategy was a good one.

The myths in this chapter have developed as marketers tried to decide who would be the best prospects for the company's product or service. The firm may be marketing to consumers or to other businesses, it may be a giant corporation or a small entrepreneur, the question is the same: Who's our target?

Most of these myths represent the conventional ways that companies make market segmentation and targeting decisions across a broad range of product categories. We'll tell you why these decisions are often dumb: They're based on mythology.

At the end of the chapter, we'll discuss two myths that capture the essence of how targeting decisions are made today in organizations large and small, from New York to Tokyo, Anchorage to Sidney. In our refutations of these myths, we'll share our experience and give you our best judgment as to how targeting decisions should be made.

Let's open this chapter with a discussion of one of the all-time most popular targets—heavy users—and tell you why selecting this target may be one of the *least* profitable decisions you can make.

Now we know that included among our readers are marketers, consultants, and advertising agency executives who have never selected a target *other* than "heavy users." Please don't stop reading to write a belligerent letter. Hear us out. We're not saying you're irresponsible or engaging in malpractice.

We are saying that, like early twentieth-century physicians who didn't know any better and who treated patients with lobotomies and leeches, your practices may be dangerous. They may be killing your patient.

Myth 57: Heavy buyers (also known as "heavy users," "high rollers," "big spenders") are the best target for most marketing programs.

Truth: Why are they the best target? Companies inevitably answer: Because they use more product than anyone else, dummy.

One can trace this idea to Dik Warren Twedt, a researcher who coined the term "heavy-half" in 1964 to describe the market segment that, relative to total sales, accounts for a large portion of an item's volume.

Almost always, a small segment of the population accounts for the most sales in a product category. This is the ubiquitous 80/20 Law—the 20 percent of the beer drinkers who consume 80 percent of the beer—applied to marketing.

But heavy users are often price-conscious, deal-prone, and consequently disloyal to the brands they buy. Winning them today with a great offer is no grand accomplishment, because you'll lose them tomorrow to a competitor's deal.

Other heavy users are psychologically locked into a competing brand. They are perfectly happy with the brands they currently buy. They are somebody else's best customers. They are very difficult to move.

Suppose a homemaker buys 20 jars of prepared spaghetti sauce a year, and the average is 5. Is that person a great target for our sauce? Not if she is buying the cheapest jar on the shelf and ours is expensive. Not if she is a vegetarian who cares about smooth texture and we feature chunky beef and vegetables. Not if she is so loyal to the brand she's been using that she would switch stores before she would switch brands.

Heavy users may also have demographic and media-usage profiles similar to everyone else in the category.

Most target groups—18-to-49-year-old women, Heavy Users, Baby Boomers, Gray Foxes, Belongers and Achievers (to mention two well-known psychographic segments)—are far more heterogeneous than homogeneous. Significant differences hide behind a superficial veil of similarity.

When a company considers a target such as heavy buyers, it is asking in effect, "Are these people different in terms of anything other than the variable that defined them in the first place?" If heavy buyers of spaghetti sauce watch daytime television—to make up an example—and light users do not, the company then knows how to reach them.

Unfortunately, these people generally are *not* especially different in terms of anything other than the variable that defined them in the first place. We cannot define them by income, education, age, the television shows they watch, the magazines they read, their attitudes toward cooking, or anything else. Heavy packaged goods buyers are rarely very similar in terms of anything other than their usage patterns and, perhaps, family size—big families do tend to buy more spaghetti sauce, toothpaste, detergent, television sets, and long-distance services than individuals living alone. But aside from that, the only thing that clearly distinguishes women who buy a lot of prepared spaghetti sauce from women who don't buy much prepared spaghetti sauce is that they buy a lot of prepared spaghetti sauce.

But other than the heterogeneity question, a company should ask, "Are heavy users different from light users in terms of how they act in the supermarket?" This is a question of behavior rather than of demographic, psychological, or geographic characteristics. And all too often, the answer to this question is "No."

Yes, it is true that heavy users gravitate toward cheaper, more heavily promoted brands, but then again today *most* brands are heavily promoted. As a result, the brand-buying behavior of heavy users is more similar to light users than many of us would like to think in categories as different as milk, light bulbs, long-distance services, and, yes, spaghetti sauce.

A company can learn fairly easily that heavy users of spaghetti sauce (or whatever) buy more spaghetti sauce than light users and nonusers. But that hardly helps. What a marketer really wants to know is *which* people in each group—heavy users, light users, and nonusers—can I induce to buy *my* spaghetti sauce? How much business can I generate from this group, and what will it cost me to do so?

The following is an illustration of this phenomenon from a recent analysis of a product category that must remain unnamed. The client loved heavy users, so we examined heavy users versus more than a thousand alternative target groups in terms of three criteria:

- Sales potential (which reflects purchase rates and prices paid)
- Profit potential (which takes into account the likelihood of winning and keeping each customer)
- Return on investment (which indexes the ratio of profit potential to the expected media cost of achieving that potential)

Target Group Profitability Analysis

Target type	$ Sales potential	$ Profit potential	ROI index
Heavy users	330M	18M	40
"Family-oriented"	228M	29M	75
30-to-59-years-old	72M	42M	79
"Macho" personality type	107M	45M	88
Moderate users	85M	36M	116
Middle socioeconomic status	211M	104M	133
"Prestige-conscious"	125M	72M	158
Young professionals	114M	55M	212

We examine only 8 of approximately 1000 targets in this table. Note that heavy users account for the lion's share of the sales potential ($330 million), yet only a small share of the profit potential ($18 million). The index, which is based on all thousand-odd targets, reveals that their profitability is forecast to be only 40 percent of the average target. How come?

Because in this case the heavy users, given their profit potential, are simply too difficult to dislodge (they are reasonably happy using a competitor's product), too sensitive to price promotion, and too expensive to reach with media.

The "winning" target, we might add, is not shown here. Needless to say, it was even more profitable than the "young professionals."

Does this mean that heavy users are always a poor target? No! We can think of times in our own consulting practice when heavy users turned out to be an excellent target, including the Schaefer Beer example cited earlier. *There is, on the other hand, no reason to believe a priori that heavy users are a great target.* Only hard thinking and thoughtful analysis can provide the answer.

Myth 58: Because most consumer packaged goods companies target their advertising to 18-to-49-year-old women, they must be a good target.

Truth: This must be the ultimate knee-jerk decision in marketing. Packaged goods giants routinely target this group after thinking about it for six seconds. Who, after all, spends the most time walking up and down supermarket and drug chain aisles? Who would argue with such overwhelming empirical "evidence"?

Some marketers do realize that 18-to-49-year-old women may not be the optimal target. When we told a major packaged goods marketer not long ago that repeated use of 18-to-49-year-old women makes little sense, the executive stared us straight in the eye and said, "We don't target 18-to-49-year-old anymore. We've had a breakthrough." There was a moment of tension until he said, "Now we go after 25-to-54-year-old women." We all laughed.

What's wrong with this target? The same things that are wrong with heavy buyers. A huge group of people such as 18-to-49-year-old women is more heterogeneous than homogeneous. Once you define them by demographics (age and sex) or by buying habits (they buy spaghetti sauce), you have probably exhausted all the factors that link them. Depending on the product or service, 18-to-49-year-old women are frequently as similar to women 55 years and older or to 18-to-49-year-old men as they are to each other.

Moreover, the chances are extremely high that every other packaged goods company in the country is targeting them as well. No marketer, therefore, has an opportunity to preempt the field.

This is not to say that targeting 18-to-49-year-old women will never pay off. Like everything else, it depends on the product and the situation. But with all the targeting options to choose from, most marketers who lock on to this target without any thought or research will be bitterly disappointed. Why marketers persist in choosing 18-to-49-year-old women, like lemmings rushing to the sea, is one of nature's great unsolved mysteries.

Myth 59: A business should invest more money in finding new customers than in further developing current customers.

Truth: This myth is so rampant that we have coined a name for it: "The Death-Wish Paradox." Marketers large and small, consumer and industrial, product manufacturers and service providers, seem to put the bulk of their marketing efforts into acquiring new customers whose value to the company is often very low.

The Death-Wish Paradox

Customer type	Marketing effort	Value to marketers	Cost of programs
New customers (acquisition programs)	High	Low	High
Current customers (retention programs)	Moderate	High	Moderate
Current customers (expansion programs)	Low	Moderate	Low

Surprisingly, there seems to be a sense in marketing that finding and closing new customers (acquisition programs) is more exciting than holding on to current customers (retention programs) or increasing business volume among current customers (expansion programs). As an illustration, in our marketing consulting business we estimate that for every 10 clients who ask us how to build trial (increase the number of first-time customers), we have only about 4 who ask about repeat purchase (retention) and 1 or 2 who are concerned with increasing usage level (expansion).

One reason this myth persists is that, in our experience, most companies don't know what a loyal customer is worth in dollars and cents. They spend most of their marketing budget and attention on obtaining new customers, relatively less on satisfying and retaining old ones. This is a mistake. For in most businesses, whether we are talking about packaged goods, retail apparel, or heavy tractors, current customers generally are worth five times more than new customers.

Fortune magazine recently put a dollar figure on exactly how much repeat business can be worth. MBNA Corporation, formerly the credit card operation of the Baltimore-based MNC Financial (which was in turn a division of Maryland National Bank), reported that it cost $100 on average to acquire a new credit card customer. By contrast, a customer MBNA has had for 5 years represents about $100 a year in profits; a customer the firm has had for 10 years represents, on average, $300 a year. Stew Leonard, the embattled head of a giant Norwalk (Connecticut) dairy and food retail business, estimates that a loyal customer is worth $50,000 in sales over a 10-year period.

The heavy focus on new customers might make sense if the probability of attracting a new customer were considerably greater than the probability of holding a current one, or if the cost of maintaining loyalty were considerably greater than the cost of acquiring customers. But neither of these assumptions is true.

Across a range of product categories, the cost of "holding" a current customer is often only 25 percent of the cost of "winning" a new one. Moreover—assuming a reasonable marketing program—the probability of holding on to a current customer is better than 60 percent, while the probability of acquiring a new one is less than 30 percent.

Thus the "Death-Wish Paradox" really is a paradox.

Myth 60: A company's best prospects for a product or service are people who "look" very much like current customers.

Truth: This is the axiom that drives much of direct marketing prospecting. It assumes that to grow, a company should simply find more of the same kind of people who now buy the firm's products or services. If you are, say, *The New Yorker*'s circulation director, the theory is that you have to learn as much as possible about current subscribers and then find more people like them. The technology exists to do both.

While this may be appropriate, it may also be a waste of time and money, depending on the situation. Take American Express. Its customers are high-income people who travel a great deal for business or pleasure. Its prospects—no surprise here—are high-income travelers.

People who resemble American Express card members but do not have an American Express card are, for that reason alone, fairly unusual people. They have been the target of heavy advertising and promotion for years. They know what "Don't leave home without it" means. They regularly frequent restaurants or airline ticket offices where they reach for a credit card. Why don't they carry an American Express card?

Perhaps American Express alienated them at some point. Perhaps they feel the annual fee is excessive. Perhaps they want the option to pay only part of the monthly bill or are entirely satisfied with their Visa card. Are they a viable target for American Express? No, even though they may look just like American Express customers.

If a company really wants to know who its best prospects are, it has to study its target in great depth. The marketer cannot assume the best prospects are heavy users, 18-to-49-year-old women, prospects rather than customers, or people who look like current customers.

Myth 61: The way to build the business is to bring nonusers into the product category.

Truth: Not long ago we visited one of our clients to talk about different targets for a $300 room air cleaner. The meeting's objective was to identify the key targets and then rank-order them so that we could follow up with a research study that would provide more information about these groups.

After a two-hour discussion, the management supervisor of the account from the advertising agency, someone who had been presented to us as a marketing genius, pointed out that we had missed perhaps the most important target of all. Everyone sat back to await his wisdom and he said, "What you've missed are the nonbuyers, nonusers."

He went on to say that by "nonbuyers, nonusers" he meant people who were not currently users or owners of an air cleaner—totally new prospects for the category. He went on to hypothesize that perhaps these people were nonbuyers, nonusers because the current product configurations and the message strategies employed by other air cleaner manufacturers were not compelling enough to bring these people into the market.

The company executives nodded their heads in agreement. We could imagine them thinking, "My God! He *is* a genius! That's why he's at this meeting! How could we have overlooked something as enormous as this? Given that only 24 percent of the population owns an air cleaner, this guy has the answer."

Before they had a chance to carry him about the room on their shoulders, we pointed out that if we are the Republican Party in a two-party campaign, and it's necessary to win 51 percent of the electorate to elect a candidate to office, we will branch out to people who had never voted before and win at least half of them. If we are Coca-Cola and want to increase our share of the cola category, it's necessary to reach out to rich and poor, young and old, black and white, cola drinkers and nondrinkers to dominate the category.

But since our client's sales represented less than 10 percent of the industry total, and since the industry's market penetration was less than 25 percent (with 1.1 air cleaners per household), it was very, very difficult to conceive of developing an advertising strategy that would build our client's business by educating consumers about the value of air cleaners—a product category more than 20 years old—and motivate them to do things they have never done before.

Time and again, across a broad range of product categories, clients set as a marketing objective the goal of attracting new people to the product category. We're going to bring in new users of microwavable entrees! We're going to bring in people who have never eaten popcorn! We're going to expand the market for soft drinks by introducing Zippy Cola! We're going to increase the number of people who buy personal computers for their home! The list is endless.

In study after study of category after category, we have found that unless the category is very new or changing quickly (or both), the likelihood of attracting new users is very, very slim. This discovery holds for new products and services as well as established ones. For almost two decades, we have been doing new-product research in which the objective has been to assess the new product's penetration among that product category's nonusers, nonbuyers, or both. Clients are always hoping that their product will perform a magical feat: attract and add new buyers to the category.

Unfortunately, the findings of this research show otherwise. Rarely—again, the exception comes in new or rapidly expanding product categories—does a new product franchise include more than 5 to 10 percent of previous nonusers.

To repeat, it is a rare case when more than 10 percent of the buyers of this new product come from outside the category. And this dismal performance is for *new* products. For an established product, it's even less likely that it will attract new buyers.

Given that the nonusers of many product categories are a larger group to go after than users, they're more expensive to reach than the users. To take valuable company resources and allocate them against this group, who are difficult to change if only because they avoid frozen entrees, don't like popcorn, prefer water to soft drinks, are not interested in a personal computer, or have no need for an air cleaner, is ridiculous.

Which is not to say there are never circumstances in which, for strategic reasons, a company would position a product against the product category's nonusers.

It makes perfect sense, for example, for Apple and other computer manufacturers to offer special prices to schools and college students. *Seventeen* and other magazines for young people are filled with ads targeted at nonusers. We've told the story in Chapter 5 of American Express going after young professionals. And most automobile companies offer special purchase/lease deals to recent college graduates. All of these make good business sense.

One must distinguish between these examples, however, and the kind described in our air cleaner anecdote. Trying to attract to the product category people who are younger than, say, 18, young people who have never used an air cleaner or a personal computer, never owned a credit card, never prepared a meal from scratch, is a sensible strategic goal.

Trying to attract *adults* who have never used a computer or an air cleaner, do not believe in credit cards, have deeply ingrained food preparation habits, is an entirely different story. Trying to convert into a fax buyer a 49-year-old steelworker who has never purchased nor has any interest in a fax machine is like trying to teach a pig to sing. It wastes your time and irritates the steel worker.

Myth 62: Big customers are the best customers.

Truth: Many companies do believe that big customers are their best customers. They believe it because big customers account for a disproportionate share of the sales volume of the company. The firm typically has had the longest relationship with those customers. They are a stable revenue source the firm can count on over time.

And yet Philip Kotler, distinguished professor of marketing at Northwestern University, recently discovered, when he undertook an analysis for one of his clients, that big customers are not the most profitable customers. They often are the most demanding in terms of both price and service. They demand the lowest possible price and they demand the highest level of service. They usually obtain both because they know they are so important to the business.

When firms actually analyze the profit contribution per unit for different kinds of customers, in our experience they often discover that their big customers are not the most profitable after all. Sometimes they're not profitable, period. Take a look at Exhibit 8.1, where for selected companies we have displayed the relationship between customer size and profitability.

What we have discovered is that the largest 10 percent of all customers are not the most profitable. Indeed, the relationship between size and profitability is not as pronounced as we had expected at all.

In addition, the more a supplier depends on a single customer, the more vulnerable it is to business reverses. Consider Murray Becker Industries, Twinsberg (Ohio), which manufactured framed pictures it sold to Kmart. According to *Business Week,* in October 1990, Kmart increased the number of outlets MBI supplied from 450 to 650. The company hired new staff and invested in additional machinery.

The following March, Kmart dropped MBI. MBI alleges the move came without warning. The break forced MBI into insolvency, since

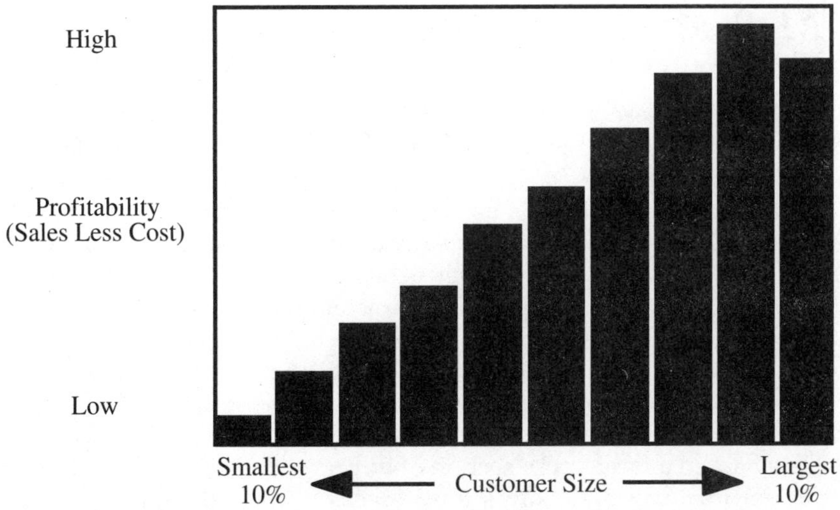

Exhibit 8-1 The relationship between customer size and profitability.

Kmart had accounted for 80 percent of its business. MBI sued Kmart for breach of contract in federal court, seeking more than $2 million in damages. Kmart denied that it had wrongfully terminated MBI, contending that MBI lost an announced 1991 competition among vendors. Kmart's response argued further that its contract with MBI allowed it to terminate the contract with 60 days' notice.

Tom Melohn, the former head of North American Tool & Die, tells the story of a CEO newly arrived at one of NATD's major customers. "Just remember," this executive said at a meeting of the firm's key supplier executives, "we're your sole source of income."

Although the CEO spoke lightly, his meaning was no joke; his minions understood him clearly enough. The company's purchasing people began to turn the CEO's insinuation into action. Checks came more slowly. The corporation's sole purchase criterion became the lowest price. Product designs changed repeatedly while in preproduction at NATD. These added costs became a significant expense. If NATD wanted to continue to enjoy the customer's continued business, NATD was expected to absorb these charges.

"After a candid discussion with the corporation's purchasing personnel," says Melohn, "I informed this customer that NATD no longer wished to 'enjoy' their continued business. It just wasn't worth the constant hassle and reduced profit. They were bullies. It was obvious their one-sided demands would never end." NATD ultimately dropped them as a customer.

Myth 63: Needs-based segmentation strategies are the most profitable way to segment and understand a product's market.

Truth: These are strategies that identify different market segments on the basis of what buyers need or desire. Dr. Russell Haley's seminal 1968 paper in *The Journal of Marketing* laid the foundation for what has come to be known as "benefit segmentation." Haley, one of America's premier marketing consultants, demonstrated that segmenting markets in terms of consumer needs was superior to segmenting markets in terms of psychographic characteristics.

Different people, Haley argued, want different things from a product. In a toothpaste, for example, some people are interested in decay prevention, others are concerned about the brightness of their teeth, still others want sweet breath, and some are concerned only about price.

Haley asked a large cross-section of buyers to rate 50 to 100 different benefits (for example, "stops tooth decay") and attributes ("tastes great") of a toothpaste in terms of importance (extremely important to not important at all).

Haley then used a statistical tool called "cluster analysis" to group people into categories or typologies. Indeed, any time you hear a marketer say something like, "There are five types of buyers in the luxury car category," or "There are three types of detergent users," you can assume the firm has done a cluster analysis.

Haley employed cluster analysis to group people into "benefit segments" (that is, segments looking for similar things in a product). The procedure was logical—discover what different segments want—and could be applied to every type of business: consumer and business-to-business, product and service.

It was so logical and convenient it became the preferred segmentation methodology among marketers for almost two decades. Benefit segments have been researched and revealed in product categories as diverse as airline travel, beverage alcohol, credit cards, computer software, frozen microwave entrees, heavy industrial equipment, lawnmowers, office equipment, small sailboats, soft drinks, telecommunications, and tractors.

Unfortunately, benefit segmentation has a serious problem. Unfortunately because (a) the method is so popular, and (b) so much about it makes sense. But here's the problem.

Assume for a moment we are executives at American Airlines. We have commissioned a benefit segmentation study. One segment interests us particularly: "The Time Conscious." These are people most concerned about on-time arrival; they represent 37 percent of all business travelers and 61 percent of all airline dollars.

What our benefit segmentation doesn't tell us (unless we do much more to the data) is that these travelers have two favorite airlines, Delta and United, and that they are very satisfied with both in terms of on-time delivery. An American advertising effort directed at this target is not likely to nudge many of them in our direction. Worse, American likes to spend its advertising money on television commercials, and on-time travelers tend to be intellectual and sophisticated and watch little TV.

A frontal attack on this superficially appealing segment is likely to fail because both the message and the media strategies will be wrong. It is not enough, in other words, to identify and label interesting segments. We have to know much more about them before we can actually select an intelligent market target.

And *sometimes* when we do this we discover that the benefit segments aren't very profitable after all.

Myth 64: Psychographic segmentation is a useful tool for segmenting markets.

Truth: This is actually a myth about modes of segmentation, about ways to define target markets.

Rather than believe the myths about certain target groups, some marketing executives believe myths about ways to segment and identify target groups. The favored way could be product usage patterns, demographics, attitudes and values, attributes/benefits, multiple trade-off utility values—there are any number of possibilities. But when a marketer falls in love with personality types or other variables in the domain of psychologists, that is what we are calling psychographic segmentation.

Our first experience with this kind of research goes back many years ago to a time when John Sculley (until his resignation in June of 1993, emperor of all things at Apple Computer) was marketing director at Pepsi Cola and BBDO was (still is) the advertising agency, and Clancy was the agency research maven on Pepsi.

Sculley had asked for a new campaign, so Clancy decided to emulate some of the early psychographic segmentation work that Al Achenbaum, Shirley Young, and a young Russ Haley had done at Grey Advertising in the mid-sixties.

To help kick off the study, Clancy invited Dr. Ernest Dichter, a Viennese-born psychoanalyst and a pioneer in motivation research to meet with the creative people at the agency to review a reel of Pepsi commercials and stimulate some discussion. The good doctor stopped everything when, after the third commercial, he said in his heavily accented English, "Kevin, stop! You are showing Pepsi in all these commercials with ice...served with ice...cans *encased* in ice! You must not do this. Ice is the symbol of death. You are associating your client with death!"

What Dichter's words killed was any interest in the agency in psychographic research. As one creative group head said, "This is too nutty for us and for the client. Can't we do something else?"

We did do something else—work that led to one of the most successful ad campaigns of the past three decades: "You've got a lot to live and Pepsi's got a lot to give." But that didn't stop us from doing psychographic segmentation for other accounts, and it certainly didn't stop psychographic segmentation from becoming a popular methodology.

It is not difficult to divide the population into personality types. Ask some personality questions, do a cluster analysis, and usually the results are fascinating. People are always interesting. The company does an analysis to figure out how many people "fall into" each segment (for example, 35 percent are neurotic; 12 percent psychotic; 17 percent manic-depressive, etc.).

The marketer judges the best segment, based on that one mode, for the product or service. When the brand manager begins to talk about "Neurotics" as the preferred market target for, say, the company's over-the-counter analgesic, the process has ended. Regrettably, the results have questionable real-world value, if only because personality by itself has little or nothing to do with market behavior.

More than 20 years ago, three academics—William F. Massy, Ronald E. Frank, and Thomas Lodahl—reported in *Purchasing Behavior and Personal Attributes* that personality does not explain what people buy. The variability in purchasing behavior that could be explained by personality traits was at most 7 percent. This finding has been confirmed over and over again, for two decades, in the academic and applied marketing literature. Nonetheless, it has not changed the attitudes of many marketing executives.

A psychographic study among approximately 1000 recent diners at fast-food restaurants reveals as an important target "The Child Centered" (33 percent of the population), people primarily motivated by the need to please their children. Other segments include: "The Health Conscious" (30 percent), people highly concerned about the nutritional, fat, and caloric content of what they consume; "The Lonely" (18 percent), people who live alone and often dine alone; "The Health Oblivious" (12 percent), people seemingly unconcerned with the health and nutrition attributes of the food they eat; and "The Cleanliness Conscious" (7 percent), people seemingly more concerned about the cleanliness of a restaurant's bathrooms and parking lot than with the food.

This is interesting stuff, and it sounds like a valuable breakthrough. But what happens when we look at product usage among these five segments? We find that there isn't a large difference between them. For example, while only 41 percent of the Health Conscious eat large burgers, 59 percent of the Health Oblivious order them (the other groups fell between these extremes). Purchases of soft drinks are flat across all five targets. Children's meals do peak among the Child Centered, to no one's surprise, and the Lonely's contribution to sales per order taken (low) or table time occupied (high) are equally predictable.

In other words, while it is possible to divide the American public into different segments psychographically, it's often of no practical use. The consumer-behavior, demographic, and media profiles of the five different fast-food psychographic segments are more similar than different. Unfortunately, this is a common finding within this research genre. The only person in the organization pleased with the result is the consulting psychologist called in to interpret the results.

Unfortunately even improved, psychographic variables are at best only remotely related to consumer behavior and market response. If a marketer using a psychographic segmentation study asks tough questions, such as, "How much of the variability in behavior or market response can these segments explain?", the answer is almost always 7 percent or less (we're back to the extensive academic literature on this topic). No off-the-shelf segmentation scheme can be as good as a customized segmentation study done for a specific product or service. Psychographic methods can break the world into pieces, but the pieces may or may not have any relevance to any one product or service.

Myth 65: Attitudes are an excellent way to segment markets.

Truth: Attitude segmentation represents a hybrid between the attitude/benefit and the psychographic modes of segmentation that we have just smacked around. A typical study asks buyers to rate 30 to 80 different statements using rating scales such as: "strongly agree," "somewhat agree," "neither agree nor disagree," "somewhat disagree," "strongly disagree." Each of these statements theoretically captures an attitude toward the product category or a need of the buyer.

This approach assumes that the researcher/consultant "knows" the critical attitudes underlying behavior in the category (usually 10 or more different "factors") and that each of these has been reliably and validly measured (by using at least four attitude statements to "capture" each factor).

The study's analysis stage employs clustering tools—just as in attribute/benefit and psychographic segmentation—to group people into different segments. Those in each segment represent people with similar attitudes.

J.D. Power and Associates recently reported the results of an attitudinal segmentation study in the automobile industry. Although their methodology was strange—they used only 16 questions, far too few for reliable, valid measurement—the results are interesting.

The study revealed six segments. "The Epicures" (25.9 percent of all drivers) are people who like stylish or elegant automobiles; "Road Haters" (25.9 percent) are fearful about driving and consequently are particularly concerned about safety; "Gearheads" (16.7 percent) are automobile enthusiasts; "Negatives" (15.8 percent) view cars as necessary evils; "Fuctionalists" (11.8 percent) are practical drivers who are very conservative about speed limits and who care about courtesy; and "Purists" (4.2 percent) are unimpressed and skeptical about auto manufacturers.

Although the Power people did not provide us with enough information to evaluate their study, we suspect that they experienced the same problems as other researchers in the 25-year history of this approach. Similarly to attribute/benefit and psychographic research, the segments tend to be very different in terms of the variables from which they were constructed in the first place (the attitude statements) but similar in terms of everything else—demographics, behavior patterns, media exposure, etc. As a result of these and other problems, the question is: What action can you take based on the information?

Attitude segments, if measured well and combined with other types of information about a consumer—such as demographics and behavior patterns—*can* become the basis for an effective targeting strategy. But only if the organization evaluates them using criteria related to profitability, as we will discuss in the next two myths.

Myth 66: There really are only a few different market targets to choose among in my product category.

Truth: This seems to be the myth underlying most targeting decisions. How else can you explain why so many companies quickly select a target as they cry, "Look, Ma! No thinking!"

Yet every product and every service has at least 10,000 possible target markets, and perhaps 100,000 or more. Consider just some of the targets this discussion has suggested. Heavy, medium, light users (3 targets); 18-to-49-year-old women, 18-to-49-year-old men, older women, older men (4 targets); people who look like your current customers, people who don't (2); current buyers, nonusers (2); big customers—the largest 10 percent versus nine other customer size groups (10); five different benefit segments (5); five different personality segments (5), and six different attitude segments (6).

That's 37 different target groups. Consider further all combinations of two different modes of segmentation, as in 18-to-49-year-old women who are heavy users. They could be the best target. All realistic combinations of two targets comes to 573 targets.

How many companies seriously investigate 573 targets when they can just choose one? Answer: hardly any at all. As we demonstrated in *The Marketing Revolution,* every product or service has thousands of different targets that the company can evaluate, and few companies seriously consider more than a handful.

One might plausibly maintain that the United States offers 275 million target markets—the U.S. population. Most of the time—although not always—a company will want a larger target than one individual.

Like most marketing issues we talk about throughout this book, some of these targets are excellent, some are atrocious, and most fall somewhere in between—once again we're talking about a standard bell curve. The trick is to find the most efficient, scientific way of segmenting the market, and to choose a target group based on its potential profit contribution. Which leads immediately to our next myth.

Myth 67: Since a marketer can't evaluate target groups in terms of profit potential, only seasoned judgment can help.

Truth: Most marketers would agree that when choosing a target market a company ought to consider the prospects' profitability. What will it cost to reach these people? How many will buy our product or service? How much money will they give us?

In practice, marketers almost always ignore profitability. They select a target group on the basis of "face validity," that is, because the target seems to make sense (if not to the marketer, who may know better, then to his or her boss).

We asked consulting firms that had recently undertaken segmentation studies why they had selected one group over another. Reasons included: "The best target had the heaviest users"; "These people are looking for product benefits our client's brand can deliver"; "More women 18-to-34—the group the client has always gone after—were in this target segment than in any other."

Marketers and researchers ignore profitability because, we believe, few know how to take the large cross-sectional surveys most major advertisers conduct for market segmentation purposes and run them through the computer to answer the question, "Which target group is the most profitable?"

Managers who choose 18-to-49-year-old women (even 25-to-54-year-old women) or who select "The Child Centered" as the company's target market are not thinking about profitability at all.

Market segmentation researchers often neglect the following criteria when they evaluate target markets, perhaps because they make the calculations even more complex. Nonetheless, these factors make the difference between a profitable and a middling target:

- *Responsiveness.* The more a target group responds to a company's marketing efforts, the greater its value to the company.

- *Sales potential.* A target group that buys or uses more of the company's product is more valuable than one that buys less.
- *Growth potential.* A growing target is more desirable than a static or shrinking group.
- *Common motivations.* The more homogeneous and preemptible a target's needs are, the greater its value.
- *Decision-making power.* The more responsibility the target prospects have for making a buying decision, the more significant they are to the company.
- *Retention potential.* The more likely it is that a target can be economically sustained and, therefore, retained over time, the greater its value.
- *Media exposure patterns and media costs.* These are important because it usually makes little sense to define a target a marketer cannot reach through media, or that is impossibly expensive to reach (for example, by looking up every prospect's number in the phone book).

Before we make any decision, therefore, we apply these seven criteria to each target group in the study. We use them to answer questions such as: How many people in each group have positive attitudes toward the company and would therefore be more responsive to its marketing program? How many people, because of their expected greater responsiveness (because they have a positive attitude) can we expect to buy the product, and therefore what percentage of total potential revenues do they represent? And what would it cost to reach each group? We express this in cost per thousand (CPM) and in gross rating points (GRPs), figures that come from the company's advertising agency.

When we went through this exercise not long ago for a client, we segmented the market 8515 ways and examined 42,575 targets. The group that the client's marketing manager loved—those people who accounted for the market's greatest dollar volume—turned out to be very expensive to reach, did not make decisions, and disliked our client. But out of the analysis, we found one group of people that was forecast to be eight times more profitable than management's favorite, the so-called "hot prospects."

Companies sometimes act as if they don't want to know what happened when their marketing plans were taken into the marketplace. Surprising as it might seem, managements do not hold marketers accountable, if only because they have no way to measure consequences.

We know that current approaches often yield disappointing, if not depressing, sales results. Companies choose their targets without too much brain power, and their programs reflect it. We've seen campaigns that have a greater effect on light users than on the heavy users for which they were intended. We've seen attribute/benefit campaigns that had more effect on people out of the target group than those in it. The efforts might have had results, but they were not the results management expected—and in those terms, the campaigns were failures. And we've seen campaigns, far too many campaigns, that have had no effect at all.

Our recommendation, as we've stated it before and will continue to argue throughout this book, is that marketers make the targeting decision only after gaining a fresh perspective, a "clean-slate" orientation. In every product category there are hundreds, thousands, even tens of thousands of targets to choose from. An organization can evaluate all of them using criteria related to profitability. The era of choosing, merely out of habit, heavy users, 18-to-49-year-old women, big customers, or new customers is coming to a close.

"When I left my last agency, I promised myself that I would help create an agency with a powerful, preemptive, unique positioning. That's why here at Pierce, Brod our slogan is, `We Make Ads.'"

9
Myths about Positioning

Positioning is something all marketers talk about, but rarely do anything about.

"Positioning," according to Ries and Trout in their classic book on the topic, "starts with a product...but positioning is not what you do with a product. Positioning is what you do in the mind of the prospect. That is, you position the product in the mind of the prospect."

Sometimes the positioning can be as short as one word. Remember the "Uncola?" Some brands are associated with one-word or one-thought positioning strategies: Volvo—safety; Marlboro—masculinity; Pepsi-Cola—youth; Mercedes—engineering; diamonds—forever; Charmin—soft; Compaq—performance; Clorox—brightening; Heinz ketchup—thick. Others are tied to more complicated but nevertheless compelling ideas:

Visa—accepted everywhere they don't take American Express

Apple computers—easy to use

BMW cars—the ultimate driving machine

L'Oreal—because you're worth it

Crest—fewer cavities

Federal Express—trust us to get it there overnight

Sure—confidence and security

Tylenol—safer than aspirin

United Airlines—friendly skies and friendly service

In talking about positioning, marketers and agency folks define it in different ways. It's "the story you want to imprint in people's minds about your product and why it's better"; "the solution your product is offering to address buyers' problems"; "the bundle of attributes and benefits you want to tell people about" or, simply, your "unique selling proposition"—"the reason consumers should buy your product rather than someone else's."

But all these definitions have something in common. They recognize that in a cluttered environment where buyers have little time to ponder product decisions, it is highly advantageous for a marketer to stand for something important, to be remembered for something significant. To have a powerful positioning is clearly a good thing.

Why then do so few companies, products, brands, and services enjoy a strong positioning? The myths in this chapter go far toward answering that question.

Myth 68: Most marketers know what positioning means and how important it is. As a result, most established products and services are clearly if not powerfully positioned.

Truth: Ries and Trout say that "you position the product in the mind of the prospect." We should, therefore, begin to look for positionings in the minds of customers and prospects.

We've conducted that search, and believe us, if most products and services are positioned at all, it's strictly in the minds of their marketing managers.

For two decades we've investigated a broad range of product categories where we asked consumers and industrial buyers to tell us about positioning strategies on an unaided (that is, completely volunteered), partially aided (that is, with some clues) and fully aided (that is, completely prompted) basis. Here's what we've found.

When we survey a national cross-section of buyers in a product category, say ground coffee or soft drinks, financial services or airlines, copying machines or personal computers, and ask on an unaided basis what each of the five leading brands in the category stands for—what they communicate about themselves that makes them different from other brands—the findings are startling. Fewer than 8 percent of the respondents associate anything with the brands that we could begin to call "positioning."

This dismal performance is not consistent across all product categories. In high ad-spending categories such as automobiles, credit cards, and beer, and in categories with relatively few dominant brands, unaided awareness of a positioning is higher—about 12 percent. Given the amount of money involved, we find those figures appalling.

But let's assume that buyers aren't paying much attention; after all, they do have more on their mind than brands and positioning. So we give them clues. We call these "tracer elements." We give people a slogan or a positioning for the brand—the essential positioning statement—and ask, "Which brand of [say, automobiles] do you associate with [we then read the positioning statement]?" Or a different question: "Which brand of [automobile] says [we read the slogan] in their advertising?"

Here are a few examples: "Which brand of automobile do you associate with `significant improvements during the last few years'?" "Which brand of automobile uses the slogan 'Have you driven a \_\_\_\_\_\_ lately?' in their advertising?" "Which brand of batteries lasts for a long time, and uses a bunny beating a drum that `keeps on going and going'?"

Even with clues as obvious as giving away the positioning/message strategy or the slogan, respondents correctly identify the advertising with the positioning only about 16 percent of the time.

What happens when you give away the store? When you give buyers the positioning or the slogan and ask if they've ever heard it? "Have you ever heard Coke use the slogan 'It's the Real Thing'?" Here's a positioning that achieved 92 percent recognition at the height of its power (remember that less than 100 percent of the American public knows who our President is at any given time). Or "Have you heard or seen any Visa Card advertising in which they show a successful business such as a restaurant or a retail store and they say 'and they don't take American Express'?" (It achieved 78 percent recognition the last time we looked).

The average, fully prompted, completely clued positioning awareness score for the top five brands in most product categories is *less than* 30 percent.

If there are more buyers in a product category who aren't aware of a brand's positioning than buyers who are aware, that's a problem.

There are three possible reasons for this problem:

1. The company never clearly developed a positioning strategy for the brand in the first place.
2. The company did not clearly articulate and communicate the positioning strategy to buyers in marketing communications.
3. Insufficient media weight or a weak media schedule failed to carry the message to buyers.

As discouraging as this news from the front lines of research may be, it shouldn't be a surprise to marketers at businesses large and small. Many brands today have a confused or no positioning. Weekends at one time were made for Michelob, but what is Budweiser's positioning? Bud Lite's? Miller Lite? For these brands and thousands like them, companies seem to advertise nothing more than the brand name. And while it's important to reinforce the brand name, it's also important to position the product in the consumer's mind.

This problem is not restricted to packaged goods categories. We challenge anyone to articulate the positioning strategies for leading fast-food companies, airlines, or major clothing retailers/department stores—unless you were to answer, "We've dropped our prices."

Indeed, "We've dropped our prices" has become the number-one positioning strategy in America. Companies are fighting to "out-cheap" everyone else. Unless our economy perks up, the 39-cent meal, the 82-percent-off air fare, the free-suit-with-every-one-you-buy (limit six per customer), all begin to seem likely.

Even advertising agencies, who should know better, have positioning problems. A while ago, we did a study for Jack Connors of Hill Holliday Advertising. Connors wanted to know how the agency world was segmented in terms of positioning strategies. We gathered annual reports and corporate brochures on the top 50 agencies and were disturbed but not surprised by our findings. We identified 6 agencies with what might be called a positioning strategy—the rest were a blur. If they had a positioning, it was, "We make ads."

But take the problem beyond major advertisers and their agencies and think small businesses. Are there two restaurants in your community with a clearly defined positioning? If so, is the positioning other than the menu—the type of food? How about a dry cleaning establishment or a service station, a food store or a tire business, a movie theater complex or a video store? We doubt it.

Talk about positioning seems to produce more smoke than fire. This is too bad, because a strong positioning strategy is as indispensable to a strong brand as a strong military is to our national defense.

Myth 69: Most new products and services are based on positioning strategies for which they have an advantage in highly motivating features or benefits or both.

Truth: You'd think so. After all, isn't the point of introducing a new product or service to launch something better than what currently is available?

Yet if most new products and services were based on powerful preemptive strategies, would the new product/new service failure rate hover between 80 and 90 percent? No. As we discussed at the beginning of Chapter 7, the autopsies of new product/services failures suggest that 3 out of 10 times the cause of death is a weak positioning.

This could not have been more clear to us than when we examined the strengths and weaknesses of new products and services run through the Yankelovich Clancy Shulman simulated test market research system. Simulated test marketing, as many readers know, is a research tool designed to forecast a new product marketing plan's performance in a fraction of the time and for a fraction of the cost of a real-world introduction.

Each new product study we did included consumer ratings of how the new product compared with its competitors on 20 to 30 product attributes and benefits in the product category, and how motivating each of these attributes and characteristics was to buyers. What we discovered is shown in Exhibit 9.1.

Most new products fell into what we labeled "the zone of normative failure." Consumers perceived them as offering attributes and benefits that (a) were not terribly motivating and (b) were not much different from competitors'.

With such a positioning, is new product failure a surprise?

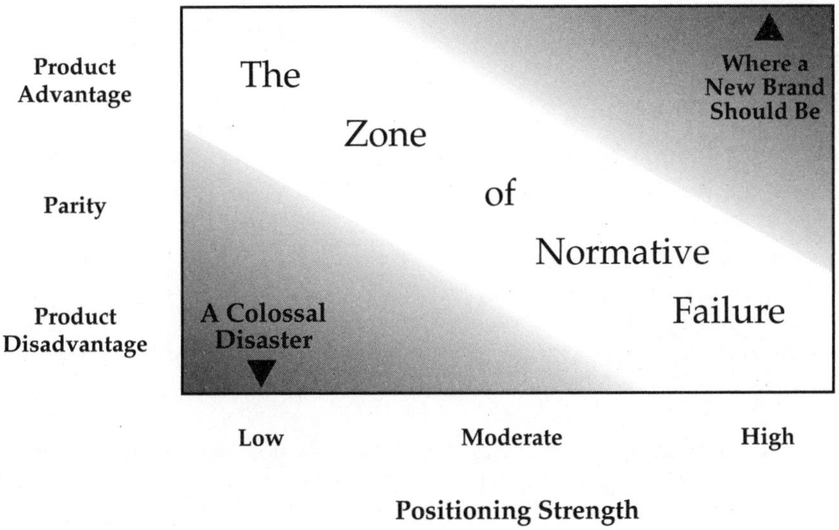

Exhibit 9-1 Positioning for new products.

Myth 70: Powerful positioning strategies can be based on ethereal, intangible attributes rather than real product differences.

Truth: Another version of this myth goes something like: Emotional advertising works better than feature/benefit advertising.

There is the apocryphal story of the client who tossed two brand-new 50-cent pieces on the advertising agency president's desk and said, "Mine is on the right. Prove it's better."

If you're in a product category where there are no product differences and no opportunity to create product differences, a generic product category where yours is the one on the right, you're stuck trying to find ethereal, intangible ways of differentiating your brand. Theodore Levitt's book *The Marketing Imagination* has a wonderful discussion of that.

But in our experience, it is more likely there *are* real product differences the company can promote. As we have said elsewhere (and will probably be saying again), the most successful products and marketing programs are those designed to address consumer problems. Some of these are real problems, some are intangible problems, but if the company's product or service addresses a rational problem with a real difference, it is likely to be successful.

Myth 71: Problem detection is the best way to develop a positioning strategy.

Truth: In the early 1970s, BBDO Advertising had a clearly articulated positioning strategy based on a four-point process: know your prospect; know your prospect's problems; know your product; break the boredom barrier. Some of the most memorable ad campaigns of the decade were based on this process, including those for Pepsi ("The Pepsi Generation"), Burger King ("Have It Your Way"), Campbell Soup ("The Manhandlers"), and Tupperware ("Lock in Freshness").

A problem was that the agency did not have a research process that would help it figure out the prospect's problems in a particular category (nor did anyone else, for that matter). Bob Wachsler, then agency research director, passed this challenge along to a trio of Ph.D.'s in his department, Kevin Clancy, Larry Krueger, and Larry Light, and "problem detection" was born.

Until that time, agencies tended to use importance ratings—what the consumer thinks is important in a product or service—to develop positioning strategies. If "good taste" is the most important thing in a soft drink, then you positioned your new soda as having good taste.

Clancy believed—and still does—that a positioning based on importance ratings runs several risks. For one thing, it turns out that what's most important to consumers tends to be generic to the product: great taste in a soft drink, fast action in an analgesic, breath-sweetening in a mouthwash, clear picture in a television set, and so on.

These attributes and benefits nearly always return to the product's essential function, to attributes and benefits that give the product category a right to exist.* They represent the standards to which consumers hold every product in the category. A refrigerator must preserve food; a paper towel must absorb liquid; a deodorant must inhibit odor.

"Our new underarm deodorant stops odor!" Claims like that are unlikely to encourage the consumer to switch brands, since the positioning offers no attribute or benefit that the consumer's current brand does not already offer. ("Buy our new deodorant because we're nicer guys than the folks who make your current brand!" is not an effective sales appeal.)

Also, when a company asks consumers to identify the product attributes and benefits they consider important, people usually play back what they've learned from advertising. Ask enough consumers what's important in a dentifrice, and you'll end up with every other toothpaste marketer's advertising claims. Just as consumers in focus groups do not produce original insights, consumers in importance studies rarely come up with product attributes the marketing and advertising specialists don't already know about.

Consumers *can* tell the specialists about their problems, however. They can talk, often at interminable length, about the difficulties they've had with a product, a brand, or both.

Recognizing this, BBDO New York developed a research method to identify consumer problems, and within a few years many researchers around the world had adopted the technique.

The agency defined a problem as a frequently occurring, important source of dissatisfaction. In an ideal situation, the agency identifies not only a problem but a solution that preempts competitive brands. That is, the agency comes up with a solution the client brand's competitors do not actually offer, or a solution consumers do not realize the brand's competitors could offer, but don't.

Problem detection begins with a list of possible problems. This first

*Occasionally manufacturers will introduce a product or create a product category that has no right to exist. It solves a need that consumers do not have (or not enough consumers have to make a viable business). The vaginal deodorant spray is one example; the electric salad spinner is another. There are many more.

phase is critical, since a company must develop as long a list as possible for the method to work properly. The longer the list, the better the study. A company can obtain problems from retailers, wholesalers, its advertising agency, researchers, and company employees. Often a company conducts focus group or individual interviews in which consumers express the full range (or rage) of dissatisfaction with the product or service in their own words. By the time this phase ends, the company has 60 to 80 problems—and often as many as 150 to 200 or more.

The next phase determines which problems really vex the prime prospects. These are the problems that offer real opportunities for the company. To learn this, researchers ask 200 or more prospects three key questions:

1. How often does the problem occur? (Frequency)
2. How much does it irritate you when it occurs? (Bothersomeness)
3. In your opinion, which of these problems is not addressed in advertising claims by other brands or products? (Preemptibility)

Researchers calculate each problem's value by combining the three measures into a single score. The bigger the score, the bigger the opportunity.

Problem detection is a useful tool as far as it goes, but it tends to overlook product attributes that, as we pointed out above, are prices of entry into the category. A soft drink, for example, must taste good before someone will buy it twice. Problem detection will not detect "taste" as a problem among Coke or Pepsi drinkers.

If you were to ignore taste, however—the price of entry into the category— and try to develop a cola that addresses peripheral issues such as carbonation, bottle size, or label design, you'd miss the market.

Also, problem detection does not identify psychological or intangible themes as problems. Sex appeal, youthfulness, prestige, happiness, masculinity, and security are a few examples of intangible dimensions this otherwise helpful research tool will not find to be problems. Let's face it, it's difficult enough for people to tell a psychiatrist about their doubts about sexual attractiveness, their need to impress the neighbors, and their fears about street crime, without having market researchers asking them to rate these "problems" in terms of bothersomeness and frequency.

Myth 72: Positioning strategies based on gap analysis will be successful.

Truth: Gap analysis looks for gaps between what buyers need (or want) and what products deliver.

But gap analysis itself is flawed, so a strategy based on it must also be flawed.

(Important note: We are going to talk about gap analysis and other techniques as if they applied only to positioning strategies. In the real world, of course, companies use them to develop new products and for other purposes. The problems with the techniques remain.)

Gap analysis first identifies determinant attributes—those characteristics that led the consumer to buy one product or brand rather than another. For an attribute to be determinant, the buyer must consider it important *and* it must be available.

Until food companies began offering frozen entrees in microwave-safe trays, it made no marketing difference that some consumers said they wanted to nuke their TV dinners in the microwave. In microwave cooking terms, TV dinner buyers saw their alternatives as undifferentiated. The attribute could not determine a consumer's choice.

(Of course, problem detection might have found that consumers wanted to nuke their frozen entrees without having to remove them from the package. Such a finding would have given the first manufacturer to offer such packaging a serious competitive advantage—once enough consumers owned microwave ovens to make the expense economically feasible.)

Gap analysis research asks:

- What attributes and benefits do people say they want or need in a product or service?
- How well does the product or service they currently use fill these needs?
- Are there any "gaps" between what people want and their satisfaction with the product they currently use? Such a gap, says the theory, may be an opportunity to reposition an established product to fill those needs.

To determine the gaps, researchers go through the same sort of preliminary steps they go through in a problem-detection study. They first identify all product or service characteristics that might be important to existing customers, to prospects, or to both. These are both tangible and intangible attributes and benefits.

Depending on the product or service, researchers will generate a list of 20 to 200 attributes and benefits, a list that includes all those consumers believe are important. The researchers then write a questionnaire that lists all possible attributes and benefits.

Respondents representing a projectable sample indicate how important they feel each attribute and benefit is (whether currently available or not) and how well the product they currently use performs in terms of each.

Typically, gap analysis reports either the mean or the percent of respondents who fell into each attribute's "top two boxes." That is, they gave a 4 or a 5 on a scale where 5 is "most important." The attributes and benefits are then grouped into categories or "factors" in order to simplify the analysis task. Instead of looking at 100 or so attributes, the research can focus on, say, 15 "factors." Here is a typical, if truncated, example. (We've made up the attributes and the figures, but the process is actual.)

Importance/Evaluation Ratings for a New Automobile

Factors	Importance ratings	Evaluation ratings	Gap (percentage points)
Safety	96%	95%	1
Performance	82%	75%	7
Sports styling	80%	60%	20
Comfort	50%	50%	0
Engineering	30%	15%	15

These figures indicate that safety is very important to people. They also indicate that, for the most part, their current car's safety level gives them what they want. To find the gaps, one simply subtracts the evaluation ratings from the importance ratings. The larger the gap, the larger the opportunity.

This study discovered that the greatest gap exists for sports styling (20 percentage points), followed by engineering excellence (15), then performance (7). It found no gap between the importance and evaluation ratings for the comfort factor. This is such a significant finding we put a box around it.

Typically, at this point, marketing management concludes that sports styling represents the best positioning opportunity. Engineering or performance each offers some possibility, while driving comfort presents no opportunity.

And that's where gap analysis falls apart.

These conclusions will be right only some of the time, and there's no way to know which time they're right.

Erroneousness creeps in when gap analysis takes data on individual consumers, converts it to aggregate numbers—adds the individual responses together—and then uses the aggregates to draw conclusions about individuals. Aggregate figures do not necessarily reflect individual behavior. They may. But then again, they may not.

To show how this works, consider the example we've just shown. Assume that the following statements are true for the fourth attribute factor, comfort:

- Those people who consider comfort in a car an important attribute know their car does not provide it.
- Those people who know their car offers comfort do not consider the feature to be important.

(All right, we're rigging the numbers to make a point, but the example is not unrealistic. The results rarely cancel each other out quite so neatly, but the point remains valid.)

A table representing the situation we've just described would look like this:

Individuals with Different Importance-Performance Ratings for Comfort

Evaluation of current Product/Service	Importance ratings	
	Highly important	Not important
Negative	50% (Quadrant 1)	0% (Quadrant 2)
Positive	0% (Quadrant 3)	50% (Quadrant 4)

This shows that exactly half the people sampled consider comfort in a car to be important, and none of them feels that his or her current car model provides it adequately; these are the people in Quadrant 1.

The other half of the sample, those who consider comfort not important to them and feel their current car provides it adequately, are the people in Quadrant 4. The result is that the one group cancels the other.

Yet the company (or the industry) is not positioning a car with a product attribute half of the market considers to be important. Someone is overlooking a serious competitive opportunity.

Traditional gap analysis masks this opportunity by concluding that there is no "gap" in the product attribute. If this had been an actual case, the opportunities the researchers reported to marketing management—go for sports styling, engineering excellence, and performance—would have been misleading.

But this is not the only way the analysis can go wrong. Traditional gap analysis, as revealed in our example, indicated that a focus on engineering shows little value as a positioning strategy. Only 30 percent of the sample respondents said it is important to them, and 15 percent said their current car has it. When we make up a table, the information looks like this:

Individuals with Different Importance-Performance Ratings for Engineering Excellence

Evaluation of current Product/Service	Importance ratings	
	Highly important	Not important
Negative	30% (Quadrant 1)	55% (Quadrant 2)
Positive	0% (Quadrant 3)	15% (Quadrant 4)

These figures indicate a potential marketing opportunity far greater than the aggregate analysis indicated. The 30 percent of the respondents who consider engineering excellence to be important buy cars they say do not provide it (Quadrant 1).

The 15 percent of the respondents who feel their current car is well-engineered (Quadrant 4) do not consider this attribute to be important, and their responses reduce the gap.

As a result, traditional gap analysis indicates a smaller market opportunity for engineering excellence than is in fact the case. Depending on management's cutoff point—"We don't want to look into any gap smaller than 5 percent"—this might well result in a misguided decision to halt any further investigation into an engineering program. But most managements, learning that 30 percent of the company's prospects consider a feature important and are not getting it, would do something to change the situation.

Researchers who analyze aggregate data by means of traditional gap analysis will reach correct conclusions only by accident. Sometimes they're right. Sometimes they're wrong. But there's no way to tell the difference.

Myth 73: Perceptual mapping and choice modeling offer prescriptive insights that help marketers to develop improved positioning strategies.

Truth: Researchers like to show marketing managers perceptual maps. They're easy to understand—just two axes, with all competing products assigned to one of the four quadrants. For an antacid, as an example, the two dimensions might be taste (awful to good) and efficacy (works fast and well to doesn't work at all). What could be simpler?

Nothing. The problem is, it's too simple. We question the value of perceptual maps, especially when a company uses them to prescribe a positioning strategy.

Perceptual mapping's working assumption is that people walk around with pretty much the same perceptions of brands and products. It assumes that if a research company has 50 people produce 50 perceptual maps and then puts them on top of one another, they'll all be about the same.

But there is no reason to believe that's true. It contradicts all other forms of marketing research, which assume that people have different perceptions, needs, and ideas. Yet many perceptual mappers, working as if the assumption were true, justify small-scale research—15, 20, or 30 people—because they argue they don't need bigger groups. But if it's true for perceptual maps, why isn't it true for other studies?

Perceptual maps have other problems. Why are there only two dimensions? Because to communicate to marketing management, people who generally are not trained in the mathematics of mapping, researchers are forced to explain brands in a two-dimensional framework. It's easy to show two dimensions on flat paper or a screen during a presentation. If the researchers try to show the brands in three dimensions, the mapping exercise becomes more complicated, and if the perceptual space requires four, five, or six dimensions, most ordinary human managers are bewildered.

When we do a perceptual mapping study, we often discover as we are formulating the report that four, five, six, or more dimensions are required to explain differences in consumer perceptions between products. Recognizing that these incomprehensible results cannot be presented to management, researchers sometimes transform—some would say bastardize—the data to force everything into two dimensions.

Can the two forced dimensions really be interpreted? In some cases, yes; in others, no. Sometimes the researchers don't know how to interpret the map. We once did a study among heavy beer drinkers, for a major brewer who wanted to see the data displayed on a perceptual map.

When we had finished the study and plotted the map, we didn't know what it meant. We hired a top academic consultant—a perceptual mapping expert—and *he* didn't know what it meant. In desperation, we built a Tinker Toy model of the beer category and held four focus groups (one each night for four nights straight) among heavy beer drinkers. We sat around for a week after work eating sandwiches, drinking beer, pondering the model, and having the beer drinkers talk about it.

All we accomplished was to make about 40 beer drinkers tipsy. We knew less about what the map meant after the sessions than before.

It is true that a company can use perceptual mapping to obtain insight into where consumers place a brand relative to other products. This is interesting *descriptive* information.

Even if a perceptual map study cannot generalize a product's characteristics because of the problems involved—lack of representative sample, small sample sizes, artificial dichotomies—the simple description of how consumers perceive competing products can serve a purpose. But maps are nothing a sensible management would use to make a marketing decision. Description is one thing, prescription is another thing entirely.

When a company uses perceptual mapping for prescriptive purposes, to draw inferences concerning the future based on the procedure, the results can be catastrophic. Knowing where your brand is today cannot tell you where it ought to be tomorrow.

The latest fad in marketing research is choice modeling. Like most fads in the industry, it will die when marketers discover that it doesn't work. A choice modeling assignment begins when a new marketing science Ph.D. enthuses about a state-of-the-art statistical model that can predict brand choice.

Encouraged by this, company or agency researchers then interview a cross-section of consumers (or industrial buyers) and have them rate each of the category's brands on a set of 8 to 20 or more different attributes and benefits.

Respondents then rate each of these brands in terms of purchase probability. The model (one form of which goes by the name of "multinominal logit analysis") then finds which attributes and benefits predict brand choice most often. The winning attributes and benefits are the likely candidates for a positioning strategy.

Choice modeling, as it turns out, can lead marketers in the "death-wish" direction for a number of reasons.

One serious problem with choice modeling is that it assumes the set of attributes and benefits the research uses to rate each brand represents the full range of reasons—tangible and emotional—that might explain brand preference. That's hardly ever the case. And it assumes that buyers can—and will—rate the less rational, emotional characteristics with the same reliability and validity as they rate the tangible ones. They don't.

Another problem, and the scariest one, is this: This aggregate level approach assumes a causal relationship between attribute/benefit ratings and brand choice, a causal relationship that not only describes the past (that is, past brand choice) but can predict the future. Only fortune-tellers believe this assumption.

Take a very different example. Pick any product category and plot the relationship between advertising spending and sales, for all the different brands in 1993. The correlation will be very high, often .9 or higher (1.0 means a perfect correlation). Now we could assume—as some managers *have* assumed, while leading their brands to oblivion—that this relationship is causal: If you increase your ad budget, you will see a jump in sales.

This, of course, is nonsense. Ad dollars and sales are almost perfectly related, for the reasons we talk about in Chapter 11. Companies often set their ad budgets as a percentage of sales. If every firm uses the same percentage (in some industries they do), the correlation between advertising spending and sales will be perfect. In this instance, then, correlation has nothing to do with causation except in the reverse sense: Sales dictated ad spending.

This is the same issue with choice modeling. If brand attribute ratings for every important dimension were perfectly related to brand choice, and were perfectly measured (neither of which is true), what would it tell us? What could it tell us about the future? Unfortunately, not much.

If the Bill Clinton brand in the 1992 presidential campaign were discovered through choice-analysis modeling to have its strength in "empathy for disenfranchised Americans" (African-Americans, women, the poor, gays, etc.) would Clinton's chances have been improved if he had enhanced his standing vis-à-vis this factor (a choice-modeling recommendation)? Or would an even greater emphasis on this dimension have cost him the election?

Clinton was performing at close to peak performance among the disenfranchised. Substantial majorities of African-Americans, women, gays, and the like were already committed to Clinton. What he needed to do was reach beyond the barriers of conventional Democratic Party wisdom to appeal to Reagan Democrats and independents. He downplayed his attractiveness to the disenfranchised, broadened his appeal, and won the election.

Stated in choice-modeling research terms, Clinton needed to ignore the study findings, recognize that correlations based on past behavior or even current attitudes are false guides to the future, and move ahead in a different direction.

Thus a positioning focus on a dimension or trait highly related to brand preference won't necessarily help a brand in the future. Indeed, it could help kill it.

In a like manner, consider a dimension unrelated to brand choice today—a solution for a presidential candidate to an outbreak of bubonic plague moving north from Antarctica, or the FDA relaxing restrictions on antidepressants that might be added to soft drinks. Since the candidates or soft drink brands are not differentiated in terms of these new dimensions today, they would not predict current or past brand choice.

Clinton, for example, would have had no edge on Bush or Perot on the plague solution, and Pepsi would not be perceived as different than Coke in terms of its pharmacological properties. Hence, a choice model would lead to the erroneous conclusion that neither of these "new" dimensions was important. Yet everyone would argue that a preemptive strategy based around either of these could be the basis of a winning campaign.

Myth 74: An established product doesn't need a differentiated positioning strategy to be successful.

Truth: There was a time when television was new, when there were relatively few products in every category, and when change was gradual. An intuitive flash could spawn a generation of successful new products and services.

The men and women who make marketing decisions today cannot rely on intuition or art. Market needs and whims change rapidly, competition is intense, technology constantly breeds new products and services, and costs are astronomical.

Today most products, services, brands, and businesses need a positioning.

A positioning tells a customer what a brand stands for, what the brand believes in, what the brand can deliver. It gives a buyer the raison d'être for trying the brand once and coming back to buy it over and over again. It is a one-word, one-phrase, or one-sentence resumé of why the brand should be hired. What brand can do without it?

A brand with a 100 percent share of market and no competitors on the horizon may not need a positioning. A brand in a commodity category doesn't need one if it wants to remain a commodity. A generic or store brand doesn't need one. A brand in an industry in which products are manufactured to purchasing agent specifications doesn't need one (although a company manufacturing the products may need one).

Practically everyone else does. The Democratic and Republican parties are large and established, yet they have positionings and every four years they seek to improve them. Harvard and MIT have positionings. So do Visa, Ivory Soap, Federal Express, United Airlines, Crest toothpaste, and the many other successful brands we've marketed.

Some brands had positionings and appear to be losing them. We'd put McDonald's and Burger King, Budweiser and Miller, IBM and DEC, Oldsmobile and Dodge, Pepsi and Coke, Sears and Montgomery Ward, Delta and NW Airlines into this category. They're in good company. There must be a thousand other brands that have fallen prey to this myth.

And many brands never had much of a positioning. They became big and established because they were first in the market, because of product or service excellence, because they had a terrific sales force, or distribution, or just plain luck.

But the years are numbered for products, services, brands, and businesses that fail to develop or manage their positioning strategy. An effective positioning offers a company the opportunity to both defend and attack. It helps a company hold current customers by giving them a constant reminder of why they buy, while providing protection from competitive onslaughts. And it helps break the gravitational force a competitor's brand has on your prospects; it gives prospects a rationale for moving from that competitor to the well-positioned brand.

"We can really help your company ideate for outstanding ads—we've got a guy on our staff who never lets hard data get in the way of a good idea."

10 Myths about Advertising

Few business topics interest people more than advertising. Everyone has an opinion on it. Everyone from the chairman of the board to the worker on the factory floor, from the purchasing agent in a major corporation to the housewife buying the week's groceries (even in the liberated nineties, women buy the bulk of products consumed in the home).

Advertising is exciting. It's fun; it's entertaining; it reflects and creates the culture in which we live; it brings us news about the products and services we buy. It is important, and it is in trouble.

Advertising doesn't have the cachet it enjoyed in its heyday—the 1950s through the 1970s. It is not the magnet it once was for talented young graduates. People talk less about it at cocktail parties and company meetings. Families comment less when they sit around and watch TV.

Worse, advertising's quality seems to have slipped. Campaigns don't seem to be as strong as they once were. Companies are not allocating the same budgets to consumer, trade, and other forms of advertising—and the industry seems to be in a state of disarray.

One evening stands as a symbol. "Clio Free For All," said an *Adweek* magazine headline about the June 17, 1991 event. "The industry's best-known show explodes into a frenzy in which attendees raid stage and steal awards." The story reported on the bizarre transformation of an evening that at one time was a major industry event: the presentation of awards for advertising excellence, the advertising equivalent of the Cannes Film Festival or the Academy Awards.

Seemingly unable to figure out who had won the various awards or why, the emcee, when Volvo advertising had apparently won, began to ask the audience questions such as, "That's a New York shop. Do we have anyone to accept the award?" When no one picked up an award in response to queries such as this, the award was given to a waiter. Eventually the audience went crazy, stampeded the stage, and grabbed whatever awards they could take.

We suspect that the problems and disarray in the industry are a result of the frustration building for years because the industry doesn't have the respect it once enjoyed. It doesn't have the respect because its work, the advertising campaigns we see every day, are not as powerful as they might be *and* should be.

They're not that powerful because they are based on mythology rather than knowledge.

Myth 75: Most advertising campaigns have a demonstrable effect on sales, if not profitability.

Truth: Companies spent approximately $140 billion on advertising in the U.S. in 1993, with little knowledge of its relationship to profitability. The same managers who can tell you to the first decimal point how their personal stock portfolios performed relative to the Dow Jones generally don't have a clue as to how their advertising budget performed relative to specific objectives (because usually there aren't any, other than perhaps "improve awareness") or ROI (because the question is rarely asked and the calculations almost never done).

We do know that when you change advertising copy for an established product or service, 9 out of 10 times nothing happens to sales. We also know that when you change advertising weight (that is, spending) for an established product or service, you will see a positive effect on sales about half the time (that's good), but the effect is usually not large enough to justify the increase in spending (that's bad).

The effects of advertising copy and weight, we've discovered, are greater for new products than old, but then again most new products and services (80 to 90 percent) fail. Since this high rate of failure can be traced about half the time to insufficient levels of awareness and a weak positioning strategy, advertising is partly to blame.

All things considered, we would say that we know little about the effects of advertising on sales and profitability, and what we do know doesn't leave us feeling very comfortable.

Myth 76: Most marketing/advertising practitioners believe that advertising has a positive effect on sales.

Truth: Think so? Here's what David Ogilvy told an interviewer not long ago, "The other day I was at a meeting where they showed me about 100 television commercials from all over the world. I was shocked. In many cases, I could not understand what they were trying to sell. They didn't tell. Neither did they say what the product was supposed to be good for. They didn't give me one reason for buying."

One does not have to be David Ogilvy to make this point. Watch an ordinary evening of television and see how few commercials actually give any reason to buy the product. The positioning/message strategies are fuzzy at best.

Christopher Whittle, founder of Whittle Communications, addressed this topic as the keynote speaker at the Advertising Research Foundation's annual meeting in April 1991.

Whittle said that about 10 years earlier he began to notice something strange about the pre/post, control/test studies of various advertising vehicles. Whittle was trying to evaluate the effects of advertising in different media. "There would be long discussions between us and our clients," said Whittle, "about whether the movements in the test cells (which measured our new vehicles) were large enough, but nothing was ever said about the fact that the control cells (which represented all other spending) almost never moved."

At first, Whittle tentatively asked his clients what they thought about this. Did it bother them that the $20 million they spent in the control cell didn't cause any apparent change? "Any time we brought this up, there was an almost noticeable discomfort, and the subject would invariably be changed."

Whittle saw the same pattern in study after study, though, and became increasingly curious. One day, during a discussion of test cell response versus control cell inactivity, he asked the client, "Why don't you just pay us based on how we perform against the control cells? If we're better, pay us more, and if we're worse, pay us less." No one, he reported, was interested.

"I began to wonder why, in 20 years in this business, no one had ever shown me a piece of research that definitively demonstrated the effectiveness of their advertising in other vehicles—if for no other reason than it would have been good negotiation. Originally I had thought they must have this information. Why would they continue to spend all this money if they didn't? Then it struck me that perhaps it wasn't there."

Over the past three years we've met privately with a number of research or media heads of America's biggest advertising spenders and with some of the heads of their biggest research suppliers. To a person, they said they no longer had any proof that the great bulk of advertising worked.

One said, "We don't measure one medium against one another, because we don't think either will work." Said another, "We stopped doing effectiveness research years ago."

Our own research among a cross-section of marketing executives is as discouraging as the words of Ogilvy and Whittle. Less than a quarter of our respondents expressed a belief that:

- Most in-market tests of advertising weight produce significant differences in sales (20 percent).
- Most campaigns designed to increase sales of established products or services are successful (17 percent).
- Most in-market tests of advertising copy produce significant differences in sales (13 percent).

This is one instance in which the experts, the practitioners, and the data appear to be in harmony.

Myth 77: Advertising budgets must be set and controlled as a percentage of sales.

Truth: This common practice is based on the related myth that it is impossible to measure advertising's effect, so there's no way to analyze, plan, and control advertising expenditures rigorously.

This idea also—as Dartmouth professor Fred Webster points out—leads to the silly conclusion that *sales cause advertising:* the more you expect to sell, the more you can afford to advertise.

If the company chooses the percentage based on an industry norm, which is often the case, then it is also based on the assumptions that competitors know what they are doing (an idea we refuted in Chapter 7), and that common practice is also the optimum. It may be, but who knows? (And in our experience, it's probably not.)

In many product categories, including some very large ones such as cigarettes and soft drinks, companies do set their advertising expenditures based on last year's sales.

Since market share doesn't change by more than a few tenths of a share point from one year to the next, the numbers that companies budget are relatively static, affected only by category sales increases.

In the fast-food category, for example, companies allocate approximately 3 percent of sales to advertising. Deodorant and antiperspirant brands, on the other hand, allocate more than 15 percent of their sales dollars to advertising. In other product categories, individual companies set relatively fixed ratios of advertising to sales. These are based not on any normative category standard, but rather on the company's history and tradition: "We always allocate 8.5 percent of last year's sales to next year's advertising."

Obviously, it's easy and comfortable to set ad budgets based on sales. In fact, companies that set ad budgets based on sales often set other budgets the same way—the promotion budget, the manufacturing budget, the R&D budget, almost every item except executive compensation.

It's like the U.S. Federal Budget. We don't know what we should be spending on education or on the military or on health care, so over long periods of time we develop budgets as a ratio of, in this case, the total gross national product. Then each year Congress and the Administration fight over whether the figures should be increased a little, trimmed a little, or left the same.

Regrettably, the Federal Government doesn't know how much money it needs to spend on education or the military, just as the Cokes and Citibanks and local dry cleaners of this world don't know how much money they should spend on advertising.

One should approach the problem by trying to determine the correct relationship between advertising spending and sales. In general there are two ways to do this, experimentation and mathematical modeling.

With experimentation, the company goes into different markets and, employing scanner data, tests different days or different weeks, with different levels of advertising. The company varies spending levels over a period of six months to two years to learn the optimal advertising level.

With mathematical modeling, the company feeds experimental data into the computer, and we'll talk more about this when we discuss simulated test market research in Chapter 19.

A third way is through some combination of experimentation and modeling. But advertisers large and small *can* figure out the right advertising budget.

Myth 78: Share of voice determines your share of market.

Truth: Advertisers define share of voice as the advertising percentage individual companies spend in the market. If *all* the companies in a product category spend $100 million in advertising a year, and one company spends $15 million, it has a 15 percent share of voice.

The myth arises because one day, after a few drinks at lunch, a company research director looks at a graph that plots the relationship between share of voice and share of market, finds it's perfect, and communicates the information to a product manager.

The product manager, who knows nothing about econometric statistical analysis, concludes that correlation here means causation. Changes in share of voice imply—or determine—changes in share of market. If you want to have a 20 percent share of market, you have to have a 20 percent share of voice. That's when everything begins to fall apart.

The correlation is perfect, because every company has set its advertising budget the same way. Assume that there are six brands in a product category. Their market shares are 40, 30, 20, 7, 5, and 3 percent respectively. Assume each sets its advertising budget as the same percentage of sales. Each share of voice will be the same percentage as the company's share of market. Perfect correlation, but not because one is causing the other.

In fact, in product categories with similar ratios of sales to advertising budgets, the correlation between share of voice and share of market is close to perfect. One example is retailing: Department stores routinely allocate 4 percent of sales to advertising. More sales, more advertising.

This dumb approach begins to take on the air of science when marketers planning new product ad budgets begin to talk in terms of ratios: "We need two times our anticipated share of market in terms of our share of voice to launch this new brand successfully."

Some companies talk in terms of a two-and-a-half times or a three-times share of market, but they are all rules of thumb, with no more basis in truth than the widespread belief in Cambridge (Massachusetts) that a macrobiotic diet will cure stomach cancer.

Myth 79: The only formula a retailer can use to calculate advertising is one based on the number of stores in a market.

Truth: Conventional wisdom in retailing today is that to be successful you have to saturate a market with advertising. That in turn is driven by media. A company must have *X* number of stores to justify the cost per thousand in newspaper and radio and TV advertising.

We argue that media isn't the only vehicle to drive retail. Does a retailer have to be an advertiser on radio or television or in the newspaper to drive people into the store? No.

But if not advertising, what?

The retailer must have a product concept that generates word-of-mouth commentary. It could be direct-response, mailings-based customer lists. It could be telemarketing. It could be creative promotion—the dry cleaner with the car wash. The appliance dealer with the furniture retailer.

It's a myth that success in retail is driven by advertising, by conventional mass media. Other things can bring people into the store.

Myth 80: Major brands, once launched and successful, can cut back advertising spending to maintenance levels.

Truth: We're not sure what a "maintenance level" might be. In the case of some companies like Scott Paper, they decided a decade ago to cut back advertising on their major brands altogether. This often has very adverse consequences, because the goodwill a brand has built up over time can soon deteriorate.

The world is a nasty place. Many competitors want the brand's business. Each competes for the consumer's share of mind and dollars. To the extent that one brand cuts back its share of voice, other brands are ready to step in and replace it.

In 1992, IBM decided to cut back on its advertising substantially, while Compaq decided, despite the fact that its sales were not especially strong, to fill the void. IBM declined considerably and Compaq moved up rapidly in terms of buyer awareness, favorable attitudes, and, ultimately, sales. While IBM is currently floundering, Compaq is having difficulty keeping up with demand.

A brand that cuts back on its advertising, loses share, and then decides to return to the former level finds it exceptionally difficult. At that point, the brand has lost its luster. Many people now think of it as an old, outdated, dying brand, and are now interested in new brands—the brands that are advertising. As a result, the company must spend more money to return to the place it was when it decided to cut than it would have spent to maintain its position all along.

That's the Scott Paper story. Scott was a famous brand name in the 1960s and 1970s—Scott Towels, Scott Toilet Tissues, Scotties. They were eclipsed by Bounty, Northern, Charmin, Cottonelle, Kleenex, and other brands, and now they are rediscovering advertising.

Myth 81: Advertising works best in markets where a brand is doing poorly.

Truth: Why, you ask, would anyone *want* to advertise in markets where the brand is doing poorly?

Because those are the markets in which the company can affect sales the most. Many brand managers would rather take credit for increasing a brand's share from 2 to 6 percent than for increasing share from 17 to 17.5 percent. And many advertising agencies are delighted to help the company buy the advertising.

In our experience, many advertisers launch campaigns to correct sales deficiencies in poor markets. They also—a different, but related, issue—direct their advertising efforts to target groups whose sales are weak.

But this is the same issue we discussed in Chapter 8: the idea that the company can bring nonbuyers, nonusers into the category. It was a myth two chapters ago, and it is still a myth for the same reasons.

In markets where the company's products sell well, the brand is being distributed. Buyers are promoting the product by good word of mouth.

In markets where the company's products do poorly, it's not just because the advertising is poor or because the company hasn't spent enough money. Often there's a constellation of reasons: The sales force is weak, distribution is inadequate, consumer tastes are different, competitors are entrenched...dozens of reasons.

Elsewhere, we've talked about this issue as "the death-wish paradox." The company spends money to find new customers and does not spend enough money to keep and influence current customers. All the evidence we've seen shows that it is less expensive—sometimes dramatically less expensive—to keep existing customers than to bring new prospects through the door.

In any event, many experiments by many companies over many years have revealed that you do better in markets where you're already doing well, and that your advertising is more effective among target groups with whom you presently enjoy a reasonable franchise.

Myth 82: Pretests of advertising copy predict real-world sales performance.

Truth: During the last 50 years, a subindustry has developed in the United States dedicated to testing print or television advertising copy prior to its introduction into the real world. This industry has bred two schools of thought as to what makes for effective copy.

One school, the persuasion school, argues that, to be effective, advertising must change people's attitudes; it must persuade them to buy. The prototypical research method for advocates of this perspective involves testing viewer attitudes and buying intentions after exposure to a new commercial in a laboratory setting.

The other school is the recall score school, which takes the view that advertising must be remembered (that is, recalled) before it can change behavior. Therefore, proponents of recall use methodologies that test what people remember about a television commercial or print ad, often after a "natural" exposure to the advertising in their own homes.

Because there was so much controversy over advertising testing, the Advertising Research Foundation decided in 1980 to launch the biggest study ever to establish the validity of different advertising research tools. The study designers, Clancy among them, believed that, to demonstrate copy-testing validity, the ARF would have to compare advertising research scores with real-world sales results. Such comparisons would uncover the advertising research methods and measures that predict marketplace results.

At first they felt this would be easy. Presumably many different campaigns were producing different performance levels for the same product; it should be possible to identify them. Advertisers were quite positive; a large number said they had two different campaigns that produced different results. But when the ARF tried to obtain the campaigns and the evidence that one was indeed better than the other, it ran into problems. Not that companies refused to cooperate—the campaigns simply did not exist! It took the ARF five years to find just five cases in which two campaigns for the same product produced significantly different sales results.

This is a sad commentary on the state of advertising. If advertising is as powerful and as effective as many people believe, it should be easy to find hundreds—thousands—of such campaigns.

In January 1990, Professor Russell Haley reported the first evidence that there is indeed some relationship between testing and sales performance. Interestingly, this relationship is much weaker than was anticipated and weaker still for the conventional persuasion and recall measures, a finding we will discuss further under the next myth. Also, and equally important, the relationships were discovered only for established packaged goods, consumer nondurables. Therefore we cannot know whether these results have any bearing for industrial advertisers, for service advertisers, or for consumer durable advertisers.

The ARF's finding was not unique. The Magazine Publisher's Association spent months pretesting magazine ads to use in a print/TV advertising effectiveness study. It finally found three—Kraft

Miracle Whip, Reynolds Plastic Wrap, and e.p.t. Pregnancy Test—that showed enough power to communicate any message.

Myth 83: It does not matter whether people like your advertising or not.

Truth: What matters, says this myth, is how persuasive or memorable it is.

This certainly could have been the theory behind the series of six print ads the Benetton Group introduced in February 1992. The images included a dying AIDS patient surrounded by his family, the shrouded corpse of a Mafia hit victim with a relative's face reflected in a pool of blood, and an African armed with an automatic rifle and holding a bone big enough to be a club. The only copy was a box that read, "United Colors of Benetton." Only an art director could like this ad.

The campaign's critics suggested that Benetton was more interested in attracting attention than in selling products, a charge that Oliviero Toscani, the firm's in-house creative director, did not deny: "Sometimes I've thought a certain image we used would shock more," he said in *Advertising Age.* "But everybody uses emotion to sell a product. The difference here is we are not selling a product. We want to show, in this case, human realities that we are aware of." Right . . .

Last summer it found a new reality. It bought two pages in the Paris daily *Liberation* to run 56 color photographs of male and female genitalia. As Kathryn Tolbert wrote in *The Boston Globe,* the photographs "might be described as the `before' shots for a Fruit of the Loom campaign." Toscani told the Italian press that the photos were not meant to provoke, but to show people as they were, disassociated from anything that could connote their economic or social standing.

Did the advertising accomplish anything? Perhaps they did in relation to the terms set by Luciano Benetton, a company vice president and president of the U.S. unit: "We didn't sit down in a room and strategically plan everything. We wanted to create something different, something new."

Did the ads do anything for Benetton's sales? "Does it hurt? Does it help? No one knows how controversy works," said one retailer who operates a dozen Chicago-area Benetton stores.

Benetton's U.S. sales dropped more than 50 percent in 1992, from an estimated $300 million to $112 million, according to *Brandweek* magazine. Part of this was the result of a plunge in the number of Benetton stores—from 700 in 1986 to 250 in 1992. Benetton tacitly acknowledged that its advertising had problems in early 1993 when it changed campaigns. "We are overjoyed that Benetton will advertise product," said the Chicago retailer.

Perhaps the Benetton example is extreme. What about Pepsi's memorable ads? During 1991, Pepsi ran some of the best-recalled advertising on television. The "Summer Chill Out" campaign caught viewer imagination. The Diet Pepsi campaign inspired millions to sing along with Ray Charles and his rendition of "You've Got the Right One Baby, Uh-huh." Pepsi's ads routinely rank No. 1 in viewer recall, according to market researcher Video Storyboard Tests, while Coke usually ranks fourth or fifth.

For the year as a whole, Pepsi's domestic soft drink net sales were $5.2 billion, up 2.3 percent from 1990's according to the annual report. According to *BusinessWeek*, Pepsi's stagnation helped Coca-Cola to increase its share of the grocery store market from 34 to 34.1 percent at the expense of Pepsi. This may not sound like much, but in the soft drink industry each tenth of a share point represents $44 million.

The ARF study found, to everyone's surprise, that the single best predictors of sales effectiveness were attitudes toward the commercials. The more people liked them, they better they worked. The particular scale used ranged from, "I liked it very much" (5) to "I disliked it very much" (1). Recall scores and persuasion scores were far behind.

Moreover, there were two specific measures that worked very well as well, and those measures were attitude toward the commercial in terms of its entertainment value and in terms of information content.

That is to say, the more people who say they like the commercial overall, and the more who say it informed them and/or it entertained them, the more likely it is that it moved the needle in terms of sales.

When there's only one program and you're forced to watch it, the commercial's task is primarily to communicate information about the product and to motivate people to buy. But the first task today is to get people to watch the commercial. If they don't watch it, it can't possibly have any effect. And to be *truly* watched, it apparently needs to be liked.

Therefore, since more and more people are grazing ("Hey, hon! I set a new record tonight—watched 27 different shows and no commercials in an hour"), the likability of advertising is an increasingly important factor to be considered.

Myth 84: Given enough cues and prompts, most people remember something about your television commercial the day after they watched it.

Truth: We have clients who are convinced of the power of television advertising. When they drop a commercial into a program, they're working under the assumption that most people watching pay at least *some* attention to the advertising. These people, they are certain, will remember something about the spot if asked the next day.

We argue that it's far more likely that you'll find *no one* who remembers your advertising than that you'll find people who do.

The average prime time rating today for network television is about 6 percent. Six percent of the households in this country watch a given show on ABC, CBS, or NBC. (For a single 30-second commercial on this show during the fall and winter of 1992, the cost was about $135,000.)

Telephoned the next day and given many, many cues and prompts—right down to the level of "Did you happen to see a commercial for Pepsi-Cola last night while you were watching *Murphy Brown?*"—20 percent of the people who say they watched the show will answer, yes, they saw the commercial.

In fact, many of those people who claim to have watched remember virtually nothing about the commercial when the researchers probe in more detail.

But assuming that's not the case, that's still just 20 percent of 6 percent, or only 1.2 percent of the households with anyone who can recall seeing a specific commercial. Twenty-four hours later, something like 30 percent of that 1.2 percent evaporates as people forget what they've seen, and in another day, yet another 30 percent evaporates.

It turns out that, if a company runs a commercial during a prime-time program on a given night, only a small percentage of the night's television audience remember anything about it the next day. By the end of the week, virtually no one remembers it.

So the television advertiser has two problems: (1) getting anybody to watch the commercials in the first place, and (2) having them recall anything about the ones they actually did watch.

We are not saying here that recall is the significant measure. Likability remains the important thing. But if the viewer remembers absolutely nothing about the commercial, the carryover effect of liking it is not likely to exist.

Myth 85: Associating a brand with a social cause is a good way to revitalize it.

Truth: Associating with a social cause *may* work.

Assume your product is a low-share contraceptive with no distinguishing characteristics, purchased, according to syndicated research, by upscale, liberal consumers. Associating the product with the National Organization of Women, contributing 5 percent of sales to NOW, and obtaining NOW's endorsement, could enhance sales.

Ben & Jerry's, on the other hand, has been doing it all wrong for years. Knowing little about the socio-, psycho-, demographic profiles of ice cream consumers, they have successfully positioned themselves as the ice cream store for people who are far out. They are prosperous in spite of their social efforts, not because of them.

To the extent that a brand is large, its buyers heterogeneous, and its cause narrow, a company that associates itself with a social cause will only antagonize prospects rather than attract customers.

Consider the following social causes: happy, healthy children; a cleaner environment; abortion on demand; gay rights. This depicts a move from broad appeal to narrow, but the broader the appeal, the less compelling the strategy. The more narrow issue is the more compelling one, but also the one more likely to offend more people.

Associating a brand with a social cause may revitalize it, but it also may kill it.

Myth 86: The more messages you pack into a television or print ad, the more effective the advertising.

Truth: One of the first things advertising researchers learn working at agencies is that the number of words and the number of messages packed into the copy influences a copy strategy test.

Researchers often do copy strategy tests by exposing 100 to 200 different buyers in the product category to a description of the product or service. The words and the phrases that describe the product vary. One concept may emphasize taste, another stress health and nutrition, a third play up convenience.

We learn, however, that if one concept has 50 words and talks about 5 attributes and benefits, it generally scores higher than a concept that has 25 words and talks about 2 attributes and benefits.

Stated differently, copy concept-testing studies show that the more words and phrases, and the more attributes and benefits the copy employs, the greater people's interest in buying the product.

This tells us nothing, however, about the relationship between the number of words and phrases, attributes and benefits, and how effective the copy is in the real world. In the real world, consumers tend to forget long and complicated advertising copy that talks about many attributes and benefits; they tend to remember short and punchy copy that discusses only one or two claims.

A more important issue, however, is how to combine attributes and benefits into an overall advertising message. Traditional trade-off analysis has a simple answer: Add up the effects. The winning concept or message is the one with the highest value.

Indeed, many marketers take this approach. They take the same 20 or 30 attributes or benefits they've always had, then test them to see which the advertising should include and how many each ad should contain.

Here are data that show that as the company moves from 1 message—from 1 attribute or 1 benefit—to 20, consumer "would buy" scores increase from 26 to 91 percent:

Relationship between Message and Purchase Intention

Number of attributes and benefits	Percent "would buy"
1	26%
2	39%
3	55%
5	73%
8	80%
12	86%
20	91%

One marketing director looking at this table decided that the 8-message strategy was the most efficient and went with it. Eight messages...80 percent "would buy." It has a nice ring. This kind of thinking turns up in much direct-mail soliciting. The envelope contains so many messages, so many attributes and benefits, so many features that they stumble over one another.

This is not advertising; it's a list of goodies the company produced in the hope that if someone reads the list he or she will find something appealing.

True, it helps to know each attribute and benefit's main effects, but there's more to effective advertising than simply adding them up to find the highest value.

Consider the two interesting, but conflicting, relationships illustrated in Exhibit 10.1. The left chart (one way to illustrate the table above) indicates that demand rises as the number of messages within a

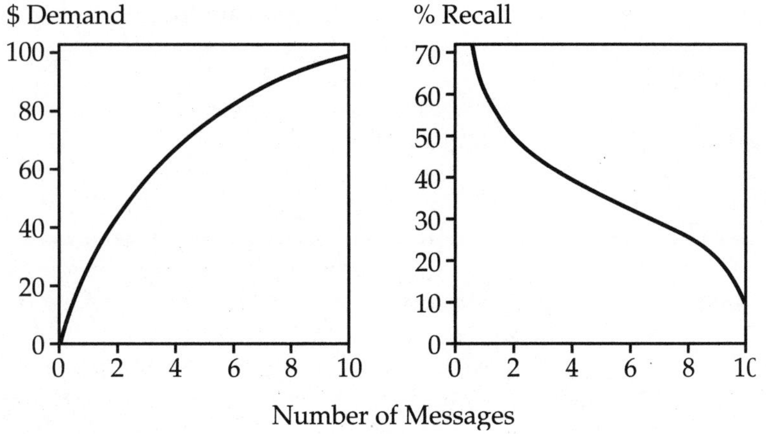

Exhibit 10-1 Two conflicting relationships.

concept increases. This occurs in every trade-off study. Not surprisingly, the more a company promises, the better the numbers.

But the chart on the right shows an equally interesting relationship. Real-world data suggests that the more messages a company packs into an advertisement, the lower the expected recall of any one message and, in some cases, the advertisement as a whole. Simple-minded stories may not be the most persuasive, but they are the best remembered. We suspect they are the best liked as well, because they're less confusing.

These curves, by the way, exhibit different shapes for print advertising and television commercials, and different shapes for low- and high-involvement decisions. Print campaigns and high-involvement decisions permit an advertiser to run more messages per advertisement than television advertising or low-involvement decisions.

Myth 87: Naming your competitors in ads is a way to distinguish yourself.

Truth: Or, more generally, comparative advertising is an effective way to communicate positive information about your brand, your product, and your people, and to disparage competitive products.

We're not saying that all comparative ads are bad.

But comparative television commercials, in naming the competition, often help the competitor as much as—or more than—it helps the bill-paying advertiser.

We believe this happens because the advertising message is so short—between 15 and 30 seconds—and drifts by in a sea of advertising and programming clutter. As we discussed a moment ago, few consumers remember anything the advertiser wants them to the next day, never mind a week or a month later. Given those constraints, it's highly unlikely that the message the advertiser wishes to convey relative to the competition will stand out. Adding another brand only adds to consumer confusion.

What about making comparisons in print ads? There the prospect can study the list of attributes and benefits and see exactly where the advertiser excels.

We've talked about low- versus high-involvement consumers. One characteristic of high-involvement decision making is that people pay a lot of attention to the advertising. They're researching the decision. They go to the library and read *Consumer Reports.* They visit automobile dealerships. They talk to friends. They're tuned in to the total environment. Products that these high-involvement consumers buy may effectively name competitors in their print advertising.

But in general, companies have to chose the advertising execution that best meets the characteristics and needs of their customers. Advertisers usually do not have time to make another point. In television particularly—since most products bought via television reflect low-involvement decision making—competitive advertising is not as effective as the myth would suggest.

"With an ad budget of less than $100,000, I'm not sure we can hit every adult in the state three times a night for a year."

11
Myths about Media Planning and Scheduling

The point of media planning is to decide where and when to put the messages that will move the target audience toward your product or service.

Media planning raises a number of questions. Where should we place the advertising? How should we schedule it? How much should we run?

The first issue raises its own flock of questions: Should we place the advertising on television? On radio? Print? Some combination of all three? Something else?

If it's television, should we use daytime television? Should we use prime time? If it's daytime TV, should we use soap operas, talk shows, or something else? Should we use morning news programs?

The second issue involves questions like: Should we run the advertising over time, or should we buy all of the media within one month? If over time, should we spread it out evenly throughout the year? Should we buy bursts (or flights)—run ads one week and nothing for three weeks, then repeat?

Finally, whatever we do, how much advertising should we run, with how much reach and frequency? This obviously is an issue related to the advertising budgeting question we discussed in the last chapter, because there's a limit to what any company can buy.

If a company has a national brand and decides for whatever reason (probably because management didn't think about it for more than 13 minutes) to spend no more than $10 million on its campaign, and wants the advertising to run continuously throughout the year, it cannot use prime-time network television on a national basis. Perhaps we ought to say "should not," because some marketers who score low in Marketing I.Q. do spend small budgets on national TV.

That is, it should not use national television at all unless it identifies its target market as being as narrow as people who watch Rush Limbaugh. In that case, it could run a national campaign on the *Rush Limbaugh* show throughout the year.

But if your audience is broader than Rush Limbaugh's, then $10 million is not going to cut it on national television. Television is simply too expensive.

Myth 88: Media planners at advertising agencies know a great deal about the relative effectiveness of print, television, and radio advertising.

Truth: Because these people are experts, the theory goes, they can decide quickly which media vehicle best suits a given advertiser's situation.

In fact, media planners don't know a great deal about the relative effectiveness of different media, because there's little available data that compares the relative effectiveness of different media types.

Researchers did more work on this topic in the 1960s and the 1970s than they've done since, and the results of that past work are ambiguous.

One of the larger basic research studies of all time on this topic was the *Life* magazine study in the late 1960s that tested the weekly *Life* magazine against prime-time network television. The research discovered that television and *Life* were comparable in terms of recall scores a day later.

Despite what evidence about effectiveness does exist, media planners tend to decide whether a company should go with one vehicle or another based on audience characteristics. If a corporation is looking for upscale business executives to whom it wants to display its corporate image, or if it wants to sell personal computers, it does not run on many television programs. Television program audiences, with the exception of *60 Minutes, Face the Nation,* and a handful of other exceptions, do not include many upscale business executives.

Even the exceptions include numerous people who are not in the target audience but whom the company has to pay to reach. Advertising in the pages of *BusinessWeek, Forbes, Fortune,* or *The Wall Street Journal,* on the other hand, will give the advertiser a greater concentration of upscale business executives.

So planners base their media decisions partially on the medium's efficiency in reaching the advertiser's target group. This is particularly true for high-involvement purchases, where marketers assume that the buyer is searching for information. They believe that, based on the search, the buyer is more likely to read in-depth advertising that provides a great deal of detail about the product or service.

But when it comes down to two different media vehicles that have the same cost per thousand (CPM) and audience profile, one planner will gravitate toward a 30-second television spot while another may choose business publications—not based on facts or knowledge, but on the basis of management judgment.

It's hard for us to envision that an oil company would drill in the North Sea or in the New Mexican desert without research that suggests they are likely to strike oil. It's hard for us to imagine an oncological specialist recommending a radical mastectomy, radiation, or chemotherapy without hard information about the relative consequences of those treatments.

Similarly, it's hard for us to imagine that 50 years after the introduction of commercial television we still know so little about the differential advertising performance of television versus radio versus print, hard for us to believe that media planners are making these decisions on the basis of judgment alone.

But they are.

Myth 89: The more deeply people are involved in television programs, the less likely they are to pay attention to advertising.

Truth: A corollary to this theory is that high-involvement programming results in low-impact advertising.

During the past 40 years, two contradictory theories of viewer involvement evolved, the "negative effects hypothesis" and the "positive effects hypothesis."

The first says that the more deeply involved viewers are in a television program, the more they like it, are held by it, are tuned in to it, the weaker they respond to the commercials. A strong program has a "video vampire effect": it sucks the life out of the commercials.

This happens, say some consumer behavior theorists, because consumers need "closure" in their television viewing just as they do in everyday life. Since commercials interrupt programs, they interfere with the drive for closure. They annoy viewers, and this irritation carries over to less attention paid to commercials and lower ad effectiveness.

The positive effects hypothesis argues the opposite. It says that involving programs keep viewers glued to the screen, and these people have more favorable responses to commercials the programs carry. The more involving the program, the more positive the ad response.

Over the last four decades, more than 30 research studies testing media environment effects have turned up evidence for both positions. Researchers, however, used different methodologies, and most of the studies measured recall only, not a full range of advertising response indicators.

Working with David Lloyd, then a doctoral student in marketing at Boston University, we decided to design a study that would overcome these drawbacks, beginning with two hypotheses:

1. One can measure "program involvement" reliably, validly.
2. Involvement is positively related to advertising response. The greater the viewer's involvement in a program, the stronger the effects of advertising shown in that program.

We exposed a randomly selected sample of female heads of households to programs and commercials, in conditions that mirrored normal in-home viewing conditions as closely as possible.

For our program-involvement measure, we asked people to tell us their degree of agreement or disagreement with 30 statements that identify cognitive, emotionally based, behavioral, and mood-altering reactions to different programs. For example:

- "This program was a cut above the average TV show—it was thought-provoking as well as entertaining."
- "There were parts in this show that really touched my feelings."
- "I was really involved in the program. By the end I wished it had lasted longer."

While we measured many advertising response variables, five key ones were unaided recall, aided copy point recall, credibility for each message recalled, purchase interest, and pre/post buying intention changes. If we had known then what we know now about the importance of attitudes toward advertising, we would have measured that as well.

As the table shows, "program involvement" had a significant positive effect on every ad response measure. Note that for each measure, the higher the involvement, the higher the level of ad effectiveness.

Advertising Response for Television Commercials (By Program Involvement)

	Program involvement			Difference in effectiveness
	Low	Moderate	High	
Unaided recall (%)	18.4	21.0	22.2	+20.7%
Aided recall (%)	34.0	48.0	54.0	+58.8%
Copy point credibility (%)	24.0	37.0	41.0	+70.8%
Purchase interest (%)	13.2	15.7	17.0	+28.8%
Pre/post behavioral change (%)	6.4	12.6	14.4	+125.0%

Myth 90: The best way to buy media is based on the cost per thousand people exposed—CPMs.

Truth: *Why* is it the best way? Because that's the way it's been bought for 30 years, and who would argue with tradition?

Television advertisers have consciously or unconsciously assumed that, for the most part, a viewer is a viewer is a viewer. The only number that counted was the total number of 18-to-34 women, or 24-to-44 men (or some other simple demographic) watching a given program.

But if, as we just showed, program involvement enhances advertising response, and if involvement means more than simple viewership, then the cost per thousand people *involved* (CPMI) is a better tool than cost per thousand *exposed* (CPM).

Media vehicles do differ considerably in terms of involvement. An advertiser that understands this difference can use it to improve a campaign's success. The question is: How closely related are the CPMI and the CPM for the same programs? Would a company make the same media buy if the decision were based on *involved* viewers rather than the total number?

The answer turns out to be "No!" We have discovered three important things.* First, two programs with the same ratings and the same type of audience demographics don't necessarily have the same levels of involvement. Since one program may be more involving than another (audience size and composition holding constant), one program will be more effective than another in terms of advertising response despite comparable costs.

*Our description here of our data and analysis is necessarily brief, but we provide more detail in *The Marketing Revolution* (pages 191–196) and articles published by Clancy and Lloyd in *The Journal of Advertising Research, The Journal of Consumer Marketing,* and *Advertising Age.*

The second finding follows from the first. If you start with a fixed advertising budget (say, $5 million) and buy a media schedule based on cost per thousand (CPMs), then do it again based on cost per thousand *involved* (CPMIs), you end up with two *different* sets of programs.

Third, and most importantly, the estimated advertising effectiveness of the CPMI buy is far greater than the CPM buy.

Everything we've done suggests that CPMIs will be the wave of the future, while (and we quote here from Chris Whittle of Whittle Communications) "CPMs will be to advertising what junk bonds were to Drexel Burnham Lambert."

Myth 91: Nielsen's rating service—especially the people meter—is a valid indicator of the number of people and the percentage of homes watching particular programs on television.

Truth: The people meter came into existence because, with the rise of cable, paper diaries were clearly inadequate. People could not recall what they watched every quarter hour, so the meter now does it for them. The meter sits on the top of the TV and prompts the viewer(s) to enter his or her identification number when the set is on. The theory is that the meter records not only when the TV is playing but who is in the room watching. And of course the theory assumes that all consumers punctiliously punch their button as they move in and out of the TV room. If you assume this, you'll assume anything.

The networks were unhappy with the people meter from the first, and for good reason. Peter Miller, an expert on survey methodologies at Northwestern University, talking to a reporter for the PBS program *Nova,* said that in the first year of people meter operation the networks found "their predictions were not only wrong but considerably wrong, and as a result they began to criticize Nielsen heavily for the quality of the numbers they were producing." The networks have complained that people get tired of pushing the meter's buttons.

But another problem is the 4000-home panel that represents the American television-viewing universe. Ron Milavsky at the University of Connecticut points out that only 35 percent of the people that Nielsen chooses for the panel provide data on any given day. Nielsen picks a household at random—a basic sampling unit. If that household refuses to join the panel (and about half do), Nielsen picks an alternate from the same area meeting the same criteria (same number of children, same access to cable, and the like).

Theoretically, the alternate households ought to provide data similar to the basic households, but an industry study found otherwise, found more viewing. Milavsky believes that because Nielsen finds it easier to recruit alternate households than the basic households, those households are probably more committed to television and therefore probably watch more. More viewing helps the network story, but the discrepancy is one more reason to disbelieve the figures.

Even more scary is the fact that the meters don't handle the problem of "grazing" very well at all. This is the tendency to use the remote-control switch repeatedly to flip from channel to channel, looking for something better. The meter will say that the viewers watched only one show—and supposedly all the advertising carried by that show—when in fact the viewer may have grazed through 2, 5, 10, or even 47 different programs and watched no advertising at all.

David Poltrack, head of research at CBS, told Nova:

> The whole business is crazy. I don't think there's an advertising agency in the United States that could get up in front of its clients and justify the way business is being done right now. I mean, it's being done on Nielsen ratings which probably aren't representative of the real population, it's being bought on narrow-based demographics, demographic targets which are not representative of product consumption in the United States. I mean, the way television and media are bought in this country is ridiculous.

Myth 92: Three advertising exposures is an effective advertising level.

Truth: This idea originally came from a seminal article published in the December 1972 *Journal of Advertising Research* titled "Why Three Exposures May be Enough."

Dr. Herbert Krugman, a pioneer in the field of advertising research, wrote, "Let me try to explain the special qualities of one, two, and three exposures. I shall stop at three because, as you shall see, there is no such thing as a fourth exposure psychologically; rather fours, five's, etc., are repeats of the third exposure effect."

Krugman wrote that a first advertising exposure provokes a "What is it?" response from the prospect. "Anything new or novel, no matter how uninteresting on second exposure, has to elicit some response the first time, if only to discard the object as of no further interest."

The second exposure provokes a "What of it?" response. The prospect decides at this exposure whether the message has any personal relevance or not. If not, then any further exposures are, in Krugman's terms, repeats of the second exposure effect.

By the third exposure, said Krugman, "the viewer knows he's been through his `What is its?' and `What of its?' and the third, then, becomes the true reminder. The importance of this view is that it positions advertising as powerful only when the viewer is interested in the product message. Secondly, it positions the viewer as reacting to the commercial very quickly when the proper time comes around."

The point that many people missed is that Krugman was talking about *psychological* effectiveness, not *media* effectiveness.

According to Krugman, from a psychological standpoint exposure has only three levels: curiosity, recognition, and decision. This may or may not be correct, but it has no necessary connection with the number of times an advertiser runs a commercial. It has nothing to do with media frequency. Nevertheless, Krugman's argument was so interesting that virtually the entire advertising industry adopted the mistaken idea that you need to expose a target audience to a commercial or a print ad three times for it to be effective.

Since 1972 when Krugman published his paper, of course, the media landscape has grown more confusing. The concept of advertising exposure had more meaning during the 1970s when we knew what an ad exposure was—in the days before media proliferation, zapping commercials, "grazing" across channels. Advertising exposure today means less than advertising exposure in 1972; it is much more a theoretical opportunity than it was then.

If, in a given month, an advertiser is trying to communicate the existence of a new product, it takes about 10 or more exposures (in the media sense, not the psychological sense) over a relatively short period of time just to communicate the product's brand name and the product's existence to half the buying public, that is, to have them remember it.

And it takes somewhere between 12 and 15 exposures (again over a short period of time) to communicate a new copy claim to half the buying public for an established product or service.

One has to ask what three exposures were capable of accomplishing even in 1972. One might plausibly argue that for a major brand with no new copy claim to communicate, three exposures *per month* would be sufficient to remind consumers of the brand when they are ready to buy. Assuming a 100 percent reach, exposing everyone in the target audience to the advertising three times represents 300 gross rating points (GRPs) per month. Multiply that by 12 for 3600 GRPs a year, a spending level only a very few brands could afford in any medium.

On the other hand for small brands, and especially brands that are trying to communicate something new about themselves, to reposition themselves, or to launch a new product, three exposures a month probably is insufficient.

Myth 93: Flighted campaigns are better than continuous campaigns.

Truth: Twenty-five years ago Procter & Gamble marketing executives often launched front-loaded campaigns for new and repositioned brands.

By "front-loaded" we mean that the bulk of the advertising ran early—often within three months of the product launch. By doing so, the brand manager could be assured that brand awareness and trial (that is, penetration) would peak within the first six months after launch.

For some reason or other, the front-loaded campaign dogma spread from the consumer packaged goods industry to other industries like an infectious disease. As a result many marketing programs have died that might have survived with a different media schedule.

We have been using simulation technology for years to examine the relationship between type of media schedule (front-loaded, pulsed, or continuous), type of product (new or established), purchase cycle (once a week, once a month, six times a year, twice a year), and other factors. The results are fascinating.

Front-loaded and flighted schedules work best for fast-turnover, new products, products the consumer buys one to four or more times a month. Continuous schedules, in contrast, work best for slow-turnover products, those the consumer buys twice a year or less frequently, and this is true whether they are new or established products.

These, of course, are just examples. In truth, agencies and advertisers often build media schedules without much science but by means of hunch, experience, and mythology. Yet a company can employ simulation technology to provide insights into what kind of media schedule is best for a particular product in a specific market.

Myth 94: The best way to introduce a new consumer durable product is with a heavy-up, front-loaded campaign.

Truth: As we've just been discussing, this tactic may work for a fast-turnover packaged good. It won't work for the infrequently purchased consumer durable.

The reason is simple: A front-loaded campaign will fire up awareness when people are not yet ready to buy. It's like operating the furnace on a June day. When people are ready to buy because they've finally used up whatever the new product is designed to replace, they've already forgotten that the new brand exists. When fall turns to winter, the fuel burned in June does nothing to warm a cold house.

Let's talk about the major appliance industry for a minute. How do you advertise refrigerators and dishwashers and ranges? These are products most consumers buy once every 10 or 15 years.

To start with, the company should look for product sales seasonality. Is there any particular month in which sales peak? (There certainly is for air conditioners.) Or is there any particular week? Or any particular day in which washers, dryers, and television sets are purchased more than others? If so, the company can then think in terms of that date.

But let's say that refrigerator sales are spread evenly throughout the year. The probability is 1 in 365 that a refrigerator will be sold on any given day. Which means that if the manufacturer wanted to cover every possibility, it would have to be in people's minds on each of those days. What's the most likely way to be remembered 365 days a year from a media standpoint?

Or, taking a different strategy, does the company want to position its refrigerators as the summer alternative? In that case it schedules its advertising during the late spring and summer. For years, Friedrich has positioned itself as the air conditioner to buy in the spring, before the summer heat strikes.

Or does the company want to promote its product—microwave ovens, for example—as the perfect gift for Mother's Day, Father's Day, or Christmas? In that case it concentrates its advertising on a relatively small number of days and hopes to impact consumer purchases.

There are different ways to deal with different products and services, whether the market is consumer or business-to-business. But to simply follow a knee-jerk reflex, to follow the rule of thumb that "we've got to go with a front-loaded campaign" or whatever, doesn't make much sense.

Myth 95: Working women don't watch daytime television.

Truth: The underlying assumption here is that no one but 1950's-style housewives, the aged, the infirm, agoraphobes, and household pets watch daytime TV.

In fact, "working" does not always mean a Monday-to-Friday, 9-to-5 routine. While approximately two-thirds of all women work outside the home, a large share—over 30 percent—work part-time or at night.

Also, working women with VCRs, the overwhelming majority, can view daytime television at their convenience.

According to J. Walter Thompson research, women aged 18 to 49 watch on average 5.07 hours of daytime (10:00 a.m. to 4:30 p.m.) network television a week. Women defined as full-time workers (30 hours a week), or 44 percent of all women, watch 3.25 hours. The four-week reach potential, however, for the first group is 73.1; the potential for working women is 68.9.

Daytime television, therefore, is a cost-efficient buy, even against working women. When an advertiser uses it in conjunction with other TV day parts like prime, late-night, and early fringe, it can help to extend reach among working women targets.

Myth 96: Prime-time commercials really move the brand, and prime time excites the trade.

Truth: This of course is another way of saying, "I want—and I want my management—to see this brand's advertising."

An advertiser should buy prime time only if it is strategically sound for the brand and the target. To the degree "the trade" is in the target audience, it will be reached.

Consider the following figures:

The Prime-Time "Premium"

	Early morning	Daytime	News	Prime time	Late night
Prime-time attentiveness index	119	114	106	100	106
CPM index	189	353	131	100	168
Index differential	+70	+239	+25	—	+62

Source: J. Walter Thompson

The figures indicate that if one sets the index of prime-time television to 100 for attentiveness and cost-per-thousand, other day parts turn out to be much more efficient. The advertiser who buys prime-time television pays a heavy premium for slight advantages in reach and attentiveness.

As for the argument that prime-time commercials excite the trade, the best way to animate the trade is through increased consumer demand.

Myth 97: Continuous sponsorship of a program will build frequency against the viewers of that show.

Truth: This myth assumes that the same people watch the same shows each day/each week, which is not true.

Viewers are fickle. Nielsen looked at the percentage of households that watched four out of four prime-time programs during November 1990. *Matlock* drew the highest percentage: 6 percent of the households watched every week. *Murphy Brown* and *Cheers* drew 5 percent of the households every week, while *Dallas* drew 4 percent.

These results vary by day part, and, in fact, daytime drama viewers are the most loyal. But it is a trap to think one's assumptions or personal beliefs are generally true, and buying a single program may involve a cost premium that is not worth the expense.

Myth 98: Teens are heavy users of radio. Therefore, radio should be a central part of any media plan targeting teenagers.

Truth: Teens are lighter users of every major medium—including radio. According to fall 1991, RADAR (Radio's All Dimension Audience Research) figures, adults 18 to 34 listened to the radio on average 21.7 hours a week. Adults 35 to 49 listened 20.5 hours a week. Teens listened 15.1 hours.

While radio can be a cost-efficient way to reach a teenage market, so can television (via Fox and syndication) and print (*Seventeen, Sassy,* and other magazines). Radio is not a "must buy."

Myth 99: Print is boring.

Truth: There's no question that television production is a lot more fun than print production. It's a lot more interesting to hang around watching a crew shoot a television commercial, especially when the location is exotic and the models glamorous, than it is to watch a photographer shoot a print ad. Advertising people sometimes make the psychological leap that because television production is fun for *them,* the commercials are effective with consumers.

Maybe, maybe not. Like everything else, it depends on the commercials. Print, meanwhile, offers significant media value with its reach, efficiency, and impact, especially for high-involvement buyers. Moreover, there is a vast and expanding array of marketing tie-ins that can extend the marketing program's effectiveness. As a result, a well-thought-out print campaign can improve delivery over an all-television plan.

"This is great! The coffee is $2.99 and I have $15 in coupons—they owe us $12."

12
Myths about Promotion

During the last two decades, corporations have been shifting money they spend on advertising to buyer and trade promotion and to sports and event marketing—all questionable activities masquerading as clever marketing tools. The ratio, which was roughly two-thirds advertising/one-third promotion, is now three-quarters promotion/one-quarter advertising.

At what *Brandweek* magazine described as a "pep rally for promotion," Dr. Larry Light, president of Arcature Corp., exhorted his audience to promote promotion, reinforcing the already widespread belief that the bulk of the marketing budget should be allocated to promotion. "Only with promotion," said Light, "can a brand become a market leader." He went on to argue that strong advertising can boost a brand to second in its category but that promotion can push it to first.

This is a repackaging of the market share/ROI argument we discredited in Myth 19. The thesis here is that promotion can be deployed to increase a brand's share. Then, magically, with share dominance comes enhanced ROI.

Aside from being an instant route to the glory of becoming the number-one brand, promotion has another benefit (as you may already suspect, we don't care for promotion as much as Larry does): Managers with an inability to defer gratification can see the effects of some types of promotion directly and almost immediately. Drop three million coupons offering 50 cents off your product's price into the Sunday papers, wait a while, and you'll see an effect on sales.

Advertising works much less directly, and results are usually slower to appear. When we interviewed marketing directors, more than three-quarters (76 percent) agreed that advertising is a long-term, franchise-building, strategic tool, while consumer and trade promotion is a short-term, price-driven, tactical tool.

Simply because the results appear quickly, however, does not necessarily mean they represent the outcome the company truly wants or needs. To explain and justify promotion, defenders have invented and sustained a number of myths.

Myth 100: Promotion decisions, like serious capital investment decisions, are guided by rigorous thinking, strong research, and at least one eye on the bottom line.

Truth: In many instances, promotion decisions are made without much thinking, with no research, and with a stick in both eyes.

We have seen clients who spend five months deliberating over a $10 million advertising campaign and then in five days allocate $20 million to promotion.

We have clients who demand that their ad agencies work hard to develop an efficient media schedule, only to turn around and decide to sponsor a road, automobile, or horse race (racing is in) without a clue about the delivery—forget impact—per dollar spent.

We've heard of marketers who labor over mundane advertising decisions such as type face for the disclaimers at the bottom of newspaper ad copy, who would leap at the opportunity to sponsor a "Nose of the '90s Beauty Pageant," or a mouse-wrestling match.

And we know many marketers who, though aware of the problems associated with consumer and trade, sports and event promotions, buy them anyway because they think it's the MC ("marketing correct") thing to do.

Myth 101: Couponing is good for consumers, good for retailers, good for manufacturers.

Truth: Part of this myth is true. Couponing is good for consumers, because it helps them reduce their weekly expenses. According to NCH Promotional Services, marketers distributed 310 billion coupons in 1992 and consumers redeemed 7.7 billion (a 2.5 percent redemption rate), with an average face value of 58 cents (up 7.4 percent over the 1991 average).

According to Mark Chesney of NCH, 78 percent of American consumers take advantage of coupons (the average percent of people who used at least one coupon on their last visit to a grocery store), saving $4.5 billion on the 1992 American grocery bill. That's billion, with a *b*.

But like the green stamp and plaid stamp craze during the sixties, this benefit to consumers comes at a price.

Consumers pay a price in added inconvenience (clipping, cutting, saving, sorting, carrying coupons). They have a reduced emotional involvement in brands (just at a time when people have less time to think, coupons cause them to pause for a moment as they switch back and forth between brands).

Retailers pay a price in increased checkout and handling costs, with few competitive advantages because the manufacturers, succumbing to channel pressures, offer the same deals to everyone.

And manufacturers pay the biggest price. Not only are there giant costs associated with distributing 310 billion coupons, but they reduce sales dollars by an estimated average of 4 percent.

Importantly, not every customer uses coupons. According to Simmons Market Research Bureau and NCH, 22 percent of the population doesn't use them at all. On the other hand, approximately the same percentage uses coupons for at least 3 out of every 10 products they buy. This "heavy coupon user" group accounts for the lion's share of all coupons redeemed.

Many of these heavy users are price buyers; marketers who win them today will lose them tomorrow, when another brand offers a better deal.

Moreover, marketers are *not* likely to find heavy coupon users among downscale socioeconomic, groups. Thus marketers who coupon heavily are subsidizing people who, in many instances, can afford to pay full price; people who are deal-prone and brand-disloyal. All for what?

This cost might be justifiable *if* couponing brought in enough new customers or repeat customers to offset the expenses, but as we will discuss under our next myth, this is not the case. No wonder some marketers—including Coke and Pepsi—have begun to cut back sharply on their couponing investments.

Myth 102: Consumer and trade promotions are more effective tools for building brand awareness than advertising.

Truth: Wow! Here's a myth that flies in the face of reality. Although promotion is more efficient for building brand trial, advertising is the single most powerful tool for building brand awareness.

In the following table, we have taken average brand awareness scores for 48 new products. We then grouped them into nine cells: advertising expenditures (below $10 million; $10 to $25 million; over $25 million), and consumer promotional expenditures (below $10 million; $10 to $25 million; over $25 million).

The Effect of Advertising and Promotion on Building Product Awareness

	Advertising expenditures		
Promotion expenditures	Low	Average	High
Low	14%	29%	42%
Average	21%	40%	53%
High	25%	46%	61%

The table indicates that when advertising expenditures were low and promotion expenditures high, the average brand awareness scores among these 48 brands reached 25 percent. When advertising expenditures were high and promotion expenditures low, awareness averaged 42 percent.

Not surprisingly, the combination of both marketing tools produces the greatest effect of all. But most important, awareness scores rise faster with increases in advertising than with increases in promotion. Dollar for dollar, advertising yields a greater impact than does consumer promotion.

Myth 103: Promotion is a more profitable tool than advertising when it comes to generating sales of a new product.

Truth: Most product managers would agree that the first task of a marketing program for a new product or service is to generate awareness and trial.

A company has to get people to buy (or try) the product once, and clearly promotion is an effective way to do so. It's effective because the company is either giving the product away in the form of a sample or selling it at a hefty discount through a coupon.

Advocates of promotion argue that promotion is effective because people's behavior changes first and then attitude change follows. However, among the marketing managers we surveyed in a study sponsored by the American Marketing Association, more than 6 out of 10 (63 percent) believe that marketing works by changing people's attitudes or their beliefs (or both) first, and that behavioral changes follow. Fewer than 2 out of 10 (17 percent) believe that people's behavior changes first and their attitudes and beliefs follow.

If a product is tangibly different from and clearly superior to its competitors, a promotion strategy will work. If you own a restaurant that has the best food, a car repair business that offers the fastest service, a toothpaste that makes teeth remarkably white, a perfume that literally attracts good-looking men, then all one needs is to get people to try the product or service once. A significant proportion of those who try will then use the product over and over again.

Assume that a company introduces a dog or cat food that smells better, looks better, and that pets unquestionably relish more than competitors' foods. If the manufacturer motivates people to buy it once or twice, it can change people's buying behavior. The brand would enjoy an annuity. (There's plenty of opportunity to develop such a product, because canned pet foods smell and look so terrible. Because pet foods are so awful, supermarkets are always promoting them.)

But take the coffee category, where consumers cannot for all practical purposes differentiate one brand from another. In fact, in most food categories a manufacturer must do something very different to create a product that stands out in terms of taste. Few consumer taste buds or senses of smell are sensitive enough to detect product differences. Therefore with most food products, including soft drinks and beer, a marketer needs to position its brands in terms of psychological identity or packaging or both. Loyalty in these categories must be built on a foundation of positioning, unless of course a manager opts to become just another cheap brand.

There is a link, therefore, between perceived or actual comparative product superiority and the use of promotion. The more superior the product or service, the more profitable the promotion program.

When the product is simply outstanding, the marketer can and should use promotion to help buyers "break the force of inertia" and to motivate them to try the better brand.

Product/Service Superiority (Compared to Competitors)	% of All Product/Services Marketed Today	Strategic Implication for Marketers
"Very High," an Outstanding Product	5%	More Promotion to Build Trial
"High," a Good Product	15%	A Mix of Promotion/Advertising
"Normal," an Average Product	65%	More Advertising/Positioning
"Low," a Bad Product	12%	Product Reformulation/Redesign
"Very Low," an Awful Product	3%	Product Discontinuance

Exhibit 12-1 Product superiority and marketing strategy.

But most products and services are not outstanding. Most are not even superior to competitive entries. What happens then?

Advertising's role should be in the ascendancy in these cases, because only advertising can build a strong identity for the brand—a raison d'être for buying it and using it over and over. If a brand is average (or inferior), promotion is simply a vehicle for offering it more cheaply. This, as we have argued before, helps sales but hurts profitability.

The real issue is that while promotion may be effective, it's not necessarily efficient. The company may be giving away more of the product than it needs to generate consumer trial. More importantly, promotion doesn't provide any incentive to buy and rebuy the product over the long run. A company needs *both* trial and repeat purchases to be successful.

Indeed, our experience shows that differences in repeat purchase rates (that is, loyalty) explain far more of the variability in new product/new service success (or failure) than differences in promotion-induced trial. That is to say, although awareness is the first step and trial the second step, it is repeat purchase that makes the difference between success or failure, not promotion-induced trial. Almost anyone can buy trial. If worse comes to worst, just pay people to use the product.

So while promotion is a wonderful vehicle for getting that first purchase, it's not such a wonderful vehicle for getting the second, third, fourth through "nth" purchases, unless the company is willing to give the product away at a reduced price. A company requires advertising to remind people of the product's existence. To remind people what they liked about it. To remind them of its advantages over the competitors' products—not baldly stated, perhaps, but implied. A company needs this sustainable image to keep the brand going.

True, there have been wonderfully successful brands without advertising. Hershey Chocolate, until recently, was the classic example. However, most products are not so great that they stand out on their own. Most products are not so terrific that they will enjoy repeat purchase unless the marketer communicates some information about the product to consumers—communicates advantages that differentiate the product from the competition through advertising.

A product or service requires advertising to help build and develop the brand franchise and to guarantee—not so much the first purchase, because the company can buy the first purchase—but rather the second, third, fourth purchase and more.

Myth 104: Marketing managers know a great deal about the effects of sports and event marketing.

Truth: The fact is that managers know little about the audience size and composition of sports and event marketing programs, and even less about their impact.

Do marketers know anything about their sponsorship of a professional baseball team, or of an America's Cup yacht, the New York Marathon, the Professional Golf Association tour? Do they know what they're getting for their dollar when they sponsor the opening of a new museum or a symphony concert? Of course not. What about miniature tennis, hip-hop tournaments, and the Great All-American Water Pistol Shoot-Out?

All this is fine if a company's philanthropic proclivities override marketing ROI considerations. Perhaps the chairman of the board is convinced that American corporations should do more to promote art museums, or perhaps the chief executive officer is an avid yachtsman. Maybe the marketing director has been a three-point hydroplane buff since childhood, or the brand manager loves to meet celebrities at charity auctions. These may be good reasons for sports and event marketing programs, but they have little to do with marketing effectiveness.

True, exceptions to this conclusion exist that we should note. If a firm or brand is closely tied to a particular event because of the products it manufactures or its heritage, then sports/event marketing *may* make sense. Reebok sponsoring the New York City Marathon, Doyle Sailmaker's involvement with the America's Cup, or Larami Corporation's support for the Great All-American Water Pistol Shoot-Out *may* make sense. But only if serious thinking and hard research find that such involvement produces a return on the investment.

Myth 105: Promotion is an effective way to maintain existing products.

Truth: Many managers believe this because, as we pointed out at the beginning of that chapter, it's relatively easy to see promotion's effects in the marketplace and difficult to see advertising's effects. Let's face it, consumer promotion has a decided effect on sales, and the shift in marketing dollars from advertising to promotion confirms this observation.

Today, as a result, in many product categories the sales volume represented by a coupon is substantial. Information Resources Inc. (IRI) has reported that 25 percent or more of the sales of popular brands such as Scope mouthwash, Bayer aspirin, Kraft barbecue sauce, Kellogg cereals, and Wisk powder detergent come with a coupon. Moreover, a significant proportion of sales in product categories from airline travel to automobiles, fast-food restaurants to personal computers, are associated with buyer promotions.

Interestingly, the French word for *sale* is *promotion,* and promotions in America really mean just that: "on sale," "cheaper," "at a discount."

The real question, however, must be: Is this sales increase *profitable?* What do we know about the return on investment of promotional programs?

We now know it's negative. Most are unprofitable. Basically, these programs produce a one-time sales boost by lowering the product's price. At the same time they diminish brand loyalty, dilute brand equity, and take sales from future periods.

Magrid M. Abraham, president of product development and marketing at Information Resources, Inc., a Chicago-based vendor of syndicated single-source data, and Leonard M. Lodish, professor of marketing at the Wharton School, have reported in the *Harvard Business Review* that only 16 percent of the 65 trade promotion events they studied were profitable, based on incremental sales of brands distributed through retailer warehouses.

They found, in fact, that in many promotions it cost more than a dollar to obtain a dollar's worth of incremental sales.

If a company's only focus is on sales, it will see an effect from its trade and consumer promotions. But if the company's focus is on profitability, return on investment, and other good things like that, promotion's effect is negative rather than positive more often than not.

This holds true not just for packaged goods but for airlines, credit cards, banks, and other categories for which promotional strategies seem to have had great appeal during the 1980s. Is there an airline executive in America who wouldn't like to return to the days before frequent flyer programs?

The automobile industry's promotional programs have resulted in extremely deleterious effects. They have trained the consumers to buy only on deal. Nobody pays full price anymore. Today, consumers do not have to rely on their personal skill in trying to persuade the dealer's sales manager to accept something other than the sticker price, which was often the case during the 1970s. Now they're waiting for the dealer and the manufacturer to give a $1500 rebate.

An interesting case in our view of promotion gone bad, is the

American fast-food business. The fast-food companies did not seem to realize that by January 1993 the recession was in recession. They were still offering bigger and better deals. McDonald's, for example, was offering breakfast for 99 cents, and continued to offer a Big Mac for 25 cents with the purchase of two others. Wendy's had a 99-cent Supervalue Menu, and Burger King was offering a buy-one-Whopper-get-one-free promotion. Taco Bell seemed to be selling a family banquet and a plot of land in Mexico for under a dollar.

During this period, these companies' positioning strategy appeared to be no more than: "We've got the best deal!"

A peculiar way to position their businesses, when they could more profitably have promoted product advantages.

Myth 106: Trade promotion is a profitable thing to do.

Truth: Companies must believe this, or why would they be doing so much? They give the retailer an off-invoice allowance (say, 8 percent), then add another special allowance (say, 6 percent) for every thousand cases sold. Throw in an allowance for coupons, and you've got a real sale (strike that word; we mean *promotion*).

The retailer loves it. He "forward buys" (code for buying up lots of goods at a cheap price, to stock for some future time) and he "diverts" (another code word, meaning he sells the goods he bought at the cheap price to other, smaller retailers who aren't strong enough to extract the same low price from his "partner" the manufacturer). The big retailer ends up making more profit through diversion than the manufacturer made selling the goods to the retailer in the first place.

The consumer doesn't benefit. The manufacturer doesn't benefit. Only the retailer benefits. Indeed, one estimate is that 70 percent of the profits of chain food and drug retailers comes from these practices.

Myth 107: A company should increase its promotional budget if its market share is decreasing.

Truth: Although many managers believe this, the reality should be self-evident.

The only thing promotion does is drop the product's price to capture the attention of disloyal brand-switchers, who were looking for the best buy at a given time. Such a cut offers the brand no real long-term advantage.

If the brand's market share erodes, the company must find some compelling reason to motivate people to buy the brand over and over again. To make the brand, if not their favorite, at least one they seriously consider buying. Promotion does not do this, whereas a well-designed advertising campaign might.

Consider Dolly Madison snack cakes. A few years ago sales were hurting, according to *Inside Media* magazine. Because of the recession, consumers had cut back on impulse buying. They were growing more health-conscious. And competitors—value-priced Little Debbie snack cakes and family-size, multipack Hostess cakes—had become more aggressive.

As Barry Kinsey, vice president, associate media director at CME-KHBB Advertising, the agency for Interstate Bakeries Corp. (ICB), put the problem, "How does a snack cake product break through the clutter of a competitive category when the category itself is under siege?"

CME-KHBB's research showed that 18-to-34-year-old men represented an opportunity, especially if the advertising emphasized single product units (rather than multipacks) in convenience stores rather than grocery stores.

"We decided that radio would be a very effective medium for reaching this young male target, especially since it allowed us to use spot buys to skew in favor of markets where we were already an established brand," said Kinsey. Because spot radio is so much less expensive than network television, the agency was able to do much more of it—more than doubling its weeks on the air.

The agency created the "Snackin' Dude," a fictional male character and his ongoing pursuit of, and love affair with, Dolly Madison and her snack cakes.

Needless to say, the new advertising strategy was successful (or Kinsey would not have been talking about it). A happy by-product: "Dolly Madison salespeople and drivers delivering product to convenience stores greatly prefer being greeted as the 'Dude,' as they've come to be called, over 'Hello, Dolly,' as they were once known. With heightened demand, increased sales, and a campaign that is quite receptive to promotions," says Kinsey, the client's sales and delivery force gave the agency strong approval.

When a company sees market share decline, there may be external reasons—new competitors with more compelling products, lower prices, better advertising, more advertising—or internal reasons—the sales force's attention has been diverted to something else. What should the company do?

Start with a strategic investigation into what the company can do to turn around the eroding brand. The answer may be relatively simple. It may be a new positioning strategy that communicates some heretofore unknown information about the brand. It may call for something more serious, a product modification, a product improvement. It may require the company to do something new and different with the brand to solve customers' problems better.

But other factors holding constant, what a company should do, in most instances, is make its brand stronger. And promotion doesn't make the brand stronger. Promotion makes the brand weaker, albeit while producing a short-term sales burst.

If the company takes money away from a product improvement, away from a new positioning strategy, and puts it into a trade deal or a consumer promotion, it attenuates the brand image and makes the product appear eager, sometimes too eager for a sale.

Can it be true that companies simply ignore the reason that a brand is losing share and try to do something to prop up sales without trying to figure out the underlying problem?

As we said in Chapter 4 on decision making, most company managements do not focus on profitability, they focus on sales. If a company pays product managers to produce sales, the product manager will produce sales with promotional programs.

The ultimate promotion would be to give the product away for three months for free. But then the consumer's perception of the product would be that the company is so desperate, they're giving their product away. Also, company profits would suffer.

Take as a cautionary example the Maytag Corporation, which announced in April 1993 that it was taking a one-time, after-tax charge of $48.8 million in the first quarter and firing three top executives who were responsible for a company promotion in Great Britain.

In the summer of 1992, the company's Hoover Ltd. division offered two free round-trip airline tickets to several cities in Europe to anyone who bought at least £100 worth of Hoover products. It worked so well (and apparently the flaws had not yet shown up) that Hoover advertised a second promotion in December and January 1993—two free round-trip tickets to New York or Orlando, Fla., to anyone who bought at least £250 of merchandise.

Consumers in England and Ireland recognized a good deal when they saw one. A Maytag spokeswoman said that the company received as many as 200,000 applications for free flights (the figure works out to roughly one person in 300 in the U.K). This was many, many more people than the company and two travel agents, Your Leisure and Free Flights Europe, had anticipated. Hoover Ltd. had expected that commissions from land arrangements—hotel reservations, car rentals, and the like—would help to cover airline costs. But these were far less than the company had counted on, while the number of people who met the basic qualification criteria was far greater than anyone had expected.

"The promotions were flawed, and we are taking strong steps to rectify the situation," said Maytag Chairman–CEO Leonard A. Hadley in a statement. "We regret the inconvenience it has caused Hoover customers in the U.K. and Eire, and we are deeply disappointed that this charge against earnings is one of the steps necessary to address the situation."

Myth 108: Cross-promotion may be a good idea, but it's just too difficult to identify possible partners scientifically.

Truth: The reality is that an organization can enter into cross-promotion (or, as some call it, "tie-in promotion" or "collaborative promotion") within different divisions of the same company, and even between different companies. These would form joint promotional and advertising ventures to sell products that naturally go together.

The company could do this not just for the purposes of consumer and trade promotion, but for advertising as well. Most important, such a campaign need not be based on inspiration alone, but can be based on new research analyses such as "Friend and Foe Analysis," a tool that searches through more than 3500 product categories, types, and services and over 5700 individual brands to find strong links to a company's product.

CPC Products, for example, might discover using SMRB data that Skippy peanut butter buyers are also heavy users of Welch's grape jelly and whole milk. Mercedes might learn that 560SL owners frequently travel to Europe. Think of these positive linkages as "friends."

The analysis might show that peanut butter buyers, on the other hand, infrequently buy soft drinks. Mercedes families are unlikely to own either a Japanese car or to shop at Wal-Mart. Negative product linkages (that is, users of one product highly unlikely to use another) are "foes."

These complements and substitutes affect most products. Usually companies identify these friends and foes from the manufacturer's perspective. They tend to use nominal industry or product category designations (or both) to pinpoint competitors who sell products that are intuitively related.

This approach may be effective in certain situations, but it often overlooks other important friends and foes that intuition cannot discover. Perhaps Holiday Inn vacation travelers are not only heavy users of Kodak film but also relatively heavy purchasers of U.S. Savings Bonds; perhaps they make relatively less use of first-class air travel and relatively few of them own laser printers.

Identifying a product's friends and foes can have many benefits:

- Lead to cooperative advertising in the form of joint advertising or promotion, or bundling products or pricing, or sharing other marketing and sales activities. The goals could be to enhance sales, reduce certain expenses, or both.
- Identify channels of distribution. Researching your friends' channels may reveal additional distribution options.
- Reveal previously unknown complementary relationships. Knowing about these may allow the focal product/brand to educate consumers as to the viability of this complementary consumption and thereby promote additional sales.
- If a company sells both the focal product/brand and its complements, it may use its better-known brands to enhance the image of the lesser-known brands; through bundling, differentiate itself from competitors who do not have corresponding complementary products/brands; determine the price leader, to thereby maximize profit.
- Pinpoint which competitors are worth monitoring more closely. This will allow more efficient use of marketing intelligence activities; assist in identifying the underlying factors that affect the performance of product lines; aid in early detection of future competitors, especially examining data over time; facilitate in making pricing decisions, by watching competition's actions more closely.
- Identify substitute relationships among focal brand's own product lines. This, in turn, enhances promotion scheduling.

Examples of Cross-Promotion/Advertising

Marketer	Conventional intradivisional	Emerging interdivisional	Revolutionary strategic alliance
Promotions	Buy a Compaq 486 computer and receive 20% off a printer	With every 24-can case of Pepsi, one medium package of Frito-Lay chips	25 cents off Skippy Peanut Butter, tied to purchase of Welch's Grape Jelly
Advertising	"Put our team to work for your team."	"The perfect complement for an energy break"	"Nothing makes your child happier than Skippy and Welch's on bread"

Our recommendation is simple. There is a constellation of opportunities in the marketplace made possible by cross-promotion and collaborative/cooperative advertising. Today there are ways to scientifically select which combinations, which marriages make the most sense.

Think of "Friend and Foe" as a computerized product-dating service.

"Chief, right now we've got a small p.r. problem someone ought to look into. Long term, this enviromania will go away."

13
Myths about Public Relations

Too many business people think only of press releases when they think of public relations (when they think of public relations at all).

When small business managers think of public relations, too many think only of high-priced PR consultants.

Public relations does include both releases and consultants (high-priced and otherwise), but that's much too narrow a concept. PR's most important function is to communicate truthfully and accurately to all the organization's publics, and, to a lesser degree, to effectively get the organization's message out into the world.

That, at least, was the opinion of 92 chief executive officers, representing both not-for-profit and for-profit organizations, surveyed in the summer of 1992 by the Public Relations Society of America. Out of 10 corporate functions, they rated public relations third for "return on investment" (behind customer service and sales/marketing).Three-quarters of these CEOs felt that public relations is important to an organization's reaching of its objectives, and, not surprisingly, given its importance, they spend between 10 and 50 percent of their time dealing with PR issues.

These chief executives are chiefly interested in seeing their public relations activities help their organizations to develop mutual understanding with their various publics: customers, prospects, employees, shareholders, potential investors, the general public, community residents, community leaders, the news media, industry and professional leaders, and local government officials. They are less interested in persuading these publics to accept their organizations' point of view.

But if these are the general truths of public relations, what are the specific myths that managers believe in?

Myth 109: A company cannot measure the effect of public relations and other forms of corporate communications.

Truth: Nonsense.

One way to measure the effects of public relations, corporate communications, and event marketing activities is to analyze stories from television programs, radio shows, and newspapers and magazines. These are articles about the company or the company's brand that ran during a time period, often one quarter.

At present it's possible to look at 47,000 different media vehicles in the U.S. alone, each one of which may have carried a story. A company such as PR Data Systems in Norwalk (Conn.) analyzes these stories in terms of what messages they communicated about the company. Was the message positive or negative? What was the message's emotional impact? What would be the message's equivalent advertising value?

In this way it's possible to show, for example, that the target media mentions of a particular company increased 32 percent from one quarter to the next. Moreover, following the launch of a reasonably priced public relations program, researchers might tell you that the bulk of the second quarter's stories concerned the company's new product and that 87 percent of them were highly positive.

One interesting by-product of this type of work is that it helps to establish the public relations message's equivalent advertising value—the dollar value of the space in magazines, newspapers, radio shows, etc. that the company received for "free." We have seen a case in which a public relations investment of less than $10,000 provoked the equivalent of $4.2 million in advertising.

Equally interesting, some firms are beginning to track the performance of public relations using survey research technologies similar to those used to quantify the effects of advertising. These companies survey by telephone a representative sample of 300 to about 1200 target group members (upscale consumers, buyers in the product category, legislators, decision makers, whatever) to ask about their magazine and newspaper readership, television-viewing, and radio-listening habits. Most important, the researchers ask questions designed to determine attitudes toward the company and its brands relative to competition, and to determine what, if any, stories these respondents remember reading/seeing/hearing about the company. Out of all this, it is relatively simple to measure the public relations effect.

Myth 110: Corporate communications and public relations may feed executive egos, but they do no real good for the company.

Truth: Public relations departments are like the Marine Corps during peacetime. Little glamour, no respect. Hollywood types who never spent a day in the military (we're thinking of *A Few Good Men*) get to portray trust-fund commando lawyers who can reduce a highly decorated, autocratic Marine colonel to incoherent mumbling.

But in wartime it's a totally different story. Were the Iraqis to launch an attack on San Francisco, New York, or Cambridge, Massachusetts, today's most vociferous military critics would be standing outside the local recruiting station pinning medals on anyone who'd volunteer to help protect their homes and families.

When there's a business crisis, when people say they've found syringes in Pepsi cans, or the *Exxon Valdez* runs aground, the unheralded public relations department comes front and center, armed and ready to protect corporate interests.

The folks in finance, manufacturing, and human resources then sit back to watch them fight on CNN's evening report.

Even in peacetime, however, corporations, like individuals, strive to manage their reputations, to have others behave positively toward them. Why? Because people make decisions every day based on the corporation's reputation. Decisions as to whether to buy the company's products or services...whether to invest in the company's stock...whether to take the company's position in a proxy fight or in a dispute with a government agency.

Yankelovich Clancy Shulman collected corporate reputation data on 489 different companies. We studied some among upscale consumers, others among corporate executives, still others among retail brokers, portfolio managers, and opinion leaders.

In one particular analysis, John Gilfeather, a corporate reputation guru, divided companies into three groups:

1. Those that scored below average on 10 corporate attributes such as "effective management," "high quality products," and "concerned about the environment"
2. Those that scored about average on these attributes
3. Those that scored above-average

Next, companies were divided based on their overall corporate reputation: neutral or negative, moderately favorable, and very favorable.

Once he had done this, Gilfeather found that two-thirds (67 percent) of companies that scored below average on corporate attributes had neutral or negative reputations. Only 5 percent had very favorable reputations.

In contrast, among companies that scored above average in corporate attributes, only 14 percent had a neutral or negative reputation. Some 57 percent had a favorable one.

Stated more generally, the impressions people have about a company are linked positively to the company's overall reputation. Positive impressions are tied to a good reputation—not always, but generally.

Does this make any difference in terms of doing business, doing things like buying a company's products—or paying more for them? Investing in a company? Recommending it as a place to work?

Not surprisingly, we have found a strong positive relationship between corporate reputation and level of supportive behavior. In another study done for Brouillard Communications, we found that when the upscale public—upscale consumers, senior executives, financial service directors of research, and portfolio managers—does not perceive a company as a winner, only 18 percent of these people report being "very likely" to buy the company's products or services. If they *do* perceive the company as a winner, 58 percent are primed to buy.

Not every winner enjoys its proper rewards, nor is every loser punished. But on average, companies with strong reputations enjoy higher payoffs than firms with average or poor reputations.

And how do you build or create a strong reputation, aside from marketing quality products, treating customers and employees honorably, paying your bills on time, and all other good things?

Corporate advertising, if done well, pays off. People remember a strong corporate advertising program. It leads to familiarity with the firm and its products, positive attitudes, and, ultimately, to supportive behavior. A weak or nonexistent corporate advertising program takes the company in the other direction.

Myth 111: Money the company spends on public relations has far less effect than the same dollars spent on conventional advertising.

Truth: This may be true in some cases, but certainly not in every case. It may not even be true in most cases.

The myth probably developed because companies felt there was no credible way to measure their public relations performance and, therefore, no way to go back to the marketing department with quantifiable results.

This is a management weakness. Most companies simply tend to continue along the same path they've always taken, and in so doing do not question the business's assumptions.

From a management standpoint, some public relations departments appear to be behind the times in terms of using modern management techniques. They simply haven't embraced them. As a result companies don't know any better and believe things like this myth or the following one, another version of the same idea.

Myth 112: Management cannot count on public relations to make a measurable contribution to the marketing mix.

Truth: The roots of this myth extend into the public relations department itself.

In our experience, public relations people do not search out new things. A company can send the public relations staff to a convention, but they'll tour the exhibit hall without much interest in learning whether anything new might apply to their function. Most do not seek out new techniques and new methods. They consider public relations an art, not a science. They believe it's who they know that's important, not the idea that they could prove their impact if they wanted to.

In dealing with marketing management, most public relations practitioners cannot articulate what they're doing in terms of the marketing mix. They cannot prove that they deliver the company's message. They cannot prove they're cost-effective. They cannot demonstrate they make a real marketing contribution, because they have not accepted the type of measurement techniques we discuss throughout this chapter.

Public relations management has convinced marketing management that no one can measure its function. (Basic tenet taught in Management 101: What you cannot measure, you cannot manage.) They say, in effect: "How can you measure open-ended news clippings, quantify them, make any sense out of them? It simply can't be done, and you have to trust that what we do makes a contribution."

True, they will paste clippings into scrapbooks and count the totals: "We got 537 mentions last year, which was up 3 percent from the year before." But a report like that does not show top management that the company is getting exposure in the top 150 ADIs or in specified markets.

Likewise, most public relations practitioners, while computer-literate, are not computer-fluent. They use computers for word processing. They may do some retrieval on the Nexus or Dialog on-line services. But mostly they buy clippings and pile them in a corner.

They've never understood how to apply computer technology to that pile of gold and translate it into meaningful information. There seems to be a feeling within the industry that says, in effect, "We've come this far without having to quantify, or to be measured."

Why does corporate management continue to employ people who do not make a measurable contribution?

Because they write the annual report and earnings statements; they do internal communication; they prepare new product releases and organize press conferences. And they protect the company in times of crisis. It's a dirty job, and somebody's got to do it.

Many public relations people began their tenures in a period when they were a kind of statesman, when the top public relations people were trusted counselors to company presidents. That seems to have gone with the wind. Even in their own publications today, PR people are concerned about their position within the corporation. They're losing their clout in many cases.

But the other problem is that the marketing people don't know how to talk to the public relations people, and the PR people don't know how to talk to marketing. The marketing executives are used to dealing with advertising and promotion people who can tell them cost per thousand, redemption percentages, and other statistical measures. It's a vocabulary that does not fit the public relations mind.

When marketing management or general management sees the kind of report we're going to talk about next, they instantly understand it, perceive its value, and love it. But the public relations people don't seek it out and would rather avoid it.

Myth 113: Public relations, because it is an art form, cannot be quantified, and thus cannot be measured.

Truth: Since we've been claiming all along in this chapter that companies *can* measure the public relations' effects, maybe the thing to do at this point is to suggest ways to do so.

You want to look at two things: Where the stories appear, and what they contain.

The first part is easy. You know from the clips which newspapers, magazines, television and radio stations carried the stories. Standard directories tell you circulations and audiences, so it is possible to see who was exposed to the message and how many of them there were.

The second part is a little harder, but not much. Break the editorial copy into explicit statements—what we call "messages." Suppose you're trying to sell a new product having four primary benefits: it's economical, it's efficient, it's scrubbable, and it's easy on the hands.

When the clippings come back, readers have a list of the four messages and they code each story to show which ones got through. You can then compare how well the message you wanted to be heard actually was heard. You can define the market for a given product, and the media in the PMSAs. This procedure can show the messages as they impact on the various markets.

This information tells the company whether it is doing better this year than last. Is the number of stories running ahead or behind? How is the company doing against competitors in terms of share of attention? Basically this is a way to quantify the news function.

Clearly this is different from advertising, where the company, because it knows the circulations and audience figures for every medium it buys, controls both the message and the audience. The only way the company can obtain feedback in its publicity effort is to measure the results.

A lot of public relations people believe that their responsibility ends once they have sent out a press release. What they send out is irrelevant. What the press uses is the only thing that counts. To know that, a company must have feedback.

Clips alone don't mean anything. One could have a clip from *The New York Times* and *The Berkshire Eagle*, but there's a huge difference in circulation and in editorial impact. The clip is the source document, and from it one can pretty much map out what's being exposed to which marketplaces.

Incidentally, this information can tell marketing management that this was the message, we delivered it here, and we're delivering more this year than we did last year. The company can see that the press seems to be responding to scrubability and ignoring price. It will document which messages are coming through. It may also show that the company has two other important messages that simply are not suited to public relations—these are the things an editor always red-pencils out.

Our point here is simple: Public relations can be measured and can be quantified effectively—just like advertising. The trick is to undertake an analysis that is far more rigorous and far more sophisticated than the one being conducted in many corporate p.r. departments.

Myth 114: A company cannot measure public relations' return-on-investment.

Truth: We know a couple of ways a company can measure the return.

Say the public relations budget is $500,000. From the analysis we've just described, the company can establish the cost of the media in which the stories appeared. It also knows the circulation and audience figures. With those totals it's possible to calculate a cost-per-thousand figure—a rough measure, perhaps, but better than nothing. Invariably the public relations cost per thousand is quite low, often under $1 per thousand, and it seldom rises to as much as $2 per thousand.

Another measure compares the cost of the space as advertising versus the cost of obtaining it through public relations. In other words, if the company actually had to write checks for the space in which the news stories appeared, what would they total? To find out, compute the newspaper lineage rate, the magazine page rate, the television time rate, to determine how much a clip was worth. If a company spends $500,000 on public relations and obtains space worth $22 million, that's not a bad ratio.

Perhaps the best way to assess return on investment is to set objectives for the public relations campaign and then compare performance against those objectives. One objective, for example, would be to "succeed in placing stories with an average value of 1.0 (where 1.0 equals a two-column, twenty-line story with headline) featuring our new financial service in newspapers and magazine that reach 50 percent of the prospective buyers." One can do this kind of analysis quickly and inexpensively.

An even more powerful approach is to set objectives based on a survey research methodology, as described earlier. One of our clients wants to know each quarter whether product awareness, familiarity, attitudes, purchase considerations, and brand preference goals have been met among people exposed to stories in targeted media vehicles.

Myth 115: You cannot measure the quality of media coverage.

Truth: Why not? Advertising people have been doing this for decades, using indices that supposedly capture the value of, say, a 30-second prime-time spot versus a 15-second daytime spot versus a full-page, four-color ad in *Time* versus one in *People.*

Not every news story is created equal. The front page of the newspaper is better than the bottom of page 44. A magazine feature article is better than a mention buried in a related story. A 3-minute clip on network news is better than 30 seconds on a local station.

Look at where the article first mentions the company or its product. The headline? The story's first paragraph? The top half of the story or the bottom? Is there a picture? Color or black-and-white? A full page or a fraction? Is the story exclusively about the company, or does it cover five other competitors?

Over and above these relatively straightforward physical measures is the message quality. As we discussed earlier, is the right message getting across? Is it reaching the audiences the company is trying to reach? If the company is trying to influence legislation, is it reaching those 47 congressmen who are important to the program?

To us these are the most important quality readings, the message and the impact on the correct audience, and it is possible to measure both.

Myth 116: Public relations cannot be used as an integrated marketing tool.

Truth: Perhaps marketing people have never seen public relations as a real marketing tool. They think that public relations is what you do when you're getting out a new product—send out a press release. Or hold a press conference. Or have an event. Most companies have separate departments, including corporate affairs, special events, publicity, and investor relations.

This points up one problem public relations people have: What's the department's function? Jack O'Dwyer, who publishes an industry newsletter, does an annual roundup of titles corporations are using to describe their public relations function. The last tally was over 40, including "marketing communications," "corporate communications," and "external affairs."

Public relations covers a broad spectrum of activities from internal communications to publicity, and on to financial reporting. Each company reflects the value the chairman puts into the function. At one company with which we're acquainted, the chairman was interested only in financial affairs. He was not much interested in the products the company was selling. He wanted to know only the financial implications of this thing called "product publicity."

Companies vary widely in the way they use public relations. Du Pont, for example, works under a marketing communications departmental organization in which product publicity is an important function. At one time, the bulk of General Electric's publicity was tied to the marketing side of the business. And there are other companies that do not put out a single release in the marketing area; they worry only about corporate and financial news.

The point of all of this is that advertising can't do everything. Sales can't do everything. Pricing can't do everything. Distribution can't... But you get the idea. To market a product or service effectively, an organization has to use every marketing tool. The best marketing executives know the contribution each element makes to the mix.

One problem is that some marketing executives have been brought up on advertising. They came out of brand management and understand advertising and promotion. That's where the real money goes. The public relations budget, if they have one, is a fraction of the advertising budget. They're not familiar with public relations and do not understand how it can contribute to marketing.

True, some bigger companies are beginning to realize they can get more mileage out of public relations than they have in the past. They're now talking about marketing communications, and including publicity with advertising. But for the most part the brand management people don't understand the function.

For years public relations people have been pushing the importance of integrated marketing and the importance of public relations. Perhaps they've succeeded to some extent. Public relations people report directly to the president in many companies. But now they have to justify that position. And the kind of research we're suggesting they adopt will help them to do so, just the way other marketing functions do.

In fact, integrated marketing is coming—not from public relations pushing for a bigger piece of the pie, but from people who represent the marketing establishment saying that public relations has a role. But it's a role that exists only when the organization can measure public relations' return on the investment.

Myth 117: A small business cannot worry about public relations.

Truth: It can, and, as we hope we've established, it must. But that leads to an immediate practical question: What can a small business do to publicize itself? There is not enough work for a public relations specialist on the staff; the firm often cannot afford an outside public relations consultant.

Public relations can be as simple as picking up the telephone and calling the editor of the local newspaper and saying, "I think we're doing something you may be interested in," and explaining what the company is doing. Ask the editor (or reporter), "Is that something you'd be interested in?" And, "How can I help you cover the story?"

Every newspaper reporter, every magazine editor, every television and radio news person is looking for a story (no story, no publication or broadcast). If your story is not one that interests them, ask what they do want; most will tell you. Every reporter needs sources, people he or she can call to ask for news, information, guidance, or all three.

Every organization is covered by one or more trade publications. Competitors read them, but so do suppliers, investors, and potential employees. How do you reach beyond these audiences to prospects for the company's products or services?

Perhaps the best way is as a by-product of what the company is already doing. During the 1992 presidential campaign, PR Data Systems, for example, studied potential bias in the news stories about the candidates—extending its expertise into a public policy area. More than 20 major daily newspapers picked up and ran the story, which PR Data now can use with prospects.

The goal is to think about your markets in terms of what media your peers read, what publications your distributors read, your wholesalers, retailers, consumers, and to think about ways of telling your story to those different publics. It doesn't require a public relations agent. It doesn't even require a budget.

Myth 118: It's better to spend money to distribute the news than to analyze results.

Truth: This is the same argument that it's better to advertise than to monitor the effects. And it's equally flawed.

Obviously if the company doesn't first distribute the news (or advertise), there is nothing to analyze. But this should not be an either/or question. Without analysis, how does the company know whether it spent the money wisely? How does it know whether the news reached the target audience?

The head of marketing has to tell the public relations person what the company is trying to sell and what management (and research) thinks will sell it. The marketing director describes the target market and the product positioning. The company gives the public relations department a budget to distribute the news *and* to analyze the results.

In our experience, public relations people are not good marketing people. Charge them to publicize a product, and their first thought is to mail a press release to every newspaper with a circulation over 50,000. They don't have the tools to select the media that serve their audiences properly.

For example, if the company wants to reach congressional influences, there are computer programs that in minutes can target every significant legislator and the media they're likely to be reading or viewing.

Public relations people tend to take the easy, the familiar course. They send the release to standard lists without attempting to discover in great detail the media that would really do the job for them. With Congress, for example, they figure they've got to place their story in *The Wall Street Journal, The Washington Post,* and *The New York Times.*

This is foolish. Aside from the difficulty of placing a story in those publications, there's the fact that the members of Congress go home and read other publications. The same with the people who buy the company's product. If you're trying to sell original equipment to the automobile industry, you find out where the buying influences live. They're in the greater Detroit area, but they're also at plant locations around the country. Once the company has found these pockets of buying influence, it can reach them via the general press. Systems exist, for example, in which a computer ensures that every release going into every market mentions the local dealer by name.

But without analysis, marketing management cannot know whether the company's story has appeared or not. It cannot know what parts of the story have been printed and what has been ignored.

The analysis will also assist public relations people in discovering exactly what they're contributing to the marketing effort. Then they can prove the value of public relations in marketing. If you can't prove that you're actually doing something, you can't have the money to do more of it.

We do see a trend toward broader thinking among public relations people. More do realize the value of setting objectives and agreeing about how those objectives will be measured. Often these directives come from the CEO, who is saying that henceforth public relations is going to be measured against objectives like every other department.

Myth 119: It's too expensive and time-consuming to target public relations to local markets and audiences.

Truth: How expensive is too expensive? How much time is time-consuming?

As we've said earlier (in Myths 29 and 76), there is no formula. The budget depends on the situation and what the company wants to accomplish.

It may be that the company wants to accomplish more than it can afford, but that is different than saying it's too expensive. And what is the alternative? Ignoring local markets and audiences, and wasting the public relations budget on improperly targeted media? Where is the savings in that?

A small business does not have to worry about 1500 newspapers, *Fortune, Forbes,* and *BusinessWeek.* The small business's public relations marketplace might be a half a dozen newspapers and a couple of local business magazines. All that is needed is somebody who's not afraid to phone the local editor and say, "We have something we thought you might be interested in."

For a larger company there are services that offer targeted media lists, so that employees don't have to burrow through phone books and media directories to build one. Services will print press releases, stuff and address envelopes, and drop them in the mail. The company can call such a service and have the story on its way the same day.

There are public relations systems that will rewrite news releases going into a community, bringing in all the local dealers or mentioning the company's decorating expert at the local lumber yard, saving the company time.

Such services can greatly improve a company's public relations mailing productivity. The computer will keep track, by subject matter, of every medium that's ever carried a piece of news about the company. If the company is sending out an earnings story, it can request every publication that normally carries its earnings stories. The computer tracks bylines and experts cited within the story.

We know one food additive manufacturer that markets a somewhat controversial product, and the company tracks accurate and inaccurate mentions. When an inaccurate mention turns up, the company sends a letter to the writer (or to the expert quoted in the story) that says in effect, "We're happy to know you're writing [or talking] about our product, but when you do, please keep this in mind...."

Such services can track negative news, giving a company the opportunity to identify the publications, writers, and sources that deprecate it. If the company has a case, it can go to the publications and say, "Hey, let us tell our side of the story."

This service could cost a major corporation as much as $40,000 a year, but the company could not put a person on staff who could come close to what the $40,000 will buy. Is it too expensive? That's a question only each individual marketing executive can answer.

"Okay, so it looks like we go with $1.79."

14
Myths about Pricing

Pricing is perhaps the most sensitive topic in marketing. How much should we charge for our product? What's a fair price? What's everybody else charging?

Price, as professors teach in Marketing 101, is an expression of value, which may or may not have any connection with reality. Is a Picasso painting worth $3 million? It is if a buyer will pay $3 million. Is a tube of toothpaste worth $4.49? Not if no one picks it off the shelf and plunks down $4.49 for it.

The trick, obviously, is to find the price that maximizes the marketer's profit. Not (usually) the lowest or the highest price possible, but the one that produces the most sales at the maximum profit. And while we can't tell you what that price should be, we *can* help you to see some of the myths surrounding pricing.

Myth 120: Because pricing is such an important component in the marketing mix, most firms have a serious pricing strategy based on businesslike pricing research.

Truth: In preparation for a major presentation on pricing at an American Marketing Association conference, we did a survey among managers to learn what is going on in America today. We found that only about 12 percent of all American companies do any serious pricing research, and a third of these have no strategy with which to use the research.

A recent McKinsey & Company survey that asked marketing managers from over 300 major North American companies whether they had done any research to "measure or predict price elasticity" in the preceding year supported our findings. Only 15 percent reported doing any kind of primary research.

It's not that marketers are throwing darts at a board to price their products, as in the cartoon. The problem is that the most common approaches are based on conventional wisdom that may have little relationship to what a real-world market will pay.

One common approach is the cost-plus pricing strategy. It falls apart because companies don't always know their costs, often because they cannot break out an individual product expense, or, if they can, they don't tell the marketing department what it is.

The corollary to the cost-plus approach is to match a competitor's price. But if a marketer doesn't know his own company's costs, how can he know his competitor's? The competitor may be just as confused, and losing money selling its product at the current price. Matching the competitor only means the company goes broke at the same rate.

Sometimes doing a *bit* of research on pricing can be almost as bad as doing none at all. Imagine a new soft drink, Zippy Cola. The commonly used multi-attribute model and theory assumes that if you add up importance scores, multiplied by brand ratings for a given attribute, they will equal the brand's "value." The product's price should be proportional to this "value." If the product's value is only half the market leader's, it should cost only half as much. Here's the kind of table such research is liable to produce:

Zippy Cola Evaluated against Pepsi and Coke

		Evaluation		
Attribute	Importance	Pepsi	Coke	Zippy
Great taste	5	5	4	5
Proper carbonation	4	4	5	5
Popular brand	4	4	5	2
Not too sweet	3	3	1	5
Deep, rich color	2	4	5	5
Weighted sum		74	73	78

This table says that on the most important attribute, "great taste," respondents gave Pepsi a "5," Coke a "4," and Zippy Cola a "5." Multiply all the evaluations by all the importance ratings and add them up, and you reach the preposterous conclusion that Zippy Cola should be priced higher than the market leaders.

While this example has been made deliberately extreme to illustrate the point, companies are today engaging in just such faulty research to establish their prices. The research is flawed because it assumes that it captures all attributes, both tangible and intangible, which it does not.

It also assumes that importance ratings really measure "motivating power," which they do not. And it assumes the company can ignore the price of entry into the category, which it cannot. Zippy Cola would be competing not only against Pepsi and Coke's taste, carbonation, sweetness, and color; it would be competing against decades of advertising.

Myth 121: Pricing is one of those factors a company cannot test beforehand. You have to pick a price and live with it.

Truth: This is simply not true. Although it's more difficult to evaluate the effects of pricing in some industries than in others, the general approach of experimentation seems to make a great deal of sense across a broad range of industries. Taking consumer packaged goods as an illustration, there are three different ways of testing different prices. One is an actual in-store test, in which different prices are employed in different stores in different markets, and those different prices are evaluated in terms of a profitability curve to find out which makes the greatest contribution.

A simpler approach is through simulated test marketing. While not quite as valid as a real-world test, simulated marketing technology, which we talk about in Chapter 19, is a useful way of evaluating in a laboratory setting (*in vitro* as opposed to *in situ*) what the effects of different prices on market response will be.

A third tool that we talked about in depth in *The Marketing Revolution* and that is very handy in terms of evaluating different prices, is a research technology called "multiple trade-off analysis." This lets you explore the effects of different product names and/or features and/or prices on consumer behavior.

This technology, also known as "conjoint analysis," enables a researcher to evaluate many different concepts using approaches borrowed from experimental psychology.

Essentially, the researcher designs an experiment to test multiple factors—name, key features, key benefits, price—by showing different combinations to different people. By analyzing these results, a company can capture the main effects of, say, seven factors, by exposing consumers to a relatively small set of concepts.

In practice, this technique permits a company to evaluate thousands of potential concepts at a price comparable to a traditional test of perhaps five concepts. The researcher's real barrier to using conjoint analysis has often been company management. Managers don't understand the procedure and often don't *want* to understand. But that's another problem.

Myth 122: A company has to accept the market price; nothing it can do will influence prices; it is the victim of its competitors' pricing.

Truth: Too many marketing managers do not understand the influence of their own pricing actions on market prices. They think of themselves as price *takers,* not price *makers.* Unfortunately, it is this lack of strategic thinking that often leads to chaotic pricing in an oligopolistic market. "The guys with this attitude," says Professor Webster at Dartmouth, "are the ones who mess things up for the rest of their competitors, by pricing that is opportunistic, erratic, reactive, and based on little information or analysis."

Even the rare company that actually begins with the consumer and the consumer's problems almost never considers profit when it evaluates prices—and in our experience this is true for companies marketing to consumers as well as those marketing to other businesses. They have a touching faith that if they price "competitively"—that is, not so high as to drive prospects away—and if the product sells at all, it will be profitable.

But this assumes that (a) the company knows what a "competitive" price will be; (b) the gross margin is adequate to return a profit; and (c) managers understand the relationship between fixed and variable manufacturing and marketing costs and sales volume. These are exceptionally dubious assumptions. Most marketing managers have no idea what the costs might be.

But even without the exact figures, most marketers can do better than the kind of educated guessing that they have been doing. For example, using a form of the decision calculus that we discussed in Chapter 4, a marketer can evaluate four prices. One price should be the manager's best judgment as to what the price should be. If you did no research at all, what would the company charge for the product?

Two other prices should be higher and lower than these two. One will be the highest possible price the manager could imagine, but one to which consumers would still respond, and the other will be a low price that would represent a good deal to customers, but be less than what the company would like to charge. The fourth price could be outrageously high or low.

Holding everything else constant (or as constant as possible in this chaotic world), estimate sales at these four prices. The manager can then fit a curve to the data and estimate sales along the entire curve, not only at the four price points. Such an analysis might well show that the company obtains maximum sales and profitability (don't forget profitability) at a price higher than the manager's original price but lower than the highest price evaluated.

Myth 123: Price sensitivity is a function of the customer's personality.

Truth: The idea behind this myth is that some people are just more conscious of price than others. Some people want the best price and they shop to find it. We tend to call these people "cheap" or "tight" and think of it as a personality issue. But price sensitivity may be a function of something else entirely.

The trouble is that price-consciousness, like most personality constructs, is difficult to measure. The problem with personality tests in general is that they tend to be unreliable. If you measure the same person twice on two different days, or sometimes during the same day (before, say, and after an argument with a spouse), you get very different scores. People who score "high" in passivity, sociability, or nurturing on one test may look more assertive, introverted, or nonsupportive on another.

Even after decades of research, researchers haven't discovered a single "price-consciousness scale" that measures price sensitivity reliably and works equally well across different product categories.

What we've discovered is that price sensitivity is not so much a reflection of personality as a function of two very different things: discretionary income, and the value the buyer places on the product purchase, the sacrifice he or she is willing to make in order to maximize utility.

Shulman is rich, with truckloads of discretionary income, so it doesn't matter to him whether he pays $20,000 or $30,000 for a new car. As a result the car's manufacturer, image, styling, performance, comfort, and other attributes are what influence his purchase, not the price. On the other hand, Shulman doesn't place much importance on the car he drives; it doesn't matter to him. Therefore, although he can afford not to care about that $10,000 difference, he does.

Clancy has limited discretionary income but is an automobile enthusiast, someone who loves cars and cares very much about what he drives.

So what happens? Shulman ends up buying a $25,000 car that his partner wouldn't be caught dead driving, while Clancy owns a 1990 BMW, pushing 100,000 miles, worth about the same $25,000.

We can express these differences with a table:

Buyer's Price Sensitivity

	Importance of product purchase		
Discretionary income	Low	Average	High
Low	Very high	High	Moderate
Average	High	Moderate	Low
High	Moderate	Low	Very low

Price sensitivity, in other words, is not so much a personality characteristic as a function of discretionary income and of the value a buyer places on the product purchase. When both factors are high, there is very low price sensitivity. When both factors are low, there is very high price sensitivity. Clancy and Shulman, though in very different positions in this matrix, both score "moderate" in price sensitivity and drive very different cars priced approximately the same.

Myth 124: Price is the consumer's "bottom line"; during a recession, price becomes the most important consideration.

Truth: During a recession price becomes a more important consideration, but not necessarily— not even customarily—the *most* important consideration.

It's clear that many marketers believe this myth, however. In the last few recessions, the critical positioning element around which companies have based their marketing programs has been price, price, price.

Many advertisers cut back on advertising during a recession because they say they can't afford it; yet if they increased share of voice during such a period they could gain an advantage they could hold for years. Marketers who maintain their prices, but offer customers product differentiation as a way to distinguish themselves from the competition, enjoy a greater probability of long-term success.

Yet in category after category we see a low pricing strategy being virtually the only form of product differentiation. The Taco Bell "Eat-yourself-sick-for-79-cents" school of promotion has caught on among fast-food marketers and automobile companies, airlines and long-distance phone services. Price has become the *key* variable that differentiates one product or service from another.

Has the consumer become so sensitive that price is the only marketing element that counts?

We do think customers are more sensitive to price when they are worrying about the economy, their jobs, and the future, but we are not sure customers are changing psychologically in terms of their value system. We've argued elsewhere that in many product categories the middle brands are thriving while the low-end brands are not.

Because the customer is more sensitive, it does not mean that a marketer must offer only price-based product differentiation. Many people will pay more, we would argue, for the charcoal-broiled burger and really tasty french fries, as a pleasant change from the grease-burger and the dried-up fries they now get. Many people will pay more for Ralph Lauren and Tommy Hilfiger clothes. Some people are paying more, the industry has discovered, for the PC loaded with product features and the new Intel Pentium chip. And a few people will even pay *much* more for a convertible that has both a driver's and a passenger's side air bag, antilock disk brakes, and a superior stereo system.

Why most brands in America seem to think that the only way they can differentiate themselves is on the basis of price, is a mystery.

Myth 125: You must match price in a competitive market.

Truth: The idea behind this myth is that our price has to be as low as—if not lower than—our competitor's. This is a version of the last myth, and it is wrong for the same reasons.

Everything we've talked about suggests that this is not the case if the company can create product differentiation. Harvard School of Business professor Michael Porter talks about different business strategies, one of them being the low-cost producer that enables the company to be the low-price provider. Yet that strategy must be built into the company's foundation; a firm does not—cannot—decide to change that strategy overnight.

The problem with trying to match the competitor's price is that a company cannot know—except at the most gross and superficial level from, say, an annual report—whether the competitor is making money. What company knows its competitor's costs, when the competitor itself may not know them? And if you don't know costs, how can you calculate profitability?

Or the company may have had a production breakthrough that it is not sharing with the world. Tom Melohn says that when he was running North American Tool & Die two of his associates created—essentially invented—a machine that improved one production process tenfold. NATD was able to underbid competition so much based on the new machine that one competitor accused him of dumping.

The point is that a business could take the same stance vis-à-vis any marketing ingredient. The management may say it has to match the competitor's advertising...product variety...square footage. But to point this out is to see it as a fallacy, because no one would argue that to compete with, say, Toys 'R Us or Wal-Mart, a store has to have as many square feet.

Companies also take a "beat it or raise it" approach to pricing, setting their prices lower or higher than competitors' because....well, because it seems like the right thing to do. We've always felt this is more like Russian roulette than poker.

A company must match price only if it cannot offer some other trade-off: features, benefits, service, format, packaging, delivery, or something else.

Myth 126: Cost-plus pricing is a sensible means of establishing product prices at profitable levels.

Truth: This, as we've said before, might be a sensible way if a company knew the cost upon which to add its profits, but that, in our experience, is where the system breaks down.

Often a company doesn't know its true costs. A product or service's *actual* cost is a major cause of "marketer headache" and is the main reason why marketers give so little attention to pricing.

It does not make a lot of sense to talk about "margin" or "markup" or "return on investment" if marketing management does not know the costs from which it is marking up, or the actual investment. Sadly, in far too many cases, that's the way the world works. Many companies simply cannot calculate their costs accurately at the individual product or item level. Those that can, either don't, or they don't share this information with marketing management.

True, even though a company may not be able to calculate exact costs it can still develop close approximations (in the past we've argued that it's better to be approximately right than precisely wrong). These estimates would be better than nothing, but to arrive at them takes both hard work and cooperation within the organization between marketing and other departments.

With such cooperation, cost-plus pricing can work, but without reasonable cost figures, the idea is a myth.

Myth 127: It's not necessary for marketing directors to know manufacturing costs; their job is to create successful marketing programs.

Truth: As we just suggested, it *is* necessary for marketing directors to know manufacturing costs if they are going to establish the most profitable prices. The "most profitable price" is a function of consumer demand (as estimated by research) and manufacturing and marketing costs.

Suppose a company has a cordless telephone it could sell at three different prices: $79, $89, and $99. The company researches the market and establishes that the phone will obtain a 10.1 percent share of the market in units at the $79 price, an 8.5 percent share at the $89 price, and a 7.3 percent share at the $99 price. Which is the best price?

Depending on the company's cost structure, the answer could vary considerably. Note the three different sets of assumptions in the following table. In each case we've assumed the same $20 million marketing investment.

How Cost Assumptions Change Profitability Forecasts

	Scenario #1	Scenario #2	Scenario #3
		Assumptions:	
Market size	10 million units	10 million units	10 million units
Manufacturing costs	$42 per unit	$42 for first 750,000, $33 for next 250,000, $30 for 1,000,000+	$30,000,000 for plant $10 per unit
Marketing costs	$20,000,000	$20,000,000	$20,000,000
	Scenario #1	Scenario #2	Scenario #3
		Profit forecasts:	
$79 price	$17,370,000	$20,340,000	$19,690,000
$89 price	$20,980,000	$21,910,000	$18,730,000
$99 price	$21,610,000	$21,610,000	$14,970,000

Under scenario #1, with an assumed fixed cost of $42 per unit, the $99 price generates the greatest contribution.

Under scenario #2, however, which assumes a variable cost structure ($42 for the first 750,000 units, $33 for the next 250,000, and $30 for all units above 1,000,000), the $89 price is marginally more promising.

Finally, note scenario #3, which assumed that the firm would have to build a new $30 million plant to manufacture the phone, with a fixed $10 cost per unit. Under these circumstances, the $79 price appears to be a winner.*

The correct decision obviously depends on the company's cost assumptions. This is a particularly troubling issue, because marketing executives in many companies do not know product cost information. Because, in short, too many companies subscribe to this myth.

Myth 128: If sales are not what they should be, the best thing to do is reduce prices.

Truth: Although this is a common myth among retailers, it is not limited to retail. It is a myth among manufacturers, among service organizations, among consumer product and business-to-business marketers. As we've said before, "out-cheaping" the competition has become the all-time most popular positioning strategy in America. Is this why Philip Morris dropped the price of Marlboro, or P&G the price of Pampers?

If a company feels it must reduce prices to help sales, it means that it believes the decision-making process most consumers go through is dominated by price.

This issue is not dramatically different from our discussion in Chapter 17 of ways to compete with a giant. If a giant's major advantage is price, then you have to compete on another basis. Does this apply to manufacturers and service companies? Yes.

*Here's the arithmetic behind the figures.

First calculate the number of units the company would sell at each price point, by multiplying the total market by the share estimates. E.g., 10.1% × 10 million units = 1.01 million units.

Next, multiply the number of units by the price to obtain a gross sales revenue figure. E.g., 1,010,000 × $79 = $79,790,000.

Next, calculate the manufacturing costs for the number of units at each price point. E.g., 1,010,000 × $42 = $42,420,000.

Finally, subtract the manufacturing and marketing costs from the gross sales figure to find a net profit figure. E.g., $79,790,000 – $42,420,000 – $20,000,000 = $17,370,000.

But if the company is going to charge more—either because the cost of doing business is higher, or because it wants to make a better margin—the trick is to offer something else, but not something that raises costs even higher or wipes out the better margin.

The store across the street sells Hanes underwear for $1.00. You sell it for $1.10. You have to do things to make the customer feel it's a wise decision to spend $1.10 for what she could cross the street and buy for $1.00. You have to offer more surrounding that product. *The trick is not only to offer more, but to offer something more that doesn't cost you an extra ten cents.*

That line of thought tends to head in the direction of intangibles, in the direction of services. In a retail business these would include return policies, clean, well-lighted aisles, and a clearly organized stock. It doesn't cost any more to have stock organized logically. It doesn't cost any more to have well-written, clear specification sheets and instruction manuals. It doesn't cost any more to have cheerful, cooperative sales associates.

The business should do things that don't cost more (or much more) but that benefit the customer to the point where the company's products or services are worth more to the customer. Will a person pay more per check at a bank if it guarantees no more than three minutes on a line? Many people will.

How does a company learn what that premium is worth? (There is, after all, a point when customers feel they would rather spend less per check, even if it means spending more time in line.) Big corporations try to discover the optimal service level and what it costs. They attempt to learn what people will pay as a premium for the service they care about.

This is what Kmart is trying to do today—run ads with the chairman of the board sitting in an office filled with antiques and talking about fashion and advanced thinking, so that when the average consumer walks into a Kmart, she feels that it's okay. She's having a different experience than a Wal-Mart experience, so she should pay a few cents more—and for some buyers it's worth it.

A smaller organization cannot do the same level of research, but the knee-jerk reaction of just lowering prices to match the competition's says that the marketer has given up on taking the initiative. That company is just following the crowd. Maybe over the edge.

"Research has discovered that customers don't trust our salespeople and they don't trust our company. I think we should cut prices."

15 Myths about Sales Force Management

Selling is a microcosm of marketing. Go back to what we've been talking about with regard to the climate, targeting, positioning strategy, designing the product, and communicating.

That's five steps, and we talk about taking them in marketing, all toward the goal of understanding customer needs and giving customers what they want. This is marketing in a microcosm.

One can think of selling as if it were a survey. What you're trying to accomplish in a survey is to understand what people want so that you can deliver it. When you ask a lot of questions and tabulate the results, it's more likely that you're going to deliver a product or service that's well suited to the prospect than if you just present products.

But one of the most common myths about sales force management is the following.

Myth 129: Selling is the only form of marketing I need.

Truth: Some marketers believe this myth so strongly that they define marketing in terms of sales, and sales force management becomes undifferentiated from marketing generally.

In truth, a business needs a balanced approach: advertising, promotion, direct, collateral, in-store displays—everything.

Salespeople, like soldiers, are only as effective as the strategy behind them and the tools the organization puts in their hands. The marketing strategist plans the attack, identifies the proper targets, decides the positioning, gives the sales force the best product possible and an advertising and promotion plan designed to support it. The marketing effort up to this point is designed to soften up the target.

We believe that selling is really education and training. When you think in those terms and think of the tools, processes, and methods used in education and training, you'll think more correctly about how to go about selling.

We all agree that the best salespeople are those that listen, understand the prospect's needs, and respond to those needs. This is so basic, it should be a given. What we're talking about is the organization's response to those needs, determining what it offers that fits the client's needs.

Sales is a subcategory of marketing. Marketing's goal is to understand what people want and give them what they want at a profit. Selling implements marketing. Selling (like advertising) persuades the customer that what the organization offers fits the customer's needs. To do that, to sell, is to educate and train the customer.

When we talk about selling to consumers, we want to be clear. A commercial for Tide on television isn't selling in the sense that we're talking about in this chapter. The salesperson in the car dealership *is* selling in the sense of this chapter. Insurance people sell directly to consumers, so there are one-on-one encounters with individual people. But for the most part we're going to talk about industrial selling.

And our basic selling premise is that everybody answers to someone else. Just like Hebrew National, almost everybody answers to a higher authority. Virtually no salesperson ever reaches the ultimate audience; the person you talk to always has to convince someone else. Even the salesperson who says, "I sell at the CEO level," has a board of directors or the shareholders standing behind the CEO.

So the process of selling is the process of educating that person about what the company is doing and how that fits in with their needs. Then the salesperson must do sales training—train that person to present this internally, to convince people of its merits, to overcome their objections, and to close the sale. Clearly this is far more than presenting something and waiting for someone to say yes or no.

Myth 130: Every order is a good order; every customer is a good customer.

Truth: We need a definition of "good customer." A good customer is someone interested in a serious, long-term relationship, someone who is willing to pay a fair price for the product or service but who expects, respects, and appreciates a reasonable level of service associated with the delivery of the goods.

Unfortunately, many customers are not good customers. They are not interested in a serious relationship. They're simply shopping around for the best deal. They're unwilling to pay quoted prices, and they extract commitments for prices that are at or below profitable levels. They are excessively demanding, sometimes distracting sales and service people from focusing on other customers' chronic issues and problems.

Not every customer values the things the firm does well. Volume-driven companies inevitably get into trouble by trying to be everything to everybody, accepting business they cannot serve efficiently and making promises to customers they cannot fulfill.

Good customers are a critical strategic resource; they ask the firm to do things it can do well and to take them in directions consistent with its strategy. They force the firm to maintain and develop its distinctive competence. Yet there are many customers who say, "I won't give all my business to one company."

We suggest that that is not necessarily a smart approach as a buyer, and it certainly isn't what you'd want as a seller. Share of market and share of customer are related ideas, but not identical ones. Share of market says you want to build as much volume as possible. Share of customer says that, rather than go after many different customers, it's better to focus on getting a greater share of the customer's dollars that are available.

That's what we mean by the notion of a good customer. The dollars being equal, we would rather see an organization earn 100 percent of a medium-sized customer's business than 20 percent of a giant customer's business.

The corollary to all this is that if you don't have a clear strategy, every customer looks like a good customer.

Myth 131: The best salespeople are those who are closest to the customer in terms of longstanding personal relationships.

Truth: Friendships, school ties, and common membership at a golf club are a valuable business asset, of course. We generally trust our friends, and trust is the biggest element in the buyer-seller relationship.

The problem comes when friendship becomes more important than the problem-solving, consultative function of the professional salesperson. In this situation, the salesperson has a hard time being both a true expert on the customer's problems and someone aggressively pushing new products and new applications.

We're not saying that building relationships is not a part of selling; it is. But if all I think I have to do is build a relationship, then I don't accept the marketing concept that says, "This person has a set of needs."

If the prospect's only need is a relationship, he should join a social club, a country club, the VFW, or place an ad in the singles section of the local classifieds. Unless the salesperson believes the prospect's only need is social, he or she misses the market.

Selling still involves persuasion and negotiation and asking for the order, activities that may violate the basic interpersonal understanding that goes along with true friendship. For this reason, it usually makes sense to reassign accounts and territories on a regular basis.

Among the liabilities of having too close a relationship is taking people for granted. Someone brought into a sales territory with a fresh perspective goes through the marketing process again. The new salesperson learns the customer's needs afresh and sees if there's a fit between the company and the consumer. Invariably, even where there's the best relationship, (assuming that the new salesperson is as competent as the old), the company will find that it can build the territory, build the client's business (share of customer) by shuffling people around. The same person left in place too long often grows stale.

Myth 132: Personal sales calls are the ultimate marketing weapon, and their use should be encouraged.

Truth: According to the last McGraw-Hill Business Information Bureau study on the subject, a personal sales call costs $251.63 on average. Given this expense, prudent management demands that salespeople make them carefully.

Are we arguing here against personal sales calls? Obviously not.

We're suggesting something similar to what we suggested in our discussion of targeting (Chapter 8). There are different prospect types who are turned on by different things and who control varying amounts of business, and who therefore need individual approaches if they are to be reached and convinced effectively.

In simple terms, there may be A, B, and C prospects, each meeting different criteria. A salesperson might have a different time schedule associated with the calls made on the A prospects, versus the Bs and the Cs. This is hardly earth-shattering news. The effective salesperson has varying criteria for whether or not to visit a customer. Those criteria come at the end of a continuum of a number of different activities the salesperson does that we call "previsit routines."

When a salesperson goes to a face-to-face meeting, he or she is doing something she could not do via preprinted materials, personal letters, fax, or the telephone, A meeting says, in effect, that an education and training session has to occur one-on-one. It means the salesperson and the prospect have run up to a hurdle the prospect is ready to jump over, and the visit will help him do so.

Myth 133: The more calls a salesperson makes in a day, the more sales he or she will close.

Truth: This myth contains two issues. One has to do with the sheer number of sales calls, the other with the quality of the calls.

We in fact would agree that, everything else being equal, the more sales calls people make the more sales they'll close.

That would argue for sheer volume. It's as if the more you advertise, the more sales you're going to get. The more money you throw at almost any problem, the more success you'll have.

We're not implying this. Nor are we suggesting the other extreme, which is that if salespeople can just find and close the perfect call once a day, or once a week, or once a year, they can be successful. That's probably theoretically true as well. One may not have to sell many nuclear submarines, skyscrapers, or turnkey computer centers to make a pretty penny. The one client that could account for enough business to satisfy the company's sales target theoretically means the salesperson only has to make one sales call. For most firms, the balance is somewhere in between.

But often, sales management thinks that success is based on sheer volume. Making a number of calls is sensible. Fewer than that number of calls, and the salesperson is underutilizing her capability. But before the calls, she has to do the prequalifying and all of the routines, which takes time. She has to be properly trained, so that when she's in front of the customer she's as effective as she can be. Otherwise it's a waste of time (not to mention the money we just mentioned in the last myth).

Truth: Make lots of good calls, all to the target market, with superior pre-call planning. The more you've done your homework, the more effective those calls will be. It's an optimization exercise again. The number of sales calls, multiplied by the preparation for those calls, puts you at the optimal level.

It's not as simple as sheer volume, and it's not as simple as one or two good customers.

Myth 134: I know my customers because I know what they buy.

Truth: You don't know them until you ask them questions.

This is a myth primarily believed in by the small retailer who has people coming through his store every day. What he's saying is, "I run my business, I know my customers. I know what they want."

Because retailers say they know the products they sell, the economics of what they sell, the management challenges of running the business, the personnel difficulties, the financial issues, they think they understand the marketing *questions.*

But do they know who their customers are? In a small business where they're talking to customers every day (this is why this is in the sales chapter), we suggest that salespeople ask customers what they need.

When was the last time your dry cleaner asked: How do you feel about dry cleaning; what do you wish you could have differently; what are you looking for in a dry cleaner? When was the last time your gas station attendant asked: How is your car running; are there any problems; is there anything you're looking for we can help you with? When was the last time your local supermarket checkout clerk—never mind a manager—asked you *anything*?

To truly know your customers you must talk to them about what they need. It's an informal process. Formally you could be surveying them on a regular basis, and even more formally you could be keeping a record of individual customer's needs, wants, and desires so that you can address them individually.

People get into a rut in running their businesses. If they want to be market-driven, they have to know their customers.

Myth 135: Knowledge of the product or service is the single most important asset an effective salesperson possesses; therefore, intensive training is absolutely necessary.

Truth: The reality is that knowledge of the product or service, advantages versus disadvantages versus competitive offerings, experience, education, personality, and a sense of urgency are all critical determinants of sales success.

Myth-busting companies give a lot of thought to sales management and to the people they hire. Mark Begelman at Office Depot says that whereas "seven years ago we *hired* people, today we're *recruiting* people, and it makes a big difference." Jack Mitchell at Mitchell's says that he no longer hires anyone who does not have a sense of urgency. "You don't have to have the intensity that I do, perhaps, but you've got to be quick. You've just got to be fast. I don't want you if you're not fast."

However, the single most important determinant for a salesperson's success is trust, signaled by effective listening. The more the buyer trusts the salesperson, the more likely the salesperson is to be successful. Trust is, in part, something that a person can learn, and reflects knowledge, experience, and education. It also, in part, reflects personality characteristics such as empathy that are relatively difficult to teach or to change.

Trust, as depicted in the following table, involves both the company and the individual salesperson. We may perceive a salesperson as being trustworthy, someone whose word we can rely on, and yet have suspicions about the company. If the company has never delivered on time, trusting the salesperson may overcome negative feelings about the company. The sale may happen, but it will be very difficult.

On the other hand, we may have implicit trust in the company to deliver the highest-quality product. Even though we don't care for our salesperson because we don't trust him—he's not smart, he's not knowledgeable, he's not experienced, and he seems a bit shifty—we may buy anyway.

		Trust in Company	
		Low	High
Trust in salesperson	*Low*	No sale	Difficult sale
	High	Very difficult sale	Easy sale

We would argue that if it were a choice between a salesperson we didn't feel great about who had a well-designed product perfectly suited and priced for our needs and budget, versus a salesperson we felt absolutely terrific about who had an ill-designed product not suited to our needs, we'd probably buy from the former. But the choice is seldom so clear.

When you trust the company *and* the individual salesperson, it's like *Candide*'s Dr. Pangloss's "best of all possible worlds." You're likely to have an easy sale.

"Well, what did you expect when you moved into the Ritz & Glitz—
zip-code cluster?"

16
Myths about Direct Marketing

Those readers who can remember the volume of mail delivered to their home every day 20 years ago, and compare it to today, already know the story of the direct-marketing industry of which all those letters, offers, and catalogs are but a part.

The last time we looked, this industry was growing phenomenally. Since 1980, for example, we've seen a compounded annual growth rate of approximately 16 percent in terms of the number of catalogs mailed to U.S. households, and about 20 percent in terms of the number of lists available to rent.

The reasons for this growth and the past success of the industry are legion: a deterioration in the quality of salespeople in retail stores; the homogenization of urban and suburban shopping malls (every mall seems to present the same stores and the same product offerings); and the increased number of women in the labor force, with less time to shop.

Perhaps the most important reason is indeed time; more specifically, the lack of it. Americans today are pressed for time, are searching everywhere for convenience, and consequently are not cruising the malls the way they did a decade ago. They're shopping from catalogs that come in the mail, and responding to telemarketers on cable television. And they're buying everything from everywhere: smoked hams from Harrington's of Vermont and beef from Omaha Steaks; gadgets and adult toys from Brookstone and The Sharper Image; upscale clothing from Saks Fifth Avenue and Bloomingdales, and outdoor clothing from L. L. Bean and J. Crew; jewelry from Tiffany and Cartier; even personal computers from Compaq and Dell. Everything seems to be available in your living room from the finest retailers in the world.

Will their growth continue, at least as we see it today? No, because there's a disease infecting direct-marketing programs that is about to become the industry's undoing. This disease is causing an exploding industry to sputter. The etiology of the disease is to be found in more marketing myths.

Myth 136: Direct marketing is growing more efficient.

Truth: As exhilarating as industry growth may be in terms of catalogs mailed and lists sold, sales of products sold through the mail have definitely slowed. More and more direct marketing is being done, but fewer and fewer people are responding to offers. Mail-order sales to households, for example, have shown a compound growth rate (in 1980 dollars) during the past decade of under 10 percent, while the offerings themselves have risen by approximately 16 percent each year. This suggests *increasing inefficiency,* not efficiency.

Myth 137: A direct-marketing effort that obtains a 2 percent return is highly successful, while one that obtains a 1 or 1.5 percent response rate isn't bad.

Truth: These percentages have been cited so often, and for so long, that it's hard to tell where they come from, but everybody uses them, and of course they're meaningless.

The fallacy lies in using averages as a benchmark. One program's response rate might be .5 percent, with that being an excellent return for the undertaking; the company would be piggish to expect more. Another program's response rate might be 20.5 percent, with that being a pitiful failure, because the firm did so many things to improve the rate.

Suppose that Steve Job's NeXT Software Company goes to a smart ad agency such as Hill Holliday in Boston and pays the handsome fee of $1 million to prepare and mail to a million "decision makers" a slick brochure for a new customer-tracking system. With a response rate of one-half of 1 percent, that's 5000 leads.

Assume further that God is very good and 10 percent of these prospects can be closed for $10,000 apiece. That's $50 million in sales for an investment of $1 million in direct marketing. You should complain?

On the other hand, if you're an Ivy League college sending out literature to help convince admitted applicants to join next September's student body, a 20.5 percent conversion rate would be a disaster; 60 percent or more is what the college expects.

Dozens of factors, after all, influence a direct-marketing program's response rate. What is the nature of the offer? Are you generating leads? Is it a free trial? Are you trying to produce an actual purchase? Are you trying to get the respondent to do something that takes a $5 commitment or a $1000 commitment?

Who are you sending the offer to? Are they prospects, people you've never written to before? Are they past customers, people you had a relationship with but don't have anymore? Or are they current customers, people with whom you have a relationship now, people who trust you? Obviously (and our experience confirms the obvious) current customers are more willing to respond to your offers because they've had some experience with you.

Did you prescreen people over the phone? This is common in business-to-business direct marketing. Did you tell recipients that something was coming? Did you tell them to expect a follow-up call? Advertising agencies are interesting direct-marketing examples, because they often put considerable money, time, and effort into generating new accounts. An agency might, as a preliminary stage, mail 100 pieces of new business correspondence to client prospects, and spend thousands of dollars on those 100 pieces. They know (or should know) exactly to whom are they sending the package; how it should be customized; and how to address each prospect's specific concerns.

The other issue buried in here, of course, is the difference between response rate and conversion rate. The agency may rate a program a failure if it didn't provoke a 25 percent response rate. It may well consider the program a whooping success if just one company responding actually buys the firm's services. Don't confuse the number of people who return a card requesting more information with the number of people who send real money or place an order.

Myth 138: You have to make specific offers to specific people.

Truth: The idea behind this myth is that it's inefficient to send mass mailings. This is one reason behind Sears Roebuck's January 1993 announcement that it was giving up its big catalog. You have to target, says the common wisdom, you have to produce minicatalogs. Look at Sears: Big books don't work.

This is a tricky myth because, like many we discuss, it contains elements of truth. Given a particular company at a distinct time in a special situation (Sears Roebuck in 1993), it may be entirely true. So we are not going to sit here and say that big books *do* work.

But we *are* going to sit here and say that technology will be turning the idea into a fallacy even as this book appears. In the not-too-distant future, information technology will make it possible for a company to catalog the entire Sears merchandise offering (words, color pictures, sound) on a medium and produce it for pennies on the dollar.

Today's CD-ROM discs (compact disc—read-only memory) hold 200,000 pages of text, but the next generation of discs will hold that much more. The time will come when a company will be able to provide the prospect with every bit (and byte) of information about what's available, while at the same time making it childishly easy to let the customer select what he or she wants.

Under this procedure, instead of the company deciding what information a prospect will receive, the company gives the customer everything and he or she selects what he or she wants to evaluate. We're touching on this today with Prodigy Information Services, CompuServe, and other on-line services, where people can sort through the information themselves to look at what they want.

So perhaps that's how the myth will evolve. Today we have to target a person and preselect the information that person receives. In time, information technology may say that preselection is unnecessary. It is efficient and cost-effective to give consumers everything and let them select the information they want.

Myth 139: By looking at your zip code, some companies can figure out what you eat for breakfast or which political party you vote for.

Truth: That was an actual headline in the December 1992 *Self* magazine.

The article was designed to warn readers that their privacy was being invaded, but marketers could read it as a ringing endorsement of zip-code marketing. Indeed, the author quoted an exuberant pronouncement of Jonathan Robbin, a founder of Claritas, the firm that divided the country into cleverly named clusters: "Geography is destiny. I can predict what you eat, drink, drive—even think." Though there is some truth to this claim, the margin of error surrounding it is often too large to make the procedure of much practical value.

The idea is that, by using zip codes, companies like Claritas can zero in on "clusters" and categorize them according to 40 socioeconomic groupings. "Young Influentials," to name one cluster, for example, drink fresh-brewed coffee, jog, travel abroad, eat yogurt, and vote Republican.

For 20 years American marketers have enthusiastically accepted the premises of zip-code marketing. The theory works like this: Similar people tend to live together. Drive around any American city and you'll find affluent neighborhoods and humble neighborhoods, good school districts and poor school districts. Similarly, people in neighborhoods tend to buy similar products. Apartment dwellers do not buy power mowers; humble families do not buy expensive imported sedans.

Assume you can find those zip codes that contain a disproportionately high number of the best prospects for your product. Once you have them, you can rank-order the country's 43,000 zip codes based on that characteristic. Voila! Market to the winning zip codes, and ignore the losers!

On the surface, this is a good idea. It makes more sense to market in those areas where you have a disproportionately high number of prospects than to spread your limited resources (resources are *always* limited) over the entire country.

The problem arises when we discover that even in the top 10 percent of all zip codes, the proportion of people who are hot prospects for a product or service is often no more than twice as high as in the population as a whole. If 20 percent of the American people are prospects for your service, ordinarily the top zip code has no more than 40 percent. Or, looking at it from the other direction, 60 percent of the people in the area with the most prospects are *not* interested in you or your product. Assume you are BMW, and only 5 percent of the people in the country are likely prospects. It means that in the top 10 percent of zip codes, 9 out of 10 people you mail to are not your target (two times 5 percent equals 10 percent; 100 percent minus 10 percent equals 90 percent).

If you mail a letter to all of the people in that zip code, it's more efficient than mailing to the entire country (indeed, it may increase the response rate by 100 percent), yet you are still wasting most of your effort on people who are not prospects for your product or service. As we'll talk about later, the future of marketing lies not in marketing to zip codes but in marketing to individuals—in finding the names and specific addresses of your prospects, wherever they live, and mailing to those individual people.

There are two simple reasons why zip-code marketing does not work as well in practice as its proselytizers say it does:

1. Demographics are generally poor predictors of consumer behavior.
2. People in a given zip code, though similar to one another, don't even have the same demographics, let alone the same attitudes and behavior patterns.

So relax. No company can, by looking at your zip code, figure out what you eat for breakfast, which political party you vote for, or where you go on vacation.

Myth 140: Privacy is such a concern among consumers and legislators that before long companies will not be in the direct-marketing business or be able to use any specialized information to talk to people.

Truth: One can visualize the direct-marketing industry as a railway accident about to happen. Heading east on the tracks is one train running at full speed gathering information, collecting data, and understanding more and more about every man, woman, child, and dog in the country.

Heading west on the same track is another train barreling along that contains consumer advocates, legislators, and academics saying, "No! No! No! You can't use this information because it invades the consumer's privacy!"

The myth is that consumers don't want companies to use information about them in their direct-marketing efforts. We think they want companies to use the information, but to use it responsibly—and we'll get into what that means in a moment—and, in a sense, to pay them for the use of the information. A company could pay them in terms of making the offer more efficient, saving them time, saving them energy. Or the company could actually pay money or credits. Given the evolving technology, there is no reason why a company could not pay a small royalty—cash, gifts, bonus points, frequent flyer miles, or whatever—to the consumer every time the company sells the consumer's name with all the information that goes along with it.

When consumers feel they will benefit from sharing information about themselves, they are more willing to give it. American Express, for example, has a program for their Platinum Card members. These customers take time to fill out a questionnaire and give the company considerable personal information. They do it because American Express already has a relationship with these people, and because the company says in effect, "We're going to use this information to be innovative about the programs we're going to offer to you." In that sense the company is paying for the information. Assuming American Express does not violate that trust, people will cooperate.

How does a company use the information responsibly? The critical question seems to us to be: Who is the privacy violation hurting or helping? If it helps only the company, then it's irresponsible and damaging. If, for example, a company employs confidential medical data to red-line potential employees or insurance customers, that's an abuse. But if the company is able to tailor offerings to help the consumer save time and money, or to otherwise enhance her life, that's fine.

Myth 141: Most retailers today send very different communications—letters, catalogs, flyers—to different customers.

Truth: Back in 1990 we were sitting around in the office talking about who were the smart and who were the not-so-smart direct marketers. And there seemed to be general agreement that Sharper Image—at that time doing very, very well—was indeed a smart marketer. All of us love their catalog. We buy stuff from it. Our working assumption was that Sharper Image mailed different catalogs to different customers, based on some knowledge of what it is that different people are looking for. We decided to test that assumption, and a telephone call to Sharper Image revealed that we were wrong. That, in fact, the same catalog goes to everyone. Not every customer receives the catalog in any given month, or in any given mailing period, but there is only one catalog. There is no segmentation of the customer base that yields different books offering different products based on the individual needs or buying patterns of the customer base.

There are some exceptions to this. L. L. Bean, one of the most sophisticated marketers in the country, has multiple catalogs—a fishing catalog, a hunting catalog, a home and a camp catalog—and different people receive different catalogs depending on what they have purchased in the past. But once again, within a given segment of the market, everyone gets the same thing. So if you're in the fishing segment, and L. L. Bean mails to all fisherpeople, you see the same book in the mail.

There's no reason why in the future, when retailers do learn a great deal about their customers, the whole direct-marketing process can't be customized so that different people receive different things depending upon what they usually use and what their attitudes, values, and behavior patterns are.

A wonderful example of this kind of thinking is represented by some supermarkets, where tracking data about individual customers is collected over time and analyzed to reveal different segments such as health-conscious customers, junk-food buyers, price-conscious shoppers, large families, and the like. The store can then offer somewhat customized advertising and promotional programs to customers of different types. So, instead of telling everyone about a given new product or making an offer to everyone, offers can be made and products can be talked about that will have particular appeal to individual customers. And given that other stores are not doing this, it offers the store in question a wonderful opportunity to develop a closer relationship with its customer.

Myth 142: Some retailers today have personalized mailings for individual customers.

Truth: Personalized/customized/one-on-one marketing is today another MC ("marketing correct") thing to do. If you're not doing it, the best thing to do is to *say* you're doing it. If we had $1000 for every manager who has told us during the past three years that his or her company engages in personalized marketing, we could retire early.

We don't know of *any* marketer who is actually doing it. Since the "truth" here is going to upset more than a few managers, we had better be very specific. By personalized/customized/one-on-one marketing we mean a marketing program directed to individual customers, with each individual treated differently, treated as if the marketer had only one customer. Consider the following letter:

> August 25, 1994
>
> Dear Mr. Wood:
>
> I would like to remind you that your wife Marian's birthday is coming up in two weeks on September 12th, and we have the perfect gift for her in stock.
>
> As you know, she loves DKNY clothing, and we have an absolutely beautiful new fall suit in a magenta red, her favorite color, in a seven, her size, priced below typical retail value of $850 at $800. Believe me, she will look simply stunning!
>
> If you like, I can gift-wrap the suit at no extra charge and mail it to you next week, so that you will have it in plenty of time for her birthday. Or if you like, I can put it aside so that you can come in to pick it up. Please give me a call within the next 48 hours to let me know which you prefer.
>
> In any event, I appreciate your business and hope to hear from you soon.
>
> Sincerely yours,
>
> Connie Lester
> Store Manager

This letter contains a great deal of information about the customer and his spouse. Not just the name and address, which many marketers have today, but preferred brand, color, size, occasion, position, etc. Was this letter actually composed by Connie Lester, the store manager? No, it was written by a new computer system that we'll describe in the next myth. But Connie does sign it, and she will follow up.

How does this compare to what managers are calling "personalized" marketing programs today?

Some firms say they're doing personalized marketing if they can get a name and address correct. They are candidates for The 1975 Marketing Hall of Fame.

Other more sophisticated marketers are taking their customer lists and segmenting them into different typologies, using the cluster analysis tool we talked about in our discussion of targeting in Chapter 8. As a result, they are able to send mailings to 3 or 5 or maybe even 20 different types of people.

These marketers are candidates for The 1985 Marketing Hall of Fame, still far from the leading edge of our discipline.

The future lies in truly individual, customer-centered communications programs, and most major marketers don't even know what this means.

Myth 143: Truly personalized marketing communications aimed at individual customers (not segments) are still a generation away.

Truth: Guess what. It's beginning to happen today, and we think we're on the front lines of the revolution. We are pleased to relay some news back from the front.

But first a story. Kevin Clancy's son David graduated summa cum laude from Dartmouth College last June, and he was promised a cheap car as a graduation gift. We were both surprised that neither David nor his dad had received any communication from any automobile company before or after graduation to acknowledge this event and the possibility of a purchase.

No "Dear Mr. Clancy. As you know, David will be graduating in June, which must make you very happy. We have a small car for him, which you would buy him as a gift if you were a loving father...." letter. Nothing. Are the auto companies asleep?

But then again, Abercrombie & Fitch, Brooks Brothers, Lord & Taylor, and Bloomingdales, where Kevin and David have shopped for years, didn't suggest a particular gift purchase either. And they certainly didn't write to David to tell him that it's time he bought a real suit. Are they asleep?

And Robert Shulman's wife Robin and daughter Molly have birthdays every year that the great marketers of America allow to pass unrecognized. Are they all asleep?

Maybe, but hopefully, not for long. There is a new approach, one marketers will find useful. The idea is to match, automatically, company inventory to prospect needs.

This is marketing software designed to increase a retailer's sales and profits. The system employs state-of-the-art automated technology combining the best of a "perfect salesman" with a "perfect advertising agency" to computer design, and implementing highly motivating, individualized, one-to-one marketing programs.

Since retail margins are being squeezed by rising costs and competition, the solution is to increase sales faster than costs, since a business's variable costs never rise as fast as sales (or if they do, the business disappears). The trick is to match customer needs and desires with store inventory.

When needs and inventory match, the store has a sales opportunity it can communicate to prospects. This, of course, is Retailing 101. But while most retailers know their inventory, few truly know their customers. This system has a customer profile that the computer can use to automatically match the inventory to the customer and generate a personal letter similar to the one in the last myth.

The customer profile includes:

- Name, home address, and telephone number
- Psychographic characteristics such as shopping attitudes, hobbies, interests, and activities
- Important dates, including the birthdays of spouse, children, and parents; anniversaries; upcoming graduations, confirmations, and the like
- Apparel needs, perceptions, and preferences, such as shopping behavior; dollar expenditures in total and by store; store and style preferences; store perceptions; and key purchases during the last six months

Customers who respond to store cards, who join a preferred-customer program, or who buy from the store, participate in the program. A retailer can offer a variety of incentives to participate: advance notice of sales, advance notice of new merchandise, special discounts or special treatment at selected times, rewards for reaching various purchasing levels.

The key differences between conventional direct response and this revolutionary approach include:

- A conventional system usually holds little to no information about the targets that can assist in developing a program. The new system has substantial information, everything from merchandise needs to the psychographics, demographics, and sociographics of the customer and her family.
- A conventional system mails a standard catalog two to four times a year. The new system sends customized letters and offerings to customers monthly.
- A conventional system offers the same merchandise to everyone. The new system offers different merchandise to different people.

The new system, in other words, offers an extremely high level of customization—a different letter to every customer. A conventional system cannot tie in with merchandise a customer purchased in the past, while the new system uses this knowledge to create mailings. Finally, the conventional system has no ability to talk to one family member about the needs of another, while this is a critical objective of the new system.

The goal of a one-to-one marketing system is to increase a business's sales and profits among selected customers; increase the number of transactions per customer; increase the average size of the transactions; help to identify the merchandise customers desire; motivate other members of the customer's household to become loyal customers; and help to optimize inventory turnover and to eliminate leftover stock.

Advertising is a distraction when you have no need for or interest in the product. A catalog is junk mail when you don't want the products. But advertising can be valuable information when you are in the market for the product. Have you ever noticed how, when you are in the market for a product—golf clubs, a car, a boat, a suit, a camcorder, a local area network, or whatever—you suddenly are seeing ads for the item everywhere? The ads have always been around, but you have been filtering them out.

As marketers, we want to reach those people who need and want our product or service. We don't want to fill the air with commercials people immediately zap, or to fill mailboxes with brochures that people toss without opening. With our ability to obtain and manipulate more and more information about more and more people cost-efficiently, we are rapidly approaching an era when we will reach only our best prospects...and leave everyone else alone.

"In this new age of marketing, we want a close working relationship with our marketing partners—and we'll do everything necessary to get it!"

17
Myths about Retailing

Let's start with probably the most common myth among retailers, that the element that makes the most difference between retail success and failure is location.

Myth 144: Location, location, location.

Truth: Or as the lead paragraph in *Advertising Age* put it not long ago, "A time-honored real estate adage is emerging as one of the most important keys to retail success: Location. Location. Location."

"There's no room for error anymore," Burt Flickinger told the *AdAge* reporter. Flickinger, described as a retail consulting veteran and principal with Booz, Allen & Hamilton, continued, "Bad decisions about where and when to open stores are costly mistakes that can drive retailers right out of business."

Forty years ago, he said, all someone had to do to find a likely retail site was to "do a survey of how many people walked or drove by a certain location each day. It was easy."

There's no question that today it's harder. But there is some confusion over the importance of location and the importance of a marketing concept grounded in customer needs.

In a relatively generic business like fast food, where few people are going to have a nervous breakdown if they have to eat at Wendy's when they had their faces set for a Whopper, a great location is a marketing imperative. For a soft drink company, where most people don't care whether they drink Coke or Pepsi, having all the shelf facings—that is, location—is a marketing essential.

But to the extent that a retailer can positively differentiate itself from the competition—the only great rib restaurant in town, the only fresh fish restaurant, the only store in town that carries Ralph Lauren or sells western clothing—people will find you rather than you finding them, and location becomes less important. So our mantra is *concept, concept, concept.*

People come from all over Connecticut to shop at Stew Leonard's in Norwalk and Danbury. An Office Depot doesn't go into a great—and expensive—location in a mall. Look at Wal-Mart, Home Depot, and Toys 'R Us. People travel from Boston to New Hampshire, where Jordan's Furniture has a colossal furniture store. Clancy travels fifty minutes to Salem, Massachusetts, to shop at a ship model store. Shulman travels anywhere to find some new golf clubs to improve his game.

On the other hand Sears has great locations, but lacking as it does a consistent and attractive marketing concept, it's losing ground. Sears is suffering, says Kurt Barnard, president of *Barnard's Retail Marketing Report,* because "consumers frequent regional malls looking for fashion-forward designer clothing. Not only is Sears not a paragon of fashion, but it also sells a broad array of merchandise not on the shopping lists of people visiting malls. When was the last time you went to a department store to buy a spark plug?"

If a company positively differentiates itself from its competitors in terms of product offering, positioning, service, or some other motivating attribute, then people—especially high-involvement customers—will travel long distances out of their way to find it.

Myth 145: Small retailers can't compete with the giant chains.

Truth: Giant chains, sometimes called "category killers," are impressive organizations. They include companies like Wal-Mart, Home Depot (hardware), Office Depot and Staples (office supplies), Toys 'R Us (toys), Best Buy (appliances, home electronics), Barnes & Noble (books), and Blockbuster Video.

The principles that follow here apply to manufacturers with giant competitors as well as to retailers, to business-to-business marketers as well as to consumer marketers, and to selling services as well as to selling products.

Admittedly it's tough to compete with a giant, but it can be done. Often the chain has rock-bottom prices (because its costs are lower than almost anyone's), offers everything the customer wants, and maintains (demands) exceptionally close relations with suppliers.

Take Wal-Mart as a representative example. Virtually no business can compete on Wal-Mart's turf—price, store size, selection. It is virtually impossible to compete with a strong business in terms of its strength. Fortunately, no business can be everything. So what the smaller competitor must do is figure out what the big boys *can't* do. What are Wal-Mart's weaknesses?

- The stores are cavernous and impersonal.
- While the stores carry a huge variety of merchandise, they offer limited selection and assortment within product categories.
- The merchandise tends to be low-end; the stores carry few higher-quality items.
- Because Wal-Mart stresses "Made in America" products, it has few top foreign brands.
- It is a mass merchandiser; there is very little sales help.
- The stores treat customers impersonally.

Kenneth Stone, an economics professor from the University of Iowa who is the country's expert on Wal-Mart's effect on small towns, advises local retailers, "You have to find a niche you can compete in. You have to get back to the basics of doing good business: having a decent policy on returns, greeting customers when they come in the store, being more careful on price."

If the big business dominates on the basis of low costs/low prices, then go for added value, create your own label, introduce service innovations. To the extent that the small business can make the relationship with the customer a personal one, create a pleasant environment for shopping, offer a broad variety of products, offer lots of convenience, it can compete.

These principles also apply to a small manufacturing or a small service business. The small manufacturer, unable to compete on price, may be able to offer just-in-time deliveries...better quality control...personal engineering consultation...or highly customized products. On the other hand, given low overhead and tighter cost controls, a small manufacturer may indeed be able to underprice bigger and less flexible firms.

The concept is pretty simple: Figure out the consumer's needs, look at the competitor's advantages or strengths; then meet those needs by doing the things the competitor doesn't do well. We realize this is far easier said than done. We also realize that many business people are mesmerized by price. A retailer, for example, who would never consider trying to compete with Wal-Mart's square footage or merchandise selection, will believe that her store *must* compete with Wal-Mart's prices.

While price is an element in the marketing mix, price is not the only element. Meet other consumer needs, and price becomes less significant.

Myth 146: Partnership marketing is the answer to the problems between retailers and suppliers.

Truth: Speakers at professional meetings, marketing consultants, and academics are fond of talking about the close relationship between Procter & Gamble and Wal-Mart. P&G has set up facilities next to Wal-Mart's Arkansas headquarters to ensure close communication between the two organizations. P&G and Wal-Mart are "partners" and partnership marketing is described as a marriage between two parties who are not adversaries but collaborators. Cooperation is the key.

But, as in everyday life, there are good marriages and there are bad marriages, as each person in a couple tries to get what they need out of the relationship. The same is true with partnerships marketing. Partnering is fine as long as it doesn't become abusive, in the same way that a marriage is fine as long as it doesn't become abusive.

Some retailers and some vendors appear to abuse their partners. It's like a woman married to an alcoholic wife-beater—not a healthy relationship. Organizations have to be very, very careful before entering into such a match.

Partnership marketing may be the single hottest topic in marketing today, but it's not the answer for everyone.

Myth 147: Don't worry too much about your profit margin, you can make it up in volume.

Truth: When a business is growing rapidly, its margins are often large enough to hide problems. The retailer has projected a cost of doing business, set prices accordingly, and opened the doors. Sales are booming, the money is pouring in, what's the problem?

The problem is that as the store expands it adds costs—a new cash register, a larger building, another delivery truck, more salespeople, increased inventory. The original cost assumptions change, and with the changed costs comes a changed business. The business may become starved for cash, because money is going into fixtures and inventory.

As long as the business continues to grow rapidly, the problems may not be serious, but when, inevitably, the growth slows, the new costs are waiting to bite the unwary.

The retailer has to watch everything all the time: sales, margins, and cashflow.

Myth 148: Retailers know a great deal about their customers.

Truth: This is balderdash. One of the most astonishing things about marketing today is how little most retailers know about their customers. Some businesses, even sophisticated businesses, don't even know their customers' names.

In 1893, a shopkeeper knew most of his customers personally. He knew what kind of clothing they bought. He knew what shoes they liked and their shoe sizes. He would call a customer if a particular piece of merchandise had arrived: the boots she wanted; the plow he had ordered; the scarf from New York; the material for curtains. That doesn't exist anymore.

If retailers do know the names of their customers, they have an address, but they know nothing about the customer's attitudes, beliefs, and values, competitive purchasing patterns, spouse, or children. They don't know what it is about the store that turns the customer on or off. They don't know what the customer likes or dislikes. They don't know which product lines that the store carries interest the customer greatly and which are of little interest. They don't know what kinds of purchases the customer is planning for the next year—an exception being Mitchell's.

Jack Mitchell points out that Mitchell's, because it maintains a record on every customer, targets what customers like in the way of clothing or in the way of services. The store's computer tracks every customer's purchase, so that it would not, say, send a Polo customer a Hugo Boss brochure. "He'd know that we didn't know him," says Mitchell. "More importantly, we try to hook up a sales associate who becomes knowledgeable about his or her customers. We'll see a customer's activity, and if he hasn't been in for a while we may call to ask what's happening." Mitchell's knows from asking whether a customer permits a sales associate to call, and when a good time might be.

"When you call, you better have a good reason," says Mitchell, "not just, 'How are you doing?' Because these are busy people. We have one sales associate who calls all the time. She does probably half her business by appointments. We're big on appointments. Every one of our sales associates quite literally is a personal shopper."

More and more retailers are going to realize that information about customers is critical, and that in some ways they will have to return to a simpler time.

Myth 149: High-end, exclusive retailers know their customers so well that they can, if necessary, duplicate the customer's last purchase.

Truth: This clearly is not true, although it should be. The more you know about a customer, the customer's needs, the customer's purchases, the more you should be able to service the customer well.

If Brooks Brothers knows that a customer likes Brooksease suits, if it knows that the customer owns a black pinstripe, maybe he'll be interested in a navy. If the store knows that the customer likes fitted shirts in size 15½, 32 sleeve, pinpoint oxford, the store can initiate a purchase by communicating to the customer that they have some new shirts in new colors.

Or the store could respond to a customer's request to reorder whatever it was he or she ordered last time. The customer doesn't have to remember size, sleeve length, or exactly what kind of shirt he bought—the store would have this information in its memory banks.

Stores without this information cannot truly serve their customers, and few stores today have it.

Myth 150: Eliminating locations is easy; find the nonperforming stores.

Truth: Right now, retail chains say that if they want to pare down, all they have to do is look for stores that don't have good sales.

This, of course, is very different from looking for stores that may have no reason to exist.

Strategically speaking, nonperforming stores could be among the chain's better stores; therefore, you don't eliminate locations just on the basis of sales to date. You eliminate on the basis of strategic review: Who is my target? Who am I going after? What is my product?

You don't eliminate just on the basis of current performance.

Retailers often look at the cost of closing a store only in terms of stemming a loss. The chain does $500,000 in sales in a store that doesn't make a profit until it does $550,000. Management decides to close the store and stop losing $50,000.

Yet the goodwill the company loses in closing that location, losing the $500,000 in sales, may be far greater in the long term than taking the time and effort to do something with the store to make it more profitable and hold on to that business. This is a typical pattern vis-à-vis a bank deciding to close branches.

It doesn't mean you don't close the weak units. It does mean you carefully consider your criteria for closing them. The one criterion shouldn't simply be current performance. Evaluation must be made on the basis of a larger strategy. A bank may decide, based on long-term strategic considerations, that it does not want branches in any town smaller than 75,000 people, because it has determined that it can't serve the needs of the people in a town smaller than 75,000 any better than local banks. That's a strategic question, as opposed to simply cutting costs.

If a store or branch is not performing well, what do you do? This brings us back to the marketing process.

There are other deleterious effects, both emotional and human, that management needs to consider. You're putting people out of work, changing your reputation. And all of these consequences need to be factored into (a) a strategic plan for the company and (b) what the real cost would be if marketing were done correctly to improve sales. We can make up a little equation here. If the losses were enormous, the human intellectual capital costs small, the cost of turnaround very high, and the strategic plan said we want to be out of these markets, then that equals a decision to eliminate stores.

Or perhaps the store will change with the community. An acquaintance of ours began working in his father's St. Louis appliance–TV dealership in the early 1950s, just as the neighborhood began to change from predominantly middle-class white to predominantly black. Rather than abandon the location where the family had done business for more than thirty years, the store changed with the neighborhood—changing the product mix, hiring black sales and management people, establishing the store's own credit company because existing retail credit companies would not extend terms to many of the store's customers. Because the business met the needs of the market, it continued to flourish.

"Our latest study shows that you can hold on to 100 percent of your customers if you give each of them a new convertible."

18
Myths about Customer Service

Clearly (and unfortunately), it's usually not enough to sell customers the company's product or service. You have to keep them happy after the sale so they will continue to be customers again and again.

Take, for example, Office Depot. Now that it is encountering other office products superstores, "our intent is to compete on a service level," says CEO Mark Begelman. "We are changing the way we do business. Seven years ago we charged customers for delivery; today, delivery is free. Seven years ago we said, `Here's our credit process; if it works for you, fine; if it doesn't, too bad.' Today we recognize that if we can give country-club-type billing, that's a competitive advantage. We now take Visa, Mastercard, American Express, and Office Depot credit cards. We have carryout service at store level, free delivery, and telephone sales—all things customers have told us are important. And this is how we develop our marketing strategies. We just ask the customers what they want—and do it."

As we have said in several different ways earlier in this book, a business's goal is to keep customers (since it's cheaper and more profitable to keep existing customers than to attract new ones) and, if possible, to obtain a larger share of their dollars.

Which brings us to customer service, a topic about which books have been written and about which, somewhere in America, even as you read these words, 27 seminars with titles like "Their Wish Is Your Command," "How To Make Your Company Your Customer's Slave," or "Reconstructing the Garden of Eden for Your Customer" are being given. One would think that with everything that's been said, there's nothing more to say.

Perhaps, but if you believe the following myth, there may be something we can add.

Myth 151: One-hundred-percent customer satisfaction is a practical, profitable objective for a business.

Truth: Waving the banner of "Total Quality Management," companies and consultants from coast to coast are preaching the joys of 100 percent customer satisfaction. Given the enthusiasm whipped up over this new corporate craze, one would think they were talking about sex. We expect a new best-seller: *How to Please a Customer Every Time.*

The underlying theory (and myth) is that offering "perfect" service will lead naturally to maximum profitability. It doesn't, and that's the problem.

Pleasing customers is, of course, something every business must do. The question is how far you take the satisfaction, and what it costs.

The late Tom Dillon, a Renaissance man in advertising if ever there was one, explained why, when he was chairman of BBDO, he ate lunch at Louis Ratazzi's New York restaurant two or three times a week, when he didn't even care for Italian food. Dillon ate there, he said, because of the service. "Louis meets me at the door, takes my coat, and escorts me to my favorite table, bringing me up to date on the latest Chicago ball scores."

Another story: Our friend John wanted to treat his wife to a special evening for their first wedding anniversary. Since she loved opera, John bought second-row seats to the New York Metropolitan Opera's opening-night production of *Salomé.* On business in Boston the day before, John noticed the perfect basic black dress at a Ralph Lauren retail outlet. Though he knew his wife's size, John also knew the dress would have to be altered, and that alterations could take up to two weeks.

He explained his dilemma to the store manager, who called the alterations department at the Ralph Lauren shop on Madison Avenue. The New York contact said, "Have your wife drop by the store by three tomorrow afternoon, and we'll have the dress altered. Someone will bring it to your hotel by 5:15 p.m." The store did what it promised. The dress was perfect. John's wife looked beautiful. They will remember the night at the opera for years. And Ralph Lauren won two loyal customers.

Louis Ratazzi and Ralph Lauren both achieved high marks for customer service by doing what every smart business should do: paying attention to individual customers. But the cost of Louis's attention to Tom Dillon and the Lauren store manager's attention to John were modest, relative to the businesses' returns. Dillon's business helped to ensure that Ratazzi's would become an agency favorite, and we've been telling John's story for two years now.

Before embarking on a 100 percent customer satisfaction program, however, a company must ask one question: What is the relationship between customer satisfaction and profitability?

When the company answers this question, it usually finds that something less than perfect service is the most profitable. The reason is simple. The average customer satisfaction level for any marketer is about 82 percent—a B grade. The marketer who improves this grade to a 90 or a 95 percent blows away his competitors and moves to the head of the class. However, the money and effort required to move from a 95 percent satisfaction level to the 100 percent level is often enormous, relative to the benefits.

If Louis Ratazzi built Dillon a private room, handed him the day's *Chicago Tribune,* and cooked him the French food he loved, would Dillon have bought lunch any more often? And even then, would these be profitable things to do?

Consider retail banking. In a time-starved world, a 30-second wait on the teller's line would be better than a 3-minute wait. But unless you know that your customers absolutely will not tolerate spending those 3 lunchtime minutes on line, cutting the wait to 30 seconds will be costly without generating more customers or more dollars.

This is not to say that better service is a bad idea. Safi Urrehman Qureshey, president and chief executive of AST Research Inc., which manufactures personal computers, told *The New York Times* not long ago, "We realized that if we upgraded all the computers that our service technicians use from 386 to 486, we could cut about 15 to 20 seconds off the time it took to get the right information to the customer. It was an added expense, but just the savings on the telephone line was worth it."

Our research suggests that as customer satisfaction increases, sales and profits increase—up to a point. But as the cost of making customers happy moves beyond, say, 92 percent, the costs associated with increasing levels of satisfaction begin to erode profits.

Myth 152: There's only one way to handle customer problems.

Truth: There are four ways to handle any problem.

(This discussion applies to much more than customer service. Indeed, the principles apply to life in general, but since this is a business book we are using customer service as the illustration. But we wanted you to know that we do recognize there is existence beyond marketing.)

You have found a problem. What do you do?

Approach #1. Deny there's a problem at all. Pretend—or convince yourself—that the difficulty doesn't exist. You hear these people on television saying, as the worst storm of the century is roaring toward them, "Don't worry about us, officer. We've seen storms worse than this, and the water's never reached our front door."

Managers who operate with this philosophy tend to get washed out to sea when there's a really *big* storm.

Approach #2. Expect that the problem will go away. If not immediately, in time. Some people take this approach as a form of time management: "If the issue is really important, it'll come back at me." It's a way to prioritize responses to what may be (or may not be) problems. Wait for the headache to come back, and if it does, it's probably important enough to deal with.

Some people don't open all their mail. They throw it in the trash. When something is stamped SECOND NOTICE, that's the signal to open the envelope. That's not an uncommon approach companies take in dealing with customer problems. The regrettable side effect is that it tends to irritate the very people on whom the business's health depends. Occasionally the problem does go away, but so does the customer.

Approach #3. Recognize that there is a problem you will have to confront shortly. Rehearse an answer.

This was the approach former President Nixon perfected during the Watergate crisis: Rehearse the response, and try to plug every avenue of confusion or every place where the bother can come back to bite. "It's not really our fault." "We were following instructions." "Let me explain...." While sometimes these excuses contain elements of Approach #1—there's really no problem—this approach does sometimes attempt to deal with what's gone wrong, but by coming up with a canned reply. The approach's weakness is that you are always reacting to the customer's ire rather than acting before it *becomes* ire.

Approach #4. When you first recognize there may be a problem, initiate the communication process. In so doing, you in effect set the agenda and level the playing field. By initiating the dialogue you can shape it, disarm it somewhat, and turn the negative around to be a positive.

A client placed an order; you promised delivery on the 15th. It's now the 13th, and you know the order *will not* go out tomorrow to reach the client on the 15th. You can deny there is any problem at all. You can wait for the customer to call. You can wait until the customer calls a second time and give your rehearsed speech: "Joe was out sick, the dog ate it, the machine went down." Or you can call the client and say, "I'm having a problem. A machine is down, and I've got three guys out sick. I can see already that your order may be late, but I wanted you to know so that it won't hurt your business and you can adjust accordingly."

Richard Freeland, at Pizza Hut of Indiana, points out that it's not the big problems that kill a business, "it's the little bitsy things every day that you keep taking care of—the ice machine isn't working, there's not enough forks—so that when performance time comes and the customer's in the door, we're ready to perform." Management has to take problems away so the employees can concentrate on the customer. "Everybody says they're number one," he says, "but there's always reasons for things to get in the way of our serving the customer."

One thing, of course, is mistakes. Freeland's business has about 1600 employees, and they make mistakes. "We have to build that imperfection into the system so that we can handle mistakes when they happen," says Freeland. "If we make the wrong pizza, or burn the pizza, or drop the pizza, or whatever, the employee knows that he or she can fix it. First, we have to go to the customer and tell them the truth. Then we have to do something appropriate that keeps her as a customer and doesn't let her walk out the door. The employee can discount the product or give the product away and apologize. The manager should be there to help apologize, so the customer understands that we do care."

Maybe Myth 152 is not myth. Maybe there really is only one way to handle customer problems, and Approach #4 is it.

Myth 153: Technology is working to distance business from its customers.

Truth: People who believe this myth point to devices such a voice synthesizers, voice mail, electronic bulletin boards, and fax machines, all of which take the human element out of business.

In fact, technology can actually help to recapture the traditional close relationship with customers.

"The new technology enables sales forces to spend more time out in the field," Barton Goldenberg, president of Information Systems Marketing, Washington, D.C., told *Strategies & News* magazine. "Here they have improved access both to getting and giving information, not only through laptops, *Windows*, modularities, and client-servers, but also with the whole concept of networks." Sales automation allows the sales force to be more productive; to provide clients (and the home office) with better information, and in turn provide better service; to enhance customer care, making it more responsive to customer needs rather than merely reactive; and to provide better communication and feedback to both the customer and the company. "All of these circle around improved knowledge of the customer," says Goldenberg.

One example of the new technology at work to improve relations between marketer and customer is the system we discussed in Chapter 16. This system "knows" each retail customer's needs and buying intentions for the next season. The system also "knows" what the retailer has in stock. Finally, the system has a logic that helps it figure out what item in stock to present to each customer—much like an old-time merchant.

Myth 154: Customer satisfaction is so easy to measure that just about any kind of survey will do.

Truth: Many American companies introduced customer satisfaction and service systems during the past decade, stimulated, in part, by Tom Peters's and Robert Waterman's *In Search of Excellence.* Satisfaction/service-tracking measurement has become big business. Some of this work is effective, much is dubious.

The questionnaires a company *mails,* for example, yield a selective sample that does not represent the firm's customer base. Americans like to cheer and love to complain. Mailed satisfaction studies produce disproportionate numbers of both cheerleaders and grouches. Those in the middle—the reasonably contented or mildly displeased—fail to cooperate, the database does not include them, and therefore does not reflect reality.

Some firms, including major companies that would not like to acknowledge service problems, use sales force downtime to contact and interview customers. This is not research; it's fishing for compliments.

Some companies talk "customer expectations" but measure something else. There has been a surge of interest among satisfaction researchers in measuring customer *expectations.* Experts have written books on the topic, and academics have published articles. Professors scour the country searching for companies that will use their latest expectation measurement models. Unfortunately, we've seen few examples of consumer expectations measured well, one notable exception being the work of Texas A&M Professor Len Berry.

Another problem is measuring company service and customer satisfaction in a vacuum. Every firm needs to evaluate its service and overall satisfaction performance compared to the competition's. Most customers have had experiences with competing firms in the same industry. People have used at least two different computers, owned two or more makes of car, flown two or more airlines, etc. A company must, therefore, build such comparisons into all service/satisfaction research.

A surprising number of studies ignore customers' needs. The researchers ask people to rate companies on a variety of dimensions without recognizing that these dimensions may motivate individuals differently. Some people may be price-conscious, others quality-conscious, still others service-oriented. All dimensions of evaluation, in other words, are not created equal, and it does not take very sophisticated technology to figure out which ones are more important than others.

Death-wish research includes all of the flaky research tools discussed in Chapters 9 and 10 when we talked about positioning and advertising. You don't measure customer satisfaction and service quality through focus groups, shopping mall samples, user conferences, importance ratings, gap analyses, and the like, unless you want to reach the wrong conclusions and make the wrong decisions.

How *should* satisfaction research be carried out? We believe a professional organization independent of the marketer should conduct any study, and should use measurement tools developed jointly by the client and the researchers. For efficiency's sake, professional interviewers reasonably proficient in the industry's vocabulary should survey respondents by phone. The sample should represent the firm's customers and be large enough to ensure the data's stability.

The questions should tap into customer evaluations of 20 to 40 tangible and intangible attributes and benefits the firm discovered by pilot testing to be related to the company's critical success factors. The research should look at the client and at least two competitors. Moreover, it should measure each attribute and benefit's motivating power for each respondent.

Satisfaction research, moreover, has to be systematic; a company should do it regularly. Companies make a mistake when they do research only when they think they've got a problem. The point of user satisfaction research is not to fight fires but to learn how the company can improve its performance and build customer goodwill.

Myth 155: We need to hold on to *all* of our customers from one year to the next.

Truth: In other words, 100 percent customer retention is a practical, profitable marketing objective.

The underlying assumption here is that all customers are invaluable (we've already demonstrated that they're not—recall the discussion of big customers in Chapter 8) and, if we could only provide the highest service level, we would retain them all.

Some management firms seeking to create a new business line for the 1990s are perpetuating this myth. These firms have discovered that if you rank-order companies in many industries in terms of customer retention, then rank-order them again in terms of profitability relative to sales, there is a strong correlation. The higher the retention level, the higher the profitability level.

This analysis, our readers will quickly note, is not dissimilar to the market share/profitability correlation we discussed in Chapter 2, in which companies drew the incorrect conclusion that market share *causes* profitability and, as a consequence, mindlessly pursued share gains duing the eighties and the early nineties.

That customer retention and profitability correlate positively is not in question. They do. The questions are: Why? What does this mean? And what are the implications for marketing/corporate strategy?

Market share and profitability are related, as we've shown, but buying market share through promotional programs or other ill-advised tactics will lead to *lower,* not greater profits, in both the short and the long run.

Is it possible that buying increased retention has the same unappealing outcome? We'll see in a moment.

Experience suggests that since most businesses lose from 10 to 20 percent of their customers each year, stopping this hemorrhaging would be a smart thing to do. The question is how far to go. If current retention levels are, say, 85 percent, then a move to 90 percent would represent a positive and perhaps profitable gain. But what about an improvement to 95 percent or, as some consultants call for, 100 percent?

Just as forest fires may be necessary in a healthy ecosystem, having some customer turnover every year turns out to be healthy in a prosperous business. Of course, we don't want this to get out of hand. We don't want to lose half of our customers, but our experience is that across a broad range of product categories a 90 to 95 percent retention level is probably normal and healthy.

We had one experience with a major bank where the corporation, inspired by the bugle call for total quality management, was interested in increasing their customer retention level to 100 percent. We were asked to develop a strategy to help them do so, and we said, "Give them all a car."

"What do you mean, 'Give them all a car'?" they asked.

We said, "If you gave every one of the customers who's dropping the bank an automobile, they'd stay on for at least another year." Since the average customer's annual value to the corporation is a fraction of the cost of a car, the client recognized the joke.

Our point is that *in every industry we've looked at, not every customer is so valuable to the company that he or she has to be retained.* Some may cost money. A company needs to do a profitability analysis of its customer base. This will determine the characteristics of customers who are unprofitable—the ones the company should not mind losing—and those of the customers it wants to hold on to.

Some customers are so demanding, require so much service, exact the lowest price, and are so distracting that, when the analysis is done, the company determines it's better to let them go than to hold them.

An American Express cardholder, for example, who hardly ever uses the card, or one who regularly fails to pay within 60 days, may not be a profitable customer. A McKinsey client who demands the lowest price for a consulting engagement and then forces McKinsey to turn itself inside out and upside down providing service is a client McKinsey may want to drop. A General Foods coffee buyer who buys only on deal and then drives the supermarket and the GF customer relations department crazy with complaints is one the marketer would rather give to Nestlé.

In some fortunate industries—insurance is one—this line of argument *may* not hold. Once you've sold a whole-life policy, you've created the closest thing to a perpetual-motion cash machine. The customer, believing that he has to stick with the company to receive the policy's full benefit, pays the quarterly premium until he drops without—and this is a key point—much intervention from the firm's marketing/sales organization. Retention in this unusual industry is easier and more profitable to achieve than most, and figures close to 95 percent may make some sense. Indeed, one management consulting firm has reported that for insurance companies, a 5-percentage-point differential in retention equals a 100-percentage-point differential in profits.

Yet even in this industry, we can imagine strategies for which total retention is not the most profitable course. If insurance firms knew how to de-market (loose translation: dump) customers just prior to their expiration (translation: death), profits would zoom. Imagine the scenario: Collect premiums for 50 years based on the presumption of a big payout at age 72 when the customer dies, then persuade the customer to drop the policy at age 71. Clearly, a scheme worthy of the 1994 Marketing Machiavelli Award.

A profitability analysis of the customer base will reveal that not all customers are worth holding on to. Many are valuable but have increasingly negative attitudes that suggest the potential for attrition:

What will it cost to make them happy? Are they worth saving? Depending on the company, the customer, and the money involved, it might in fact be worth giving them the new convertible. But without research, you'll never know.

The only thing you can know for certain is that a 100 percent customer-retention rate will rarely be a practical, profitable objective.

"I know it's a major introduction, but why do we want to waste $100,000 on a simulated market test when I know it's a go and I can take the money and do the shoot in Europe?"

19
Myths about Test Marketing

Assume a company has avoided all the myths we've discussed up to this point. It has analyzed the marketing climate, designed the product, picked a profitable target market, developed a strong positioning and advertising theme, researched the price, and all the rest. Why not just launch the product and beat the competition?

Actually that's not a bad idea, when the cost of a market test is greater than the money the company would lose introducing a product that bombs completely.

Most of the time, however, the company needs—if you'll excuse the metaphor—to test the water before plunging in headfirst.

Traditionally, companies have introduced new product into one or more markets that represent the product's national market to see how it will do. Since that is time-consuming and expensive (aside from other disadvantages we'll describe), companies are now using other methods to test a new product or service.

A simulated test market (STM) gives answers quicker (3 to 5 months versus 12 to 18) and less expensively ($100,000 versus $3 million) than an in-market test. The STM couples a research study to a computer-based mathematical model that is able to forecast what would happen if the company took the brand national.

For any business, a test's goal should be to introduce a product or service to the target audience, measure its response—by both trial and repeat purchases—and be able to project that response to the full launch. And that brings us to our first myth.

Myth 156: The simplest and best way to evaluate a new product prior to the national roll-out is through conventional test marketing.

Truth: Test markets are fraught with problems, starting with how companies select them—often because they are easy to manage, not because they represent the markets the company actually wants to reach.

Competitors do their best to confuse the test market's results. "The competition will do everything within the law to make a test tough to read," says Sheldon Roesch, general manager of the Pepsi Lipton Tea Partnership and former head of PepsiCo Inc.'s new business ventures. Competitors will flood the test market with coupons, run special sales, and have their store salespeople turn the new products sideways on store shelves or move them to other shelves where customers won't notice them.

What does a company do when a competitor is tainting its test market results?

Assume that the test market follows a simulated test market, which is often the case. The simulated test market suggested the product would be a healthy success, while, because of competitive activity, the test market suggests a major failure. The manager who is not risk-adverse will launch the brand nationally anyway.

A more risk-adverse manager might say, "Well, gee, maybe we ought to go back and repeat the simulated test market. Maybe even replicate it with a somewhat different methodology, just to see if the second STM produces the same results." After all, simulated test marketing researchers do not claim that they work 100 percent of the time, just 9 times out of 10.

If the company does the simulated test market again, and obtains essentially the same results, then it might contemplate taking the brand national. We know it's risky, but if your concern is that a competitor in test market is tainting your results, and if you recognize that they can't affect you the same way on a national scale, and if you have a better product and a strong marketing program, you might take a chance. That could be a more prudent decision than simply dumping the new product onto the scrapheap of failure.

Fortunately, what competitors can do to disrupt a test market is usually not what they can do in the national market. The country is just too big and unmanageable—which is why some companies are testing in, say, a quarter of the country. As *BusinessWeek* wrote not long ago, "Scanner data available within days can give a fix on how the product is doing in real life, not just in a pretest. In addition, the product is sold in a market too large for rivals to distort. Within a year or two, the new product hits all 50 states. That's how General Mills rolls out such products as its Multi-Grain Cheerios."

Another possibility of course is a simulated test market study, which offers several advantages we'll talk about in a moment.

Myth 157: When a new product or service fails in test market or in national introduction, there's very little you can do to rejuvenate it.

Truth: The company is better off, so goes this thesis, to walk away from the failure and do something else. Our experience finds that oftentimes an autopsy on the new product can reveal the reasons for success or failure.

Perhaps the new product failed because it generated insufficient levels of awareness. Maybe the awareness level was good, but not enough people were motivated to try the product. Possibly the distribution was poor and prospective customers couldn't find it, or there was too little promotion...or a weak positioning strategy...or not enough advertising. Maybe the media schedule was ill timed, or ill equipped to do the job. Finally, maybe the company had a good marketing plan, but the brand failed because of competitive activity.

It may very well be that a product autopsy will show that the product is dead and that there is very little hope of bringing it back to life. If customer satisfaction levels are low, one could argue that—unless the company is willing to make significant design or formulation changes—the product is a failure.

On the other hand, the company might discover that the product is simply in a coma. Properly revitalized, it can achieve success.

Take, for example, our experience with what we'll call the Ritz and Glitz Credit Card. The card promised access to top health clubs, golf clubs, tennis clubs all over the world, in addition to the kinds of benefits one might expect from a card that cost $500 a year.

The Ritz and Glitz Credit Card did not do well at all (understatement). Less than one-half of 1 percent of the target group to which the marketer mailed applications signed up for it.

Our autopsy revealed that the card had a significant marketing challenge. The company had obtained a good level of awareness among the target market, but not enough people who received the mailing understood what was new and different about the card. Without this understanding, they were not motivated to spend the $500. The card had an awareness-to-trial conversion problem. The company rewrote its direct-mail package and was able to improve response dramatically.

Myth 158: No $100,000 simulated test market study can provide the same results as a $3 million, 18-month, in-market test.

Truth: Admittedly, there's no substitute for a real-world test. For one thing, a real-world test gives a feel for the trade's attitude toward a new product. Ore-Ida once did an STM in which the company assumed 90 percent distribution. When it introduced the product, however, it obtained only 10 percent average monthly distribution, because the retail grocery trade saw the item as a once-a-year loss leader and did not want to carry it year-round.

As there is no substitute for a real-world test, so there's no substitute for a well-done simulated test market. Why?

A well-done STM reduces risk, risk that includes not only lost marketing and sales dollars, but also the capital risk—the expense of putting in production lines or building a new factory to manufacture the product. Since 9 out of 10 new packaged goods products fail, why would a company want to spend $2 or $3 million and wait a year and a half to get the news of failure, when it can spend $100,000 or $150,000 and take three to six months to learn how to fix the problems?

A STM increases efficiency. If a company has, say, three new product development projects under way, and one seems to offer more volume and greater margins, sagacious management would promote that project rather than the others. The STM can indicate the project offering the greatest return. An STM can also optimize the company's marketing efficiency with a new product it does go ahead with—to show the effect, say, of shifting a budgeted $1 million from television advertising to a coupon, or vice versa.

STMs maintain security. As soon as a company puts a product into a test market the whole world knows about it, starting with the competition's salespeople. And competitors can react either by trying to smother the new baby or by introducing their own child. Several years ago, Procter & Gamble began testing a ready-to-spread Duncan Hines frosting. General Mills saw the test and rushed out its own Betty Crocker brand, which now dominates the category.

It's not that test marketing isn't good, it's that test marketing is fraught with problems, and you simply *have* to be aware of those problems.

Myth 159: The technology does not exist to transform a failing new product or service into a winner.

Truth: Today's better simulated test markets capture every important component in the marketing mix and assess the effect of any plan on product awareness, market share, profitability, and more.

STMs can test any plan the marketer wants to consider—even a competitor's. The marketer simply enters the plan into the computer and the model forecasts awareness, sales, profits, and more.

Some STMs can go beyond a volume forecast to permit a manager to ask "What if?" questions such as, "What would happen if I decreased media spending 25 percent?" Or, "What would happen if I increased consumer promotion 10 percent?"

A good STM will recommend a plan, and we have never seen a plan an STM recommends that does not beat the one submitted by the product manager. Sometimes the margin is modest; sometimes the difference is overwhelming.

To begin an STM, the marketer must provide the researchers with a great deal of information, most of which comes right out of the marketing plan. Since these assumptions determine the forecast, the closer they are to reality, the closer the forecast will be to what really happens. Companies have a tendency to assume the best; it's a tendency to fight, because small hopes can turn into large mistakes.

The company's inputs include the market's size (in buyers, units, and dollars); copy-testing results; advertising budget for the test product and for competitors; media schedule, by month; consumer promotion, by month; trade promotion, by month; price; distribution build (the proportion of stores carrying the new product, by month); and expected marketing costs and gross margins.

The consulting firm designs a research study that simulates the likely trial and repeat purchase for the new (or re-staged) brand. To do this also requires a supply of the test product and the competitive product (or products), advertising for the test product in finished, rough, or even concept board form, and competitive product advertising.

For a simulated test marketing study, the research firm recruits approximately 500 consumers who represent the category's buyers. They answer questions about their product-related attitudes and purchase behavior, then watch a television program containing the commercial for the new or re-staged brand and for competitive brands.

They then write down their comments about the program and the advertising and visit a simulated store (a small store stocking test brands, competitive brands, and related product categories) where they can buy anything they want with either cash or coupons.

The proportion of consumers who buy the test product, corrected for category norms, is an estimate of the trial probability (given consumer awareness and product distribution) in the real world. Two to six weeks following this simulated purchasing experience, customers have an opportunity to reorder the new product. The company can use the reorder numbers, together with other attitudinal data, to estimate first and multiple repeat purchases. It can insert the trial data, repeat data, and all the marketing plan information into a sophisticated mathematical model that generates a sales and profit forecast.

Myth 160: Simulated test marketing has a questionable track record in predicting marketplace performance.

Truth: Simulated test marketing is in fact the single best-validated tool in all of marketing research. For a new packaged good, the better STMs can forecast what will happen in the real world plus or minus 15 percent.

This is not to say, however, that there are no cases where an STM result goes awry. This does happen.

The biggest failures come about because the assumptions on which the model made its forecast were flawed. For example, if a company estimates a distribution level of 90 percent and obtains only 80 percent, the volume forecast can be off substantially because, in some industries, distribution corresponds almost one-to-one with volume.

But not only may the assumptions be mistaken, the market's dynamics may change between the STM and the actual test market. The company may have a new competitor, one it did not know about when it began the simulated test market research.

We find that sometimes the company's commitment changes between the STM and the market test. Or to put it another way, in most simulated test markets, companies assume adequate marketing support, support that may disappear by the time they begin the product's national introduction. It's easy to say, in a simulated test market study, that you're going to spend $24 million on advertising for the brand, because no one has to write a check. It's something else to execute the plan.

Discrepancies arise between the simulated test market performance and the actual test market, because the real world is messier than an

STM. But discrepancies also arise between the test market and the real-world, or national, performance. Companies routinely obtain test market distribution levels that are much higher than they ever see again. Why? Because the test market sales force knows it is being watched and they work harder than usual. This sensitivity to the product's success brings results the company never sees again.

But suppose the real-world test results are significantly worse than the simulated test market research results. We automatically say to the client, "Tell us what's happening in the test market...tell us what the shelf facings are...what the distribution is...what's going on in terms of trade activity...consumer promotion...what the competition is doing...your share of voice." With these new inputs, the STM can virtually always match what's going on in the market.

At that point we can ask different questions: "Given what's going on in the market, is there anything we can do, anything we can learn from the simulation that will produce a better plan? Given that the competition has increased its advertising and promotional spending in our test market 630 percent, can we add markets until it becomes just too expensive for them to continue?"

Today's simulated test marketing research goal is not just to obtain a volume forecast. The objective is to provide diagnostic insights that will help to improve the likelihood of success. Telling marketers that they will obtain a 5 percent share or a 10 percent share doesn't make them happy. They want insight from the study that will help them build plans with an even lower risk of failure.

Myth 161: A simulated test market is only a research tool for forecasting new product success or failure.

Truth: A good STM should tell you not only how you're doing but what to do. A sophisticated decision-support system combines simulated test marketing with mathematical modeling of the marketing mix. Such a system goes beyond forecasting first-year volume potential to providing insights into improving the advertising, the concept, the product and packaging, and the marketing plan itself.

Marketers can ask the STM to evaluate every ingredient in the marketing plan in terms of effects on sales, or profits, or both. Some STM models will run hundreds—in some cases thousands—of simulations to identify those factors that most contribute to marketing success.

Not long ago we performed a sensitivity analysis on only a few variables for a new product (see Exhibit 19.1). The model showed that if the company dropped the number of prime-time 30-second commercials by

20 percent, it would save $870,000 and lose 345,000 sales units. Simultaneously, the model indicated that if the company spent approximately the same amount—$877,000—on daytime television it would increase sales 549,000 units. In other words, a switch from prime-time to daytime 30-second commercials was forecast to increase sales by 204,000 units at an incremental cost of only $7000.

Marketers can do the same sort of thing to model competitive response. Experience and past history help to assess a competitor's plans to stop the new product. The model can then help determine which offensive strategy will overcome the most likely defense.

Critical attribute analysis is another example of how simulated test marketing can improve a marketing plan. Critical attribute analysis enables a marketer to assess the attributes and benefits that most affect a customer's purchasing decision. It provides insights into the factors that contribute to or inhibit product trial. And it permits a company to evaluate how well a product or service fulfills the customer's prepurchase expectations.

Critical attribute analysis, unlike traditional research and analysis, goes beyond the customer's self-reported behavior to estimate the true

	-40%	-30%	-20%	-10%	10%	20%	30%	40%
Prime 15 Second Commercials								
Change in Sales (000s of Units)	-97	-71	-44	-27	27	44	71	88
Cost (000s of $)	-295	-222	-148	-74	74	148	22	295
Prime 30 Second Commericals								
Change in Sales (000s of Units)	-725	-531	-345	-168	168	327	476	628
Cost (000s of $)	-1741	-1305	-870	-435	435	870	1305	1741
Day 30 Second Commercials								
Change in Sales (000s of Units)	-610	-451	-301	-150	142	284	416	549
Cost (000s of $)	-877	-658	-439	-219	219	439	658	877
Consumer/Promotion								
Change in Sales (000s of Units)	-584	-434	-292	-142	142	292	434	575
Cost (000s of $)	-2570	-1928	-1285	-643	643	1285	1928	2570

Exhibit 19-1 Example of a sensitivity analysis for selected marketing components.

impact of features on brand preferences and purchasing behavior. By taking a multidimensional approach, linking feature motivating power with brand perceptions, the analysis identifies product strengths, weaknesses, and opportunities. Once a company has this information, of course, it can build on the product's strengths, work to minimize its weaknesses, and take advantage of any opportunities.

Myth 162: Simulated test marketing cannot measure competitive response.

Truth: Until recently this was no myth. Pretest market simulation systems, with a few exceptions, didn't really capture competitive response. One STM system, Litmus, did include share of voice as a parameter, but most other measures of market response assumed "normal" levels of competitive activity, an assumption clearly out of touch with marketing reality.

Because competitive response has been changing rapidly, however, researchers have begun to address this problem. We've learned, for example, that we can measure, in the laboratory simulation during the experiment, some of the "new" competitive promotional factors like featured pricing.

To understand this, it might be helpful to understand more about the simulation experiment.

In a Novaction, Yankelovich, or ESP study, people move through three stages: exposure to product advertising in a television program, or to other advertising or to promotion, or both; opportunity to buy the product in a simulated store; and follow-up phone calls to measure repeat purchase. We can measure the effects of competitive pricing strategies in this experiment with an acceptable level of validity. The procedure is very simple: Vary the prices of competitors on the shelf in the simulated store.

In a study for Hefty Steel Sack bags that led to the brand's successful national introduction, we tested three different price points for Hefty and three different competitive price points, to learn how Hefty would perform under different competitive pricing scenarios.

Other competitive-response factors require a combination of the experiment and self-reported measures included in the interview, such as competitive couponing. Most consumers don't use coupons for most purchases. To measure the effect of consumer promotion, therefore, we first need to estimate the probability that someone will use a coupon in the real world, then observe that person's behavior in the laboratory environment.

Finally, some competitive variables we wish to capture require a judgment call based on real-world data, if it's available, and the marketing/research manager's surmise. Take shelf dominance. Our clients tell us that they can estimate the share of facings they can buy as a part of trade deals. What they don't know is how this share of facings relates to sales. Since laboratory experiments do not seem to measure this variable very well, we have had to turn to judgmental and historical relationships while continuing to test alternative research methodologies.

Nevertheless, researchers can forecast sales and profits using a three-step procedure:

1. The company's marketing management creates four alternative competitive scenarios: the most likely case, a more serious case, a life-threatening case, and a doomsday case.
2. The researchers use an STM model that combines laboratory simulation, measurement, and decision calculus to estimate the effects of each scenario on each market-response parameter—for example, increasing radio advertising, reducing television advertising, dropping the price.
3. The STM forecasts awareness and profitability figures for each scenario.

The company can now develop alternative offensive plans to counter likely competitive response. Afterward, the computer can generate awareness-to-profitability forecasts for each plan. Common strategies that companies use when trying to neutralize competitive response include:

- Adjusting each component in the marketing plan up or down in terms of its budget
- Evaluating different decisions for each component; for example, new advertising copy or pricing strategy
- Modifying the introduction's schedule—choosing between the "big blast" and the "accretion" strategies
- Examining a "hold" versus "fold" position

Simulated test marketing *can* measure competitive response, and a company *can* do something with the information.

Myth 163: Simulated test marketing works only for new products.

Truth: While simulated test marketing research works best with new products, you also can use it for restaging (or repositioning) an established product, and for extending a line.

As we've said before, every three or four years, as top management notices product sales sliding slowly toward oblivion, someone says, "Why don't you turn this dying brand around?" While it's possible to use STM for a restaging effort, it's much more difficult than introducing a new product, for at least two reasons:

1. The restaged product has a history. It exists. People have bought it in the past. So the trick (and it is a trick) is to measure the difference in sales between the restaged product and what sales would have been without the restaging.
2. Often the incremental sales are so small they're hard to measure. It's hard to tell whether you're measuring an actual change or random noise. To do STM for the restaging of an existing product usually takes a much larger sample size than for a new product, and it takes much more sensitivity in the research measurement process to pick up true differences.

On the other hand, the more elements the company changes, the greater the likelihood that the restaged product will perform like a new product. We like to call this the "big-think, big-bang approach." If you change the product formulation, the packaging, the advertising, the pricing, the promotion strategy, the distribution—even the name, by calling it "new and improved"—the restaged product begins to behave like a new product, and simulated test market research can be more helpful.

Most firms that introduce a repositioned product, however, haven't learned their lesson. They change one or two elements in the marketing mix—the label and the advertising are usually not enough to make a difference—and watch the product continue its slide.

Consider: If the average, established brand in the average product category is declining by 0.3 percent of a share point every year, and if there are a dozen ingredients in the marketing mix and you change one of them, how much effect will it have? How much absolute change of sales could possibly be due to any one of the twelve ingredients in the mix? How much would be due to, say, advertising weight alone, or to positioning alone? The answer is very, very little, perhaps too little to be measurable.

Line extensions share many of the same problems as restagings. The product already exists in another form, and you're trying to measure the difference between the extension and the existing product(s). This problem is further complicated by the extension's propensity to cannibalize the existing product. The challenge is to measure net incremental sales, which is difficult but doable.

Simulated test marketing will work for repositioned products, but it is more difficult to use.

Myth 164: Marketers thank the messenger who brings bad news about a new product introduction.

Truth: Marketers *should* give thanks; the messenger may have saved the company millions of dollars spent on a failed introduction. But this rarely happens. *Messengers are drawn and quartered.*

Even though a company's marketers may do their best to define the target market, position the product, maximize its profitability, and create effective advertising before the simulated test market research, STMs, by their nature, forecast failure more often than not. A forecast of failure may not please the client, although it usually beats failing in the marketplace.

New product efforts, as we've said before, gain a life of their own. Not long ago we did an STM study for a company that was interested in introducing a cleverly positioned soft drink that had a unique bottle. To introduce this new drink, however, the company would have to build a new bottling plant, and both the plant and the equipment to manufacture the product would cost many millions of dollars.

The study went on for a long time. It was very complicated, and at every stage the marketing research director told us how important it was to come up with a good number, because an important decision hung in the balance. It seemed to us that he was saying, "Don't come up with a number that gives us the go-ahead, because if you do, we'll have to build this factory." The message he *thought* he was sending was, "Make sure you do everything you can to tease out more sales, so we can go ahead and build the factory." Companies don't necessarily hire consultants to lie, but they do want them to support their judgments.

We finally met with him and presented the STM's preliminary forecast, which said, in effect, don't build the factory. The research director became furious: "I can't present this to my management! These numbers are impossible!" And much, much more. Two days later, at nine in the morning, he walked into our office unannounced. He wanted to talk about the product. He stayed until noon, discussing the project, showing us data, going over old research reports. We reviewed our work carefully, but we could not make the forecast any better.

Two weeks later, we made the big presentation to the division head. We usually start with the forecast and then get into the nitty-gritty detail supporting it. Five minutes after we had begun, the research director took issue with our presentation and we took issue with him. After we had clashed for a few minutes, the division head said to his research director, "I don't know why you're arguing this point. All the results we've gotten at the other stages have been mediocre. We know there are a lot of problems associated with the product, so don't take it personally." At that point the research director began to quarrel with his boss.

When the dust had settled, the research director still had his job, but the company had decided to abandon the product.

Over and over we see people become emotionally involved in their products, which is probably a good thing, but not when it seriously clouds their judgment. What would have happened to the research director and the product manager if the company had built a multimillion-dollar factory and *then* learned the product was a lemon?

Another example. In early 1988 we sat through a meeting in which a major packaged goods firm presented a $25 million plan to introduce a new antiperspirant. We were there because we were to do the simulated test market research that would provide the company with early returns on the product's sales and profitability.

The product manager flipped through a chart, presenting the product's background. Researchers in the company's laboratory had developed a formulation that was 37 percent more effective than the market-leading antiperspirant. It offered 24-hour protection. "We found in a series of 12 focus groups that women remain concerned about perspiration and underarm odor," said the product manager. "They are not entirely satisfied with the products they currently use, and our new entry is designed to answer these concerns."

The target market was to be 18-to-49-year-old women, because that group accounts for 62 percent of all sales of this type of product. The product was to be positioned as an effective, convenient solution to perspiration. In all the concept tests, the product scored very high in terms of consumer-appeal scores. In product testing, the new formulation performed measurably better than the leading brands. The company planned to price the product 20 cents below the market leader. During the introductory phase, the company would drop 50 million coupons in freestanding newspaper inserts. The planned television commercials and the print advertising contained five key selling messages about the product, messages designed to appeal to most women in the target market; the advertising budget was comparable to the market leader's.

Our role in such a meeting is not to challenge a marketing plan's assumptions. The client had invited us simply because he expected us to include the plan's particulars in our simulated test market research.

Less than six months later we were back in the same conference room, with our forecast that the product would be an unequivocal failure. Hearing this, the product manager attacked us angrily: "This may not be the greatest answer to every American woman's perspiration problems, but my product—given this company's resources and experience—*is* going to be a success. I think you should seriously consider revisiting your sales and profitability estimates." ("Revisiting" is a marketing code word for revising the numbers upward.) "They're wrong! This product will perform *much* better than you've projected!"

The manager then went on to question our research methodology, our forecasting model, the data quality, and anything else he could think of that might have intervened between his hopes for a great forecast and our projections.

We said as diplomatically as we could that we had carefully followed the marketing plan's assumptions, and, while we would certainly review our work for mistakes, unless we found something unusual we could not adjust the forecast.

The product manager, growing more and more agitated, said in passing, "If this product is killed, I won't have a brand." Because this is an important client and because the product manager was so distressed, we offered to review in detail the strategy and research on which the company had placed its bet.

We spent almost a day studying the company's research and the assumptions based on the research. We discovered that at every crossroad, from original product concept to launch, the research had suggested mediocrity: most likely product failure, at best marginal success. The product, however, had taken on a life of its own, gathering momentum until nothing, not even our eleventh-hour prediction, could stop the introduction.

The company did launch the product in 1990, and all its resources and experience did not prevent a costly failure.

"Yes, we're just about ready to go with the $50 million campaign. All we need is a reality check, so tonight we're doing the focus group."

20 Myths about Measuring Marketing Performance

One of the death-wish marketing symptoms we discussed in the Introduction is the overall lack of accountability for marketing programs. Managers spend corporate monies like drunken gold-rush miners, never knowing whether the investment produces a fair return. (Marketing dollars must be regarded as investments, just like a new factory or employee training, if the business is to thrive.)

For reasons we have never been able to understand, otherwise bright and responsible people who can tell you to the first decimal point how their personal portfolios performed in 1993 know little about their marketing investment portfolio's performance. If marketers analyzed advertising, buyer promotion, trade promotion, sports and event marketing, and the sales force with the same scrutiny with which they look at personal investments in mutual funds, blue-chip equities, real estate, treasury notes, and insurance, they would demand a lot more information, make decisions much more deliberately, and institutionalize the kind of systems for monitoring marketing performance that we will discuss in this chapter.

Perhaps the lack of accountability in marketing today is due to the fact that business managers have not regarded marketing as the sun of the business solar system. If marketing is just another planet circling about finance—which it has been, in the Ptolemaic decade of the 1980s—a planet not appreciably different from human resources, management information systems, and manufacturing, it should come as no surprise that it's not taken that seriously.

After all, the focus has been on the sun—finance. We depend upon it for warmth, light, and the production of food. Since CEOs are not asking tough questions about the ROI of management information systems (companies have invested tons of money in MIS during the past two decades, without any evidence of an improvement in productivity; now the same people are suggesting that firms invest even more to reengineer the corporation, guaranteeing only their own livelihoods as a result), of manufacturing, distribution systems, strategic planning, human resources, public relations, and other business planets of smaller size and significance, why should it dumbfound anyone that they are not asking tough questions about marketing? After all, until now marketing has been to finance what Venus is to the Sun.

CEOs *may not even know the questions to ask,* a topic we will cover momentarily.

When the Copernican revolution comes to business, however, and managers begin to regard marketing and its concomitant customer focus as the true center of the business solar system, things will change for the better.

And one of the first changes you can expect is the eradication of persistent myths about the measurement of marketing performance.

Myth 165: CEOs know the right questions to ask about the marketing program's performance.

Truth: They don't. Otherwise they would have realized long before now that most of their marketing programs yield a questionable return on investment.

If marketing managers are to really concentrate on avoiding the myths of marketing, they must research and make decisions in at least ten critical areas:

1. Environmental climate
2. Market segmentation and target selection
3. Positioning
4. Product design or formulation
5. Pricing
6. Advertising

7. Direct marketing
8. Promotion
9. Distribution channels
10. Sales force allocation

A smart CEO may ask how thoroughly each of these issues has been researched and how much confidence the marketing manager has in each decision. Confidence could be expressed on an 11-point scale, ranging from 0 (no confidence at all) to 10 (100 percent confident). The manager who gives, say, pricing a 2, is saying he is 20 percent confident in the decision. Adding up all ten decisions gives a "marketing plan confidence factor" ranging from 0 to 100. Reconsider or scrap any plan with a confidence factor of less than 70.

Assuming that the manager is reasonably confident of success, the marketing plan finally is ready to be implemented. The new or repositioned product or service is launched. What happens next?

All too often, management sits back to wait for reports from distant battlefields. Sometimes the reports don't arrive for months; often a company does not (or cannot) evaluate the program's relative success for a year or more. And all too often the report comes back that the campaign failed to achieve its objectives.

How many managers invest a significant chunk of their own dollars and wait a year to learn how the investment is doing? How many mangers, investing as individuals, would take a chance if they thought the risk of failure was high? How many, even if they thought the risk was modest, would not monitor the investment's performance?

For some reason, naturally risk-averse individuals holding responsible corporate positions often begin to behave in ways that suggest that corporate bank accounts can afford major losses. We say this because corporations routinely launch $1 million, $20 million, even $100 million marketing programs before they have put systems into place to carefully track, evaluate, and help improve campaign performance.

Myth 166: Marketing programs can be evaluated without specific objectives related to profitability.

Truth: The fact is companies do this all the time—most marketing programs are not designed or implemented with specific objectives in mind. But that doesn't mean it's right. It's wrong! It's like turning your life savings over to a money manager and not asking what she plans to do (her objectives), or having any way to evaluate her performance.

Managers wouldn't behave so irresponsibly with their personal money manager. They shouldn't with the company's bank account.

This point came home to us very clearly when a business-to-business client asked us about putting together a study to evaluate his 1994 advertising program. The company is planning to spend $40 million in television and print, and provided us with details concerning media reach (92 percent of the target), frequency (four times a month, every other month), target group profiles, and all the rest.

We asked, "What are the specific objectives for the campaign?"

The answer: "To build brand awareness and corporate name recognition."

We said that those were very general objectives; did the company have anything more specific?

The answer: "No. What do you mean?"

It turned out to be an old story. Without much research and analysis, the agency had developed four different commercials and five different print ads, all of which were encomiums of the marketer's new product line.

Focus group research was the mainspring for both the copy development and the advertising testing. We said, "You can't be serious!" They said, "We didn't have time to do anything else."

We then asked, "Do you know specifically what you want to accomplish in terms of awareness, familiarity, positive attitudes, brand personality attributions, purchase considerations, preference, or sales?" They looked at us sheepishly and admitted that, sadly, they did not.

This is everyday life in Corporate America.

It doesn't have to be this way.

An organization can and should set objectives for every marketing program. An objective must be *realistic, specific,* and *measurable.* It should not be fuzzy, ethereal, or soft, such as, "Our objective is to increase the number of people who feel good about our company and its new product," or the all-time most popular objective, "Our plan is to build awareness." A bank's objective might be: "A 10 percent increase in the percentage of customers who open an IRA by April 15, 1994." A software firm might demand "800 new leads for sales calls within 90 days in California." A coffee marketer might want to increase loyalty by 20 percent, while a new product manager should set specific objectives for product awareness, trial, repeat purchase, market share, and profitability.

Once the organization has set these objectives, a research study can be designed and undertaken to measure how well the program has performed.

Myth 167: If the market program works, we'll know it. If it doesn't, we'll know that too. Tracking research is a waste of money.

Truth: The research should do more than track. It should tell you not only what you're doing, but what to do.

Most marketing programs fail for all the reasons we've outlined: the wrong target, positioning, message, pricing, and all the rest. Sometimes, tragically, they die because management did not know they were sick until it was too late to help. They might have been saved with tracking research.

Such research has a reputation for being dull, repetitive, and unenlightened, undertaken by dull, repetitive, and unenlightened researchers. The people who do it are "bean-counters" (because originally they counted canned bean sales in grocery stores, no kidding). Some companies do not budget for tracking research, because they do not understand or believe the effort can improve their marketing; some do not believe it's worth the money.

But it can be the marketing department's distant early-warning line. Take, for example, "The Death of the High Roller Credit Card." The story began when a major credit card company decided to launch a premium credit card designed for affluent Americans, people earning more than $75,000 a year. For an annual fee of $500, the card would be accepted at restaurants and hotels around the world. Of great interest to the affluent, however, the card would open the doors to private golf, tennis, and social clubs from New York to Tokyo, and provide access to a $30,000 line of credit and personal valet services in every major market. The marketer hired a well-known research company (not us) to do an elaborate and sophisticated concept test, which suggested that 15 percent of all prospects would sign up for the service.

With a 5 percent response, the new service would have broken even in the first year; a 15 percent response would have been the success story of the decade. Euphoric, the marketer put the delivery system into place, hired an advertising agency, developed a direct-mail campaign, and launched the service. The total effort cost about $20 million (in 1993 dollars).

Within six months, management knew it had launched a disaster. Fifteen percent of the prospects did not sign up. Neither did 10 percent...or 5 percent. The actual number was less than half of one percent.

Management's initial reaction: "Bad market research overstated the concept appeal." That indeed seemed to be the situation; the research had overstated consumer interest by more than 30 to 1.

At that point, in an unusual step—since most companies bury their mistakes with as little notice as possible—the company called us in to do an autopsy, to see if we could discover what had really gone wrong.

The first thing we did was a tracking study, in which we traced the various input-output relationships—the number of brochures the company mailed, the number of people who recalled receiving the brochure, and other factors, to identify the cause of death. We found only 60 percent of the target group claiming to have received the mailing. Somewhat less than half of those who actually recalled receiving the mailing, or 28 percent of all prospects, said they had read most or all of it.

Of those who read the mailing, 71 percent were aware of the new service. To estimate real-world awareness, take the 28 percent of the prospects who received and read the mailing and multiply it by the 71 percent who were aware of the new service. This calculation yields the 20 percent of all prospects who were aware of the service.

The direct-mail piece was very confusing. Even after we had read it twice, the new service's unique attributes and benefits were not clear. We found it difficult to describe this new service's advantages compared to similar services. We were not alone in this view; when we measured consumer comprehension of what the new service offered, only a quarter of the aware prospects had really understood it. Twenty-five percent of the 20 percent-aware prospects gives you a 5 percent comprehension level.

Finally, when the research focused on the people who were both aware of the new service *and* understood it, 16 percent had already signed up or were about to. Sixteen percent of 5 percent is less than 1 percent. The monitoring study and the direct-mail campaign's results, in other words, showed essentially the same thing. Researchers call this convergent validity, and everyone is happy when it happens.

But look at the following table. The figures in the right-hand column are those the marketer must have assumed, if management was expecting a one-to-one correspondence between the concept test results and real-world performance.

High Roller Credit Card Tracking Research

	Achieved	Assumed
Received mailing	60%	100%
Read material	28%	100%
Awareness	20%	100%
Comprehension	5%	100%
Conversion to purchase	16%	15%*
Sales	0.5%	15%

*The rate estimated from the concept test.

In the highly artificial, forced-exposure environment of a concept test interview, there is 100 percent reception, 100 percent reading, 100 percent awareness, and usually 100 percent comprehension. Multiplying the 15 percent conversion-to-purchase estimate by 100 percent gave the marketer the misleading sales forecast on which he based the national launch.

The preliminary diagnosis might have been "death due to research overstatement," but the true cause of death was poor marketing, a program that failed to generate a sufficient awareness and comprehension level. But the company would not have known this without the tracking study. It would have known only that its auspicious new service had died.

Tracking research done well provides a marketer with a scorecard and a blueprint. The scorecard gives the basic numbers: how the firm is performing over time, relative to its competitors. This information is essential, but insufficient. The company requires marketing intelligence to see how the marketing program can be improved to produce an even greater return on investment. Good tracking research can do this. It can answer questions such as these:

- Are we achieving our goals and objectives?
- Are we spending the right amount of money on advertising, promotion, and the other components of the marketing mix?
- How are our mass media and public relations efforts performing compared to competitive activity? What can we do to enhance them?
- Which media vehicles are working best? Which worst?
- Are we moving the needles in terms of buyer perceptions, attitudes, and performance? If not, why not? If so, what can we do even better?

Ultimately, is our marketing program producing a strong return on investment, or would we be better off writing a check to our favorite mutual fund? If it's not producing a good return, how do we improve it?

Myth 168: Automated intelligence shows little short-term promise in helping to develop and evaluate good advertising and marketing.

Truth: Every marketing manager in America sits down once a year to write marketing plans for his brand. He pulls data from multiple sources to put together a dry description of where the brand stands relative to the competition. He shows facts and figures on market penetration, brand share, competitive usage rates, and brand profiles, often comparing the current year against some earlier period such as three or even five years ago.

In many cases, the marketing manager provides detailed profiles of key target groups within a category such as heavy users. The manager profiles these targets in terms of demographic variables and, in some cases, attitudinal and media behavior patterns as well. No targeting analysis is complete, however, without a look at how the company's brand is performing in terms of these key targets when compared to competitors.

Often, writing this plan consumes a few weeks of a brand manager's (or her assistant's) time. The final report, however, is often poorly written, costly, underanalyzed, and not based on timely or—in some cases—useful information.

Today there are services available, employing automated intelligence programs, that work with one or more years of client data to search for, analyze, and write a report featuring critical, timely data, key to the developing of an annual marketing plan. The report is a finished document complete with data tables, statistical analyses, and narrative interpretation.

Another example. Not long ago we sat through a company's day of media advertising planning. The firm was not sure that its target market—executives in high-tech industries—watched television, or actually read the field's specialized business publications. The advertising agency had brought rough estimates of cable and network television reach for this group, but they had only circulation—not readership—figures for the 20 top trade publications they were considering. They did have roughly comparable readership scores for *BusinessWeek* and some of the general-audience publications such as *Time, Esquire,* and

GQ. In other words they had incomplete data, and what they had was not comparable.

We found it appalling that in 1993 executives of a major advertising agency were leafing through loose-leaf research books to find cross-tabs of media exposure patterns for men, 40 years of age and older, in high-technology industries. One ought to be able to sit at a computer and tell it: "I have a budget of $25 million. My target group consists of these kinds of people. Give me a profile of the media these folks watch, read, and are exposed to."

The machine should ask questions: "How many times do you have to reach a person each month to be successful? Do you have one campaign going, or several?" Once the company had answered the computer's questions, the computer would analyze its databases and make a recommendation. A relatively primitive expert system could provide a recommendation. But if companies buy media in terms of 18-to-49-year-old women instead of more subtle target groups such as people most responsive to the firm's marketing efforts, even a primitive expert system is probably overqualified.

The last five years have seen tremendous growth in computerized marketing decision-support systems (MDSS) that are outgrowths of corporate sales databases. The latest technology matches near real-time sales tracking information, which means that the marketing executives obtain sales data almost as fast as the sales occur, with sophisticated market modeling. For the first time, we are able to study marketing input-output relationships in depth.

The complaint of most practitioners who are struggling with implementing a marketing decision-support system is that they are drowning in data, and they have no information. Which is why companies are creating automated intelligence, or expert systems, on top of the MDSS systems. These systems can absorb the huge data stream pouring into corporate databases, winnow through the data to find the critical trends and advertising sales effects, and emerge with recommendations for action.

Tools now exist, some in the form of expert systems, that vary considerably in terms of sophistication. A device that simply takes a load of data and analyses it to ferret out the key findings is a very primitive version of automated intelligence technology. But the fact that a technology may be primitive does not make it boring or useless. Something may be very useful without requiring a great deal of technological polish.

The most advanced of these programs combine the best thinking of inspired analysts with the tireless patience of the computer. In the future, these systems will use sophisticated modeling and decision rules to identify marketplace opportunities such as local competitive vulnerabilities, long-term share-gain opportunities, or optimal pricing/dealing tactics. Once researchers have understood these effects, they can model them.

In the near future, it will be possible for most brands to "parse out" the effects of short-term sales promotions and local store activity to uncover direct short-term effects of advertising. For those who take a longer-term view, the promise of single-source panel data is the ability to track the longer-term effects of advertising on purchasing loyalty and deal sensitivity.

Not only will these expert systems work with the data that exists, they will permit human managers to study the world that could be. They will integrate marketing science modeling, automated-intelligence technology, historical marketplace relationships, and marketing mix models. These systems will take the mathematics and merge it with the wisdom of marketing experts: the experience, the rules of thumb, and the insights experienced marketing practitioners now use.

True single-source data, which merges household media exposure information with sales data for the same household, is increasingly available. Many companies are merging this new data source into their overall structure in order to evaluate advertising and, in the process, to fundamentally change the advertising evaluation system.

Some marketing people react to these changes by (metaphorically) throwing up their hands and burying their heads in the sand. They say, in essence, "So what? I don't need more and faster data. I don't know what it tells me anyway." If they don't know what the data tells them, and if they're not willing to learn, then they're right. They don't need more data, they need compassion.

Because if a company is an astute, smart, and aggressive competitor, and if its managers take the time to understand and use these new information systems, especially while its competitors are sitting back and saying, "So what?", they can gain a tremendous competitive advantage.

We've learned, in exercises designed to optimize a marketing plan, that over time the level of superiority of "machine" over "manager" goes down. The more often people use a sophisticated system, the smarter they become. The more often they use an expert system, the more they become expert managers.

So we do not really believe the day will arrive when a computer can become a marketing department in a box. The world, human beings, and reality as a whole will remain too complex.

We do believe, however, that an expert manager guided by an expert system will be a formidable competitor. Companies that adopt this emerging technology early will enjoy an edge over the competition, an edge that will be difficult to overcome. Perhaps total product failure rates, on average, will remain the same. But they will certainly decline for the firms employing expert managers and systems, even as they will increase for the companies that do not.

Myth 169: Once a marketing program dies—and most do—it can't be resuscitated. It's time to create another program.

Truth: Marketers can also use monitoring research effectively to track performance relative to competition for every objective set by management.

Take awareness. Since we know that awareness builds nonlinearly with each marketing dollar invested, a company can use monitoring study data to plot a product or service's performance compared to the competition's. The important thing is not to ask how Visa is doing compared to MasterCard, or Coke to Pepsi, or Ford to Chrysler, but to ask, how are Visa and MasterCard, Coke and Pepsi, Ford and Chrysler doing relative to the size of their marketing investment?

As companies invest marketing dollars, consumer awareness increases—just as one would hope. The computer calculates the best solution to all the data points and draws a line representing this solution, a curve on a chart. A company located right on the line is perfectly average; companies above the line enjoy greater consumer awareness than average, those below, less. A hypothetical chart (see Exhibit 20.1) might show that while American Express spends the most money, Visa has greater consumer awareness. MasterCard, which has spent almost as much as Visa, is not doing as well. If this in fact were true, MasterCard might want to develop and test alternative advertising strategies, or executions, or both.

In the same way, a company can measure every component in its hypothesized model of how marketing works. For example, the relationship between awareness and purchase consideration tends to be linear; as awareness increases, so does purchase consideration. In most product categories there must be some awareness before the company sees any purchase consideration at all. With an impulse item, awareness may not be as important.

The next step is the conversion of purchase consideration into actual buying behavior, measured in terms of share of customers. Again, it is

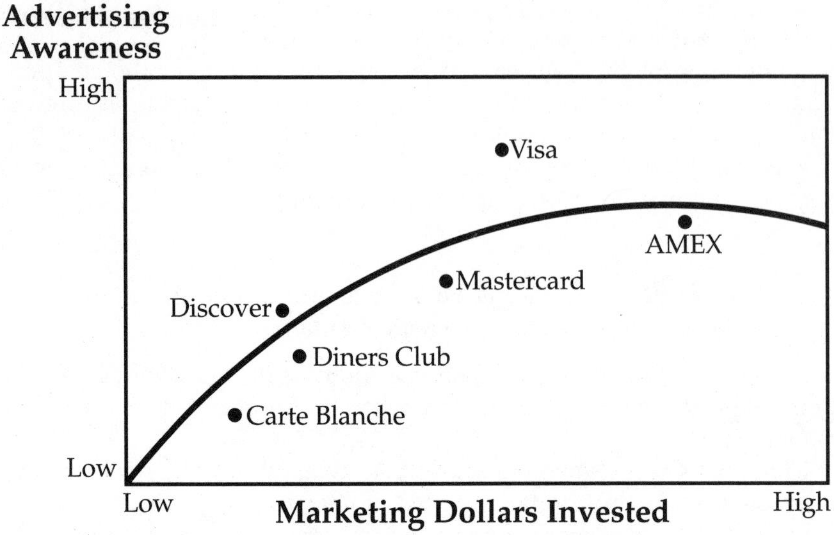

Exhibit 20-1 The relationship between marketing investment and advertising awareness.

possible to take this data, plot it on a graph, draw a line between the points to show average performance, and see instantly which companies convert a larger share of prospects into customers and which convert a smaller share.

Finally, there's the link between share of buyers and share of dollars. If the relationship were perfect, this would be a 45° line and all firms would sit right on it; as a company's share of buyers rose, its share of dollars would rise equally. The relationship is not perfect, however, because some firms have larger volumes than others. Firms above the line generate more dollars per customer than firms below the line.

Observing where the company falls vis-à-vis the competition on this line, and at all other stages in the company's marketing model, provides management with insights into the strengths and weaknesses of its marketing programs. Sometimes this intelligence can be used to resuscitate a dying brand or even resurrect a dead one.

Myth 170: You can't evaluate the performance of specific media vehicles.

Truth: Once upon a time, this was true. Today it's not.

This question comes up all the time: Can you figure out the contribution of different media vehicles? Does print, for example, work better than television, or network TV better than cable? Sophisticated tracking and analytical methodologies can answer such questions.

We recommend that the market-tracking questions contain measures of media exposure for each major medium the program employs. Then, later, at the analytical stage, the company can examine advertising effects for each vehicle separately. Exhibit 20-2, for example, for a major marketer of copying machines, shows that among both business buyers and upscale consumers an investment made in magazines, particularly business and news publications, had much more effect than either network or cable television.

For example, advertising penetration increased 63 percent among business buyers heavily exposed to business publications, and only 7 percent among business buyers heavily exposed to network television.

In contrast, in a study for a new soft drink, network television demonstrated tremendous increases in brand awareness and trial, while print performed at a mediocre level.

Our point here is not to argue for the superiority of one medium over another, but to point out that media effectiveness *can* be tracked and diagnoses made to improve campaign performance.

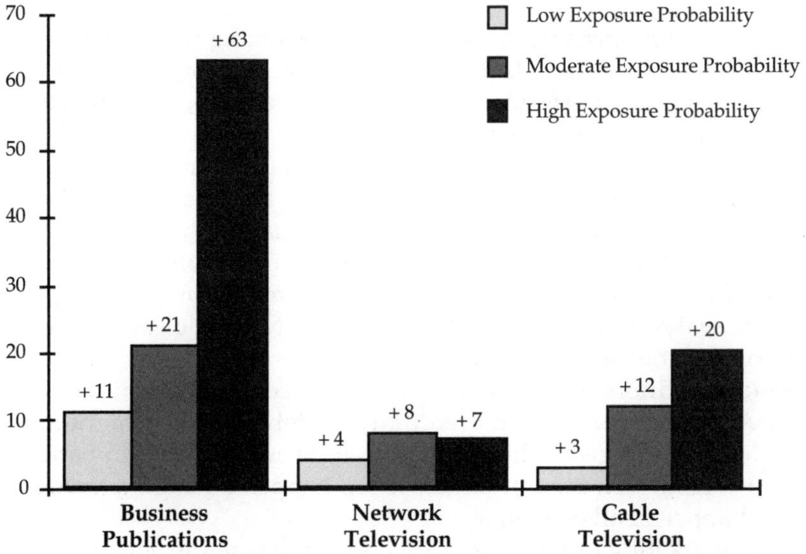

Exhibit 20-2 The effects of media exposure on advertising penetration for copying machines.

Myth 171: Auditing marketing performance in the same way that we audit financial performance is a farfetched idea that will probably never be implemented.

Truth: Every company in America, small to large, knows that once a year the auditors come in and, following a fairly standard format, assess the enterprise's financial health.

The marketing audit's time has come. We see a new kind of auditing firm coming into an organization annually to assess the firm's marketing capabilities. For example, does the organization understand marketing? What is its marketing I.Q.? What kind of intelligence is being collected about customers? What's the quality of that intelligence? Was there consensus as to the marketing plan that was implemented?

These new auditors will ask questions about the marketing plan: Were the right customers targeted? Was the product positioned correctly? Was the product designed well? How about the advertising? How was the advertising evaluated? The strategy, the implementation program, and the tracking—is each piece of the plan done as well as it might be?

Finally, and most importantly, the marketing auditor's task will be to ascertain whether the marketing plan is generating a fair return on its investment. Is brand equity being built over time? How well do the various components in the plan perform relative to objectives and relative to competitors?

We see a comprehensive marketing audit becoming commonplace as the decade unfolds, an audit by means of which an organization can assess its marketing performance in the same way as accounting auditors assess financial performance.

Who will invite such a firm in? CEOs will invite the marketing auditors in, in much the same way as they invite the financial auditors. Some CFOs would love to be in charge of evaluating their own books. It's the independent auditor's analysis that provides some insight into the way financial executives handled the firm's money during the year—an analysis that could be unfavorable. Nevertheless, the company brings in outside auditors.

Financial auditors have GAAP, generally accepted accounting principles. At the moment there aren't any widely accepted marketing principles, which is why the marketing audit is not going to happen tomorrow. And even though we say it *will* happen during the 1990s, it will not happen at all companies.

Today, marketing expenditures are one of the major expenditures of American corporations. Our view is that many are of questionable merit. We've given a lot of reasons why. It seems obvious to us that an audit of the marketing function, which is designed to evaluate what the organization got for its money and how to get more, is something in which everybody ought to be interested. Are there standard ways to do that now? No. But, GAAP didn't exist a century ago. Something will develop over time. Eventually we'll have GAMP—generally accepted *marketing* principles.

Myth 172: Even if we could do a marketing audit, it's not clear what it would contain.

Truth: Not surprisingly, it's very clear to us. It is also very clear to Professor Philip Kotler, who has been describing the need for marketing audits since 1977. The marketing audit does for the marketing department what a financial audit does for the accounting department. It is a comprehensive review of a company's marketing environment, objectives, strategies, research, and performance. The audit identifies operational strengths and weaknesses and recommends changes to the company's marketing plans and programs (one reason that some marketing people oppose such an audit). A well-designed marketing audit examines the marketing organization's effectiveness, marketing's productivity, and all functional relationships within the marketing organization.

Because a marketing audit is so comprehensive, the firm must conduct it as systematically as possible. Before the auditors examine the first document, before they interview one employee, customer, or supplier, the company prepares a detailed structure for the audit. This includes the significant points to be examined, the questions to be asked, and the types of information sought. Every audit should address 10 central issues:

1. An assessment of the key factors that impacted the business for good or ill during the past year. This should emphasize an evaluation of marketing surprises—those unanticipated competitive actions or changes in the marketing climate that affected the marketing program's performance.
2. An assessment of marketing knowledge, attitudes, and satisfaction, for all executives involved in the marketing function.
3. An assessment of customer retention and both attitudinal and behavioral loyalty, based on research among key target groups.
4. An assessment of the extent to which specific, realistic, and measurable objectives were set for each marketing program—objectives tied to profitability.

5. An assessment of the extent to which the marketing program was marketed internally and bought into by top management, marketing, and nonmarketing executives.
6. An assessment of the extent to which each decision in the marketing mix was made correctly after careful evaluation of the many alternatives in terms of profit-related criteria.
7. An assessment of the performance of advertising, consumer and trade promotion, public relations, sports and event marketing, sales force, and marketing research programs, with an emphasis on return-on-investment.
8. An overall assessment of whether the marketing plan achieved its stated financial and nonfinancial goals and objectives.
9. An autopsy of all aspects of every plan that failed to meet objectives, with specific recommendations for improving next year's performance.
10. An assessment of the current value of brand equity for each brand in the product portfolio.

For the same reason that the company hires an independent accounting firm to audit its books, an individual or organization independent of the marketing department should audit marketing performance. This may not always be possible, because outsiders may not have the necessary qualifications, in which case the company will use in-house talent to prepare the audit. Although top management cannot expect company employees to be totally disinterested, we have seen instances where a task force within the firm performed an audit professionally and evenhandedly.

We believe a company should schedule regular marketing audits, generally once a year. If a company conducts regular audits, it should find few nasty surprises uncovered by the report, and it should be able to correct problems before they develop into a crisis. If the firm waits for a crisis before initiating a marketing audit, the number of unhappy surprises may be more than management can handle.

The marketing audit is a planning tool that goes beyond the day-to-day controlling activities of management. In addition to looking at how well the firm is doing what it does, the audit considers whether the firm is doing what it should be doing at all. The results sometimes perturb top management, especially the first time a company conducts an audit. We have seen audits that uncovered substantial differences between what company management believed to be true about its marketing effort and the reality. But it is better to learn about the company's shortcomings from an impartial auditor than from an angry customer or, worse, an aggressive competitor.

The marketing revolution now taking place means that companies are recognizing changes in the marketplace and aggressively changing the way they do business as a result. They monitor their marketing effort, and they audit the marketing process. They obtain the information they need to correct small problems before they become serious crises. They move from death-wish marketing to marketing intelligence.

Conclusion

American business, as we have shown, is experiencing serious problems. Led by financially oriented managers during the 1980s and early 1990s, a frenzy of mergers and purges, acquisitions and divestitures, expansions and downsizings have resulted in zero growth in sales, profitability, and productivity.

The only thing that has grown, for reasons beyond our understanding, is the prices people have been willing to pay for stock in these companies—rising prices reflected in the Dow Jones industrial average's upward climb.

Finance, we have argued, has been the hub, the center of the business solar system for too long. It should not have been there in the first place.

Just as the Ptolemaic theory that placed the earth at the center of the universe eventually broke down—it didn't work; it couldn't explain what mankind had begun to observe in the heavens—the conventional view of finance's central importance is beginning to crack.

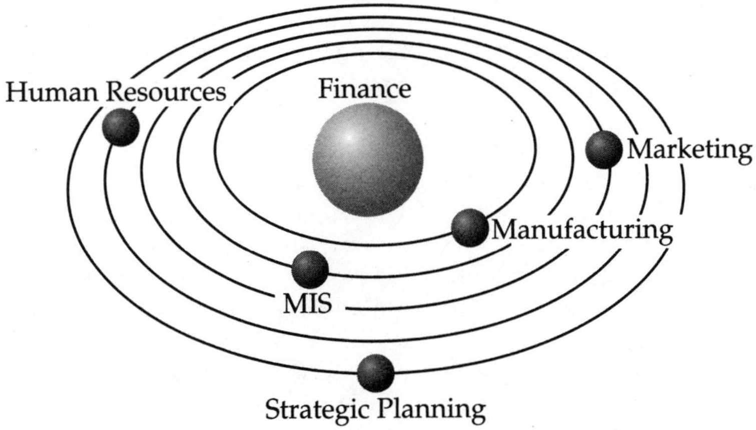

Exhibit C-1 Business in the 1980s.

Just as the Copernican theory placed the sun at the center of the solar system and eclipsed the Ptolemaic theory, a revolution will occur in the mid-to-late 1990s that will place marketing and the customer at the center of business.

Marketing, after all, is what drives business. Marketing is responsible for finding, serving, and keeping customers, and that's what every business is about. Marketing keeps financial managers and accountants and everyone else in the organization afloat. Without marketing, the business would not exist.

If a business were a household, marketing would be those activities concerned with the life, liberty, and pursuit of happiness of husband, wife, and children. Finance would be about...well, *finance*—income management and distribution, spending and investments. Marketing would be key; finance, peripheral.

A revolution is coming not simply because marketing must replace finance as the focus of business's attention but because marketing doesn't work as well as it should.

As we've shown, CEOs don't know much about marketing, and marketing managers are not particularly well educated or trained at what they do. As a result, most marketing programs have a questionable effect on sales and an uncertain relationship to profitability.

Companies large and small are spending big bucks, with little knowledge of what those bucks are paying for. With approximately $400 billion invested in advertising and promotion alone, more money than the gross national products of most nations passes through the hands of marketing managers.

Yet when asked, "What do you get for your marketing investment?", or "What level of ROI did you receive?", most managers don't know. And, interestingly, they even admit that they have grave doubts. In one recent survey, more than half reported that they "don't believe that most marketing programs produce a return on investment."

We do know that few advertising campaigns appear to have any effect on sales—never mind profitability. If you increase the advertising or change the copy for an established product or service, most of the time nothing happens.

If you develop an entirely new marketing program for an established product that's losing share—sliding downhill—9 out of 10 times nothing happens.

And if you launch a new product or service, whether a food product, automobile, financial service, medical testing device, or television program, 8 to 9 times out of 10 it will fail.

Why? What's wrong with marketing programs today? They fail because they are based on myths. Managers believe things that simply aren't true. They believe myths about the environment, targeting, positioning, advertising, pricing, and every other marketing element.

Myths are part of the "death-wish marketing" syndrome we described in *The Marketing Revolution* and in the Introduction of this book. The age of myth and ignorance in marketing is coming—must come—to an end. Marketing, no matter what practitioners thought in the past, is more science than art. It is no longer necessary to rely exclusively on hunch, hope, mythology, and divine illumination. The data and the tools currently exist to improve a company's marketing success rate dramatically. All that's required is the will to use them.

This is not to advocate abandoning such essential inputs great marketing as creativity, sound management judgment, and experience. These are absolutely essential. And no one should think we believe in slavish obedience to numbers alone.

On the contrary, we are increasingly convinced that American business needs to *balance* science and management judgment in marketing.

Effective marketing is serious business. Before the organization invests a single dollar in the annual marketing program, it should challenge the marketing manager to demonstrate the profit-directed thinking that went into each critical decision in the plan. It should demand to see the anticipated return on the organization's investment in the plan as a whole.

Starting with a perfectly clean slate, managers must analyze the environment, the target, the positioning, the product design, pricing strategy, the advertising—everything. And each of these alternatives can be—should be—evaluated in terms of criteria related to profitability.

The time is over for choosing target groups because they are frequent buyers; for choosing positioning strategies because of meaningless "gaps" or even more meaningless focus groups; for choosing product designs because they produce the highest "top box" scores. The time is over for selecting ad executions because of high-recall scores; for selecting media plans based on experience at roulette tables; for setting prices based on neither strategy nor research; and for setting consumer-service levels based on an intent to satisfy and retain every customer. The time is over for marketing plans that are based on picking one of 14 billion possible plans out of a hat.

American industry can no longer tolerate such a waste of our economic resources. We can no longer countenance routine marketing failure. We can no longer accept as the order of the day marketing-management-led light brigade charges into oblivion.

The marketing equivalent of the Copernican revolution is here. Those of our readers who embrace it will experience improved marketing programs and more profitable businesses, and thereby help to build a stronger America.

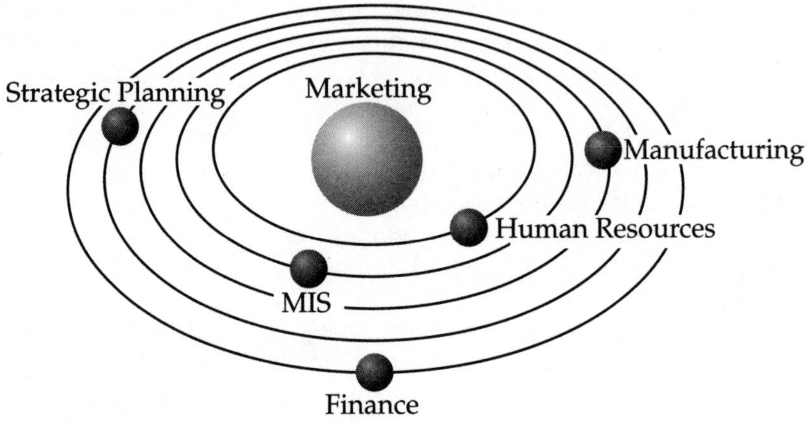

Exhibit C-2 Business in the late 1990s—and beyond!

Appendix

How to Grade Your Marketing IQ™

The "correct" answer to each Marketing IQ statement is listed below. Note that most of the statements are *false.* They are myths. After you have read the book, you will know why they are myths.

1. false
2. false
3. true
4. true
5. false
6. true
7. false
8. true
9. false
10. false
11. false
12. false
13. false
14. true
15. false
16. false
17. false
18. false
19. false
20. false

Add up the number of answers that you got correct and the number of answers to which you responded "don't know," then calculate your IQ from the scoring key that follows. After you've read the book, you may want to take the IQ test again to see how your performance has improved. With study and practice, a "genius" score is possible.

Marketing IQ Scoring Key

Number of correct responses	Number of "don't know" responses	Your IQ
20	0	160
19	1	156
19	0	152
18	2	152
18	1	148
18	0	144
17	3	148
17	2	144
17	1	140
17	0	136
16	4	144
16	3	140
16	2	136
16	1	132
16	0	128
15	5	140
15	4	136
15	3	132
15	2	128
15	1	124
15	0	120
14	6	136
14	5	132
14	4	128
14	3	124
14	2	120
14	1	116
14	0	112
13	7	132
13	6	128
13	5	124
13	4	120
13	3	116
13	2	112
13	1	108
13	0	104

Number of correct responses	Number of "don't know" responses	Your IQ
12	8	128
12	7	124
12	6	120
12	5	116
12	4	112
12	3	108
12	2	104
12	1	100
12	0	96
11	9	124
11	8	120
11	7	116
11	6	112
11	5	108
11	4	104
11	3	100
11	2	96
11	1	92
11	0	88
10	10	120
10	9	116
10	8	112
10	7	108
10	6	104
10	5	100
10	4	96
10	3	92
10	2	88
10	1	84
10	0	80
9	11	116
9	10	112
9	9	108
9	8	104
9	7	100
9	6	96
9	5	92
9	4	88
9	3	84
9	2	80
9	1	76
9	0	72
8	12	112
8	11	108
8	10	104
8	9	100
8	8	96

Number of correct responses	Number of "don't know" responses	Your IQ
8	7	92
8	6	88
8	5	84
8	4	80
8	3	76
8	2	72
8	1	68
8	0	64
7	13	108
7	12	104
7	11	100
7	10	96
7	9	92
7	8	88
7	7	84
7	6	80
7	5	76
7	4	72
7	3	68
7	2	64
7	1	60
7	0	56
6	14	104
6	13	100
6	12	96
6	11	92
6	10	88
6	9	84
6	8	80
6	7	76
6	6	72
6	5	68
6	4	64
6	3	60
6	2	56
6	1	52
6	0	48
5	15	100
5	14	96
5	13	92
5	12	88
5	11	84
5	10	80
5	9	76
5	8	72
5	7	68
5	6	64
5	5	60

Number of correct responses	Number of "don't know" responses	Your IQ
5	4	56
5	3	52
5	2	48
5	1	44
5	0	40
4	16	96
4	15	92
4	14	88
4	13	84
4	12	80
4	11	76
4	10	72
4	9	68
4	8	64
4	7	60
4	6	56
4	5	52
4	4	48
4	3	44
4	2	40
4	1	36
4	0	32
3	17	92
3	16	88
3	15	84
3	14	80
3	13	76
3	12	72
3	11	68
3	10	64
3	9	60
3	8	56
3	7	52
3	6	48
3	5	44
3	4	40
3	3	36
3	2	32
3	1	28
3	0	24
2	18	88
2	17	84
2	16	80
2	15	76
2	14	72
2	13	68
2	12	64
2	11	60

Number of correct responses	Number of "don't know" responses	Your IQ
2	10	56
2	9	52
2	8	48
2	7	44
2	6	40
2	5	36
2	4	32
2	3	28
2	2	24
2	1	20
2	0	16
1	19	84
1	18	80
1	17	76
1	16	72
1	15	68
1	14	64
1	13	60
1	12	56
1	11	52
1	10	48
1	9	44
1	8	40
1	7	36
1	6	32
1	5	28
1	4	24
1	3	20
1	2	16
1	1	12
1	0	8
0	20	80
0	19	76
0	18	72
0	17	68
0	16	64
0	15	60
0	14	56
0	13	52
0	12	48
0	11	44
0	10	40
0	9	36
0	8	32
0	7	28
0	6	24
0	5	20
0	4	16

Number of correct responses	Number of "don't know" responses	Your IQ
0	3	12
0	2	8
0	1	4
0	0	0

What Is Your Marketing IQ?

If you scored:	You are:
150–160	A marketing genius
130–149	A guru, a maven
110–129	An up-and-coming consultant
90–109	A seasoned professional
70–89	A typical marketer
50–69	A death-wish marketer
30–49	An incompetent
11–29	Dangerous to your company
0–10	Guilty of malpractice

If you scored under 130 on this Marketing IQ test, you will benefit tremendously from reading this book. Read the book, then take the IQ test again and see how your performance has improved. With study and practice, your marketing intelligence will increase significantly.

Index

About the Authors

Kevin J. Clancy and Robert S. Shulman are chairman and CEO, respectively, of Copernicus: The Marketing Investment Strategy Group, headquartered in Westport, Connecticut. Previously they held the same positions with Yankelovich Clancy Shulman, building it into one of the largest and most prestigious marketing consulting and research firms in the world. They are the authors of *The Marketing Revolution: A Radical Manifesto for Dominating the Marketplace*, a business best-seller.

Dr. Clancy is also a professor of marketing at Boston University and held positions in marketing and sociology at the Wharton School. Early in his career he was V.P. for Research Services at BBDO Advertising.

Following graduate studies in political science, Mr. Shulman rose through the ranks at Xerox Corporation to become National Accounts Manager. Later he joined the Yankelovich Organization, where he was a vice president in the simulated test market division. Mr. Shulman is a recognized expert on marketing strategy, new product evaluation, and sales management.